CW00889157

© Haynes Publishing

First published in September 2008

All rights reserved. No part of this publication may be reproduced, stored in a retrieval system or transmitted, in any form or by any means, electronic, mechanical, photocopying, recording or otherwise, without prior permission in writing from the publisher.

Giles Chapman has asserted his right to be identified as the author of this book.

A catalogue record for this book is available from the British Library

ISBN 978 1 84425 570 2

Library of Congress catalog card number 2008926354

Published by Haynes Publishing, Sparkford,
Yeovil, Somerset BA22 7JJ, England
Tel: 01963 442030 Fax: 01963 440001
Int. tel: +44 1963 442030 Int. fax: +44 1963 440001
E-mail: sales@haynes.co.uk
Website: www.haynes.co.uk

Haynes North America Inc.
861 Lawrence Drive, Newbury Park,
California 91320, USA

Designed by Lee Parsons

Printed and bound in Great Britain by
J. H. Haynes & Co. Ltd

Readers may notice that dates of manufacture in the text do not always match those shown on the front cover of the accompanying Haynes manual. This may be because the manual covers a wider or narrower range of models than is discussed in the text, or because the manual covers only those years where the particular model was imported to the UK, or because late models, certain derivatives or those with particular engines are not covered by the manual.

About the author

Giles Chapman is an award-winning writer and commentator on the industry, history and culture of cars. He began his career in 1984 in automotive consultancy, moving into magazine publishing in 1985. By 1991, he was editor of *Classic & Sports Car*, the world's best-selling classic car magazine. Since 1994, he's worked freelance across a huge variety of media. Today, he contributes to national newspapers and motoring publications, and was voted Jeep Consumer Journalist Of The Year in 2005. He's the author of more than a dozen books including, for Haynes, *TV Cars*, and *'My Dad Had One Of Those'* (co-written with Top Gear's Richard Porter) was a non-fiction hardback best-seller in 2007

THE CLASSIC CUTAWAYS

FOREWORD BY JOHN HAYNES OBE

CONTENTS
THE CLASSIC CUTAWAYS

INTRODUCTION — JOHN HAYNES OBE 6
ALFA ROMEO — ALFASUD 8
ALFA ROMEO — ALFETTA 10
AUDI — 100 12
AUDI — 80 14
AUSTIN/MORRIS — 1100 & 1300 16
AUSTIN/MORRIS — 1800 18
AUSTIN — A40 FARINA 20
AUSTIN/MORRIS/ROVER — MINI 22
AUSTIN/MORRIS — PRINCESS 24
AUSTIN — ALLEGRO 26
AUSTIN/ROVER — METRO 28
AUSTIN/MG/ROVER — MAESTRO 30
AUSTIN/MG/ROVER — MONTEGO 32
BMW — 3.0Si 34
BMW — 320i 36
BMW — 2002 38
CHRYSLER — ALPINE 40
CHRYSLER — SUNBEAM 42
CITROËN — GS 44
CITROËN — BX 46
DAF — 66 48
DATSUN — CHERRY 100A/120A 50
FIAT — 124 COUPÉ 52
FIAT — 126 54
FIAT — X1/9 56
FIAT — STRADA 58
FIAT — PANDA 60
FIAT — 131 MIRAFIORI 62
FORD — PREFECT 100E/107E 64
FORD — ANGLIA 105E 66
FORD — ZODIAC MK3 68
FORD — ESCORT MK1 MEXICO 70
FORD — CORTINA MK1 GT 72
FORD — CORTINA MK3 74
FORD — CORSAIR 76
FORD — CAPRI MK1 3000 78
FORD — CAPRI MK2 1600GT 80
FORD — CONSUL/GRANADA MK1 82
FORD — ESCORT MK3 RS MEXICO/2000 84
FORD — FIESTA MK1 86
FORD — ESCORT MK3 XR3 88
FORD — SIERRA 90
HILLMAN — IMP 92
HILLMAN — AVENGER 94
HILLMAN — HUNTER GLS 96
HONDA — N600 98
HONDA — CIVIC MK1 100
JAGUAR — MK1/2 102
JAGUAR — E-TYPE 104
JAGUAR — XJ6 SERIES 1-3 106

LADA 1500 108
LAND ROVER SERIES I-III 110
MAZDA RX3 112
MERCEDES-BENZ 250/280SL 114
MERCEDES-BENZ 250/280 (W123-TYPE) 116
MGA 118
MGB 120
MG MIDGET MK3 122
MORRIS MINOR 1000 124
MORRIS MARINA 126
NISSAN BLUEBIRD 128
OPEL MANTA MK1 130
PEUGEOT 504 132
PEUGEOT 205 134
PORSCHE 911 136
RELIANT ROBIN 138
RENAULT 4 140
RENAULT 16 142
RENAULT 5 MK1 144
RENAULT 20 TS 146
RENAULT 14 148
RENAULT FUEGO 150
ROVER 3500 P6 152
ROVER 3500 SD1 154
SAAB 96/95 V4 156
SAAB 900 TURBO 158
SKODA S110R 160
SUNBEAM RAPIER 162
TALBOT HORIZON 164
TALBOT SAMBA 166
TOYOTA CARINA 168
TRIUMPH TR5/6 170
TRIUMPH 2500 172
TRIUMPH SPITFIRE 174
TRIUMPH TOLEDO 176
TRIUMPH STAG 178
TRIUMPH DOLOMITE 180
VAUXHALL VIVA/FIRENZA 182
VAUXHALL VICTOR/VX FE 184
VAUXHALL CHEVETTE 186
VAUXHALL CAVALIER MK1 188
VAUXHALL CAVALIER MK2 190
VAUXHALL NOVA 192
VOLKSWAGEN BEETLE 194
VOLKSWAGEN 'TYPE 2' TRANSPORTER 196
VOLKSWAGEN 1600 FASTBACK 198
VOLKSWAGEN POLO MK1 200
VOLKSWAGEN GOLF MK1 202
VOLVO 144/145 204
VOLVO 164 206
AFTERWORD 208

INTRODUCTION JOHN HAYNES OBE

The cutaway illustration on the front cover of every Haynes car manual has been an unmistakable identifying feature since the very early days. The 100 cover cutaways featured in this book are just a small part of the work of Terry Davey, who in the 20 years that he worked for the company produced over 400 of these drawings and several thousand other technical illustrations.

Terry Davey was born on 29 October 1933. He attended Yeovil Technical College, leaving in 1952 to do his National Service in the RAF. After being demobbed he worked for Westlands, the Yeovil-based aircraft manufacturer, for five years. When he applied to join Haynes in 1972 he was employed as a design and display manager for a well-known supermarket chain.

Terry had a unique (and largely self-taught) ability to visualise the internal workings of complicated mechanical assemblies and to draw accurate representations of how they would look from any perspective: sectioned, or in three dimensions, or when partly stripped of their casings. His raw materials were model photographs, sales brochures and technical literature, supplemented in the Haynes tradition by personal inspection. He was a frequent visitor to the project vehicle workshop, taking photographs and making sketches of the component parts of whatever model was being dismantled that week. The annual Motor Show at Earls Court or the NEC saw him doing the rounds with his camera, picking up brochures, peering under bonnets and quizzing sales staff, many of whom turned out to have considerably less technical knowledge than he did.

A great bear of a man with his trademark pipe always on the go (the smoke alarm above his drawing board had to be disconnected), Terry was a familiar figure in the Haynes canteen at lunchtime, where he always had the full three courses. He was also a voracious reader, with a staple diet of thrillers and lurid magazines devoted to 'true' crime and murder stories, supplemented by whatever book might recently have been made into a television series. Some of his colleagues still treasure the memory of him coming into the office the morning after the transmission of an episode of *Brideshead Revisited*, saying 'Here! Did any of you lot know that Evelyn Waugh was a bloke?' We feigned surprise.

His own cars were always a source of interest and pride, though at least one (it may have been the Hillman Hunter GT) came to an untimely end. Driving home from the pub one night, Terry saw what he thought was a cardboard box in the middle of the road and decided that he could safely drive over it. The 'cardboard box' was in fact a lump of Ham building stone and the car was a write-off, though fortunately nobody was hurt.

The late 1970s and the 1980s were a period of rapid expansion for Haynes. At its peak the drawing office held four other illustrators, all of whom reckoned they could do what Terry did. Some were more justified in this opinion than others, but it is true to say that whilst some other illustrators (both at Haynes and elsewhere) have been successful in producing technically accurate cutaways, Terry's style remains unique and immediately recognisable.

Terry's health was not good in the later years and he retired in 1991. This coincided with a decision to modernise the look of the Haynes manual and the cover cutaways became less detailed; a couple of years later they began to be produced in colour. Pens, paper and French curves gave way to scanners, graphics tablets and Photoshop, and soon the cutaways were being originated from a series of workshop photos – a craft no less intricate than before, and one which has evolved over the years to produce an equally impressive result, but using a different set of skills.

All the cutaway drawings in this book were done in pen and ink, with nothing more than the traditional instruments of the draughtsman (though the keen student of detail will note the use of Letratone in some of the later examples). The hard-copy archive has been converted into electronic form by Terry's former colleague Roger Healing, who has also made good any damage. There are already literally millions of manuals in circulation bearing these drawings, and the latter now enjoy a new lease of life, gracing mugs and fridge magnets, bags and notebooks, key rings and clocks – and, of course, this book.

Terry Davey – a great bear of a man with his trademark pipe

ALFA ROMEO ALFETTA

YEARS MADE
1972–84

NUMBER MADE
440,417

ORIGINAL PRICE
£2,449 (1.8 in 1974)

MECHANICAL LAYOUT
Front engine, rear-wheel drive

RANGE OF ENGINES
1,570–1,962cc petrol, 1,995–2,393cc diesel, four-cylinder

MOST POWERFUL ENGINE
130bhp (1,962cc)

FASTEST VERSION
113mph (1,962cc)

BEST FUEL ECONOMY
27mpg (1,779cc)

WHEELBASE
2,508mm

LENGTH
4,267–4,384mm

NUMBER OF SEATS
5

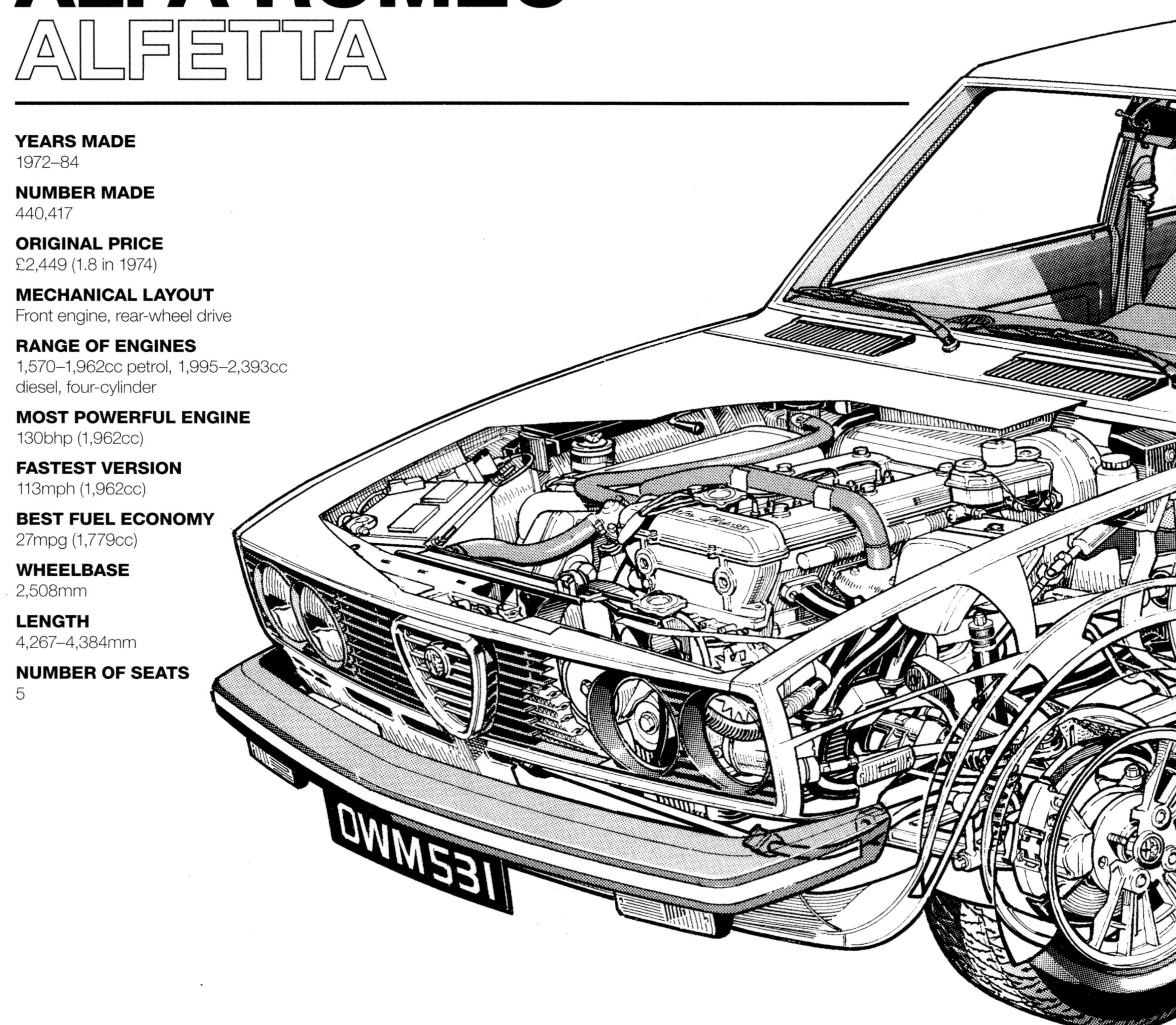

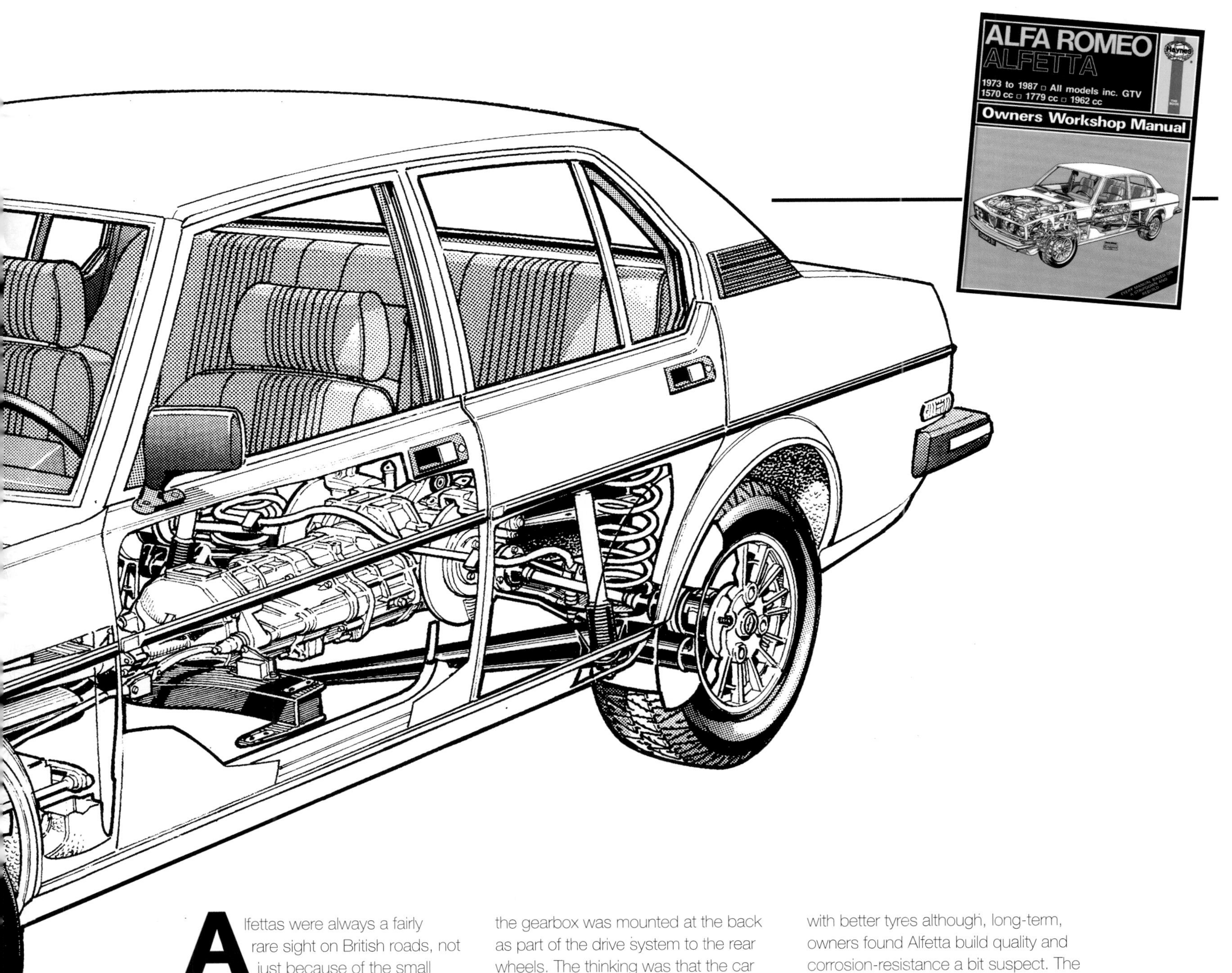

Alfettas were always a fairly rare sight on British roads, not just because of the small numbers sold but also down to the discreet, BMW-like styling. They tended to be bought by dedicated Alfa enthusiasts who were, perhaps, forced by family circumstances into driving a four-door saloon when they'd much rather have been zipping along in a GTV or a Spider.

The car did encompass some genuinely interesting thinking, in that the gearbox was mounted at the back as part of the drive system to the rear wheels. The thinking was that the car would enjoy excellent weight distribution with engine at one end and gearbox at the other. However, early cars tended to have heavy steering and a seemingly awkward gearchange with such a long linkage, not to mention slightly unruly wet weather roadholding. Obviously, Italian development engineers did most of their work on fine days…

Later cars did improve their handling with better tyres although, long-term, owners found Alfetta build quality and corrosion-resistance a bit suspect. The turbodiesels made sense in Europe, but were not sold in the UK.

Resourceful Alfa Romeo used the Alfetta structure as a basis for several other cars, including the more aerodynamic Giulietta range, the longer Alfa 6 luxury saloon and, indeed, the 1985 Alfa 90 that replaced the Alfetta itself. All are now largely forgotten, Alfetta included, and survivors are rare.

AUDI 100

YEARS MADE
1968–76

NUMBER MADE
796,787

ORIGINAL PRICE
£1,475 (100LS four-door in 1969)

MECHANICAL LAYOUT
Front engine, front-wheel drive

RANGE OF ENGINES
1,760–1,871cc, four-cylinder

MOST POWERFUL ENGINE
112bhp (1,871cc)

FASTEST VERSION
108mph (1,871cc)

BEST FUEL ECONOMY
23mpg (1,760cc)

WHEELBASE
2,675mm

LENGTH
4,590mm

NUMBER OF SEATS
5

The first Audi 100 became the turning point for the German marque, as it was the first Audi to directly challenge the premium executive car sector that was previously the preserve of Rover, Ford and BMW. What's more, it was technically more advanced than most large saloons, boasting front-wheel drive with in-line engines.

Auto Union, the Audi parent company, had been sold by Daimler-Benz to Volkswagen in 1965, and gifted with it was the Audi 100 design which had enjoyed plenty of input from Mercedes' quality-obsessed development engineers. VW, however, mainly wanted to get its hands on Auto Union's Ingolstadt factory to boost production of its own Beetle, and postponed all new Audis while the facilities were absorbed. Even though he was forbidden from working on the car, the 100's father Ludwig Kraus went on refining it and, when VW boss Heinrich Nordhoff saw the excellent result, with its sleek styling, he changed his mind and gave the car the green light.

From this single decision sprang the entire growth of Audi as a leading sports and luxury brand. Also, in introducing a thoroughly-developed water-cooled design to Volkswagen, it helped pave the way, via the VW K70 and Passat, for the Volkswagen revolution that did away with the air-cooled, rear-engined Beetle and ushered in the excellent Golf. So admire this motor car's fine features, and salute its pioneer status!

AUDI
100
1969 to September 1976
All models 1760 cc 1871 cc
Owners Workshop Manual
Haynes
Audi
H.353
OWM 162

AUDI
80

YEARS MADE
1972–8

NUMBER MADE
1,103,766

ORIGINAL PRICE
£1,544 (80LS four-door in 1973)

MECHANICAL LAYOUT
Front engine, front-wheel drive

RANGE OF ENGINES
1,296–1,588cc, four-cylinder

MOST POWERFUL ENGINE
110bhp (80 GTE, 1,588cc)

FASTEST VERSION
112mph (80GTE, 1,588cc)

BEST FUEL ECONOMY
32mpg (1,296cc)

WHEELBASE
2,470mm

LENGTH
4,175mm

NUMBER OF SEATS
5

The original 80, unveiled in 1972, gave Audi a credible small saloon in the Ford Cortina league. It was neatly designed, well built, and would entice huge numbers of new customers into the Audi arena. The range would consist, ultimately, of two- and four-door saloons and a rarely encountered four-door estate.

The 80 was, like the larger 100, front-wheel-drive and carried its engines in an in-line 'north/south' configuration. Those power units were all originated at Audi, although they were destined to be shared with other models in the Volkswagen range, especially the near-identical Passat.

The Passat also shared the 80's suspension system, with a 'dead' axle at the back supported by coil springs and trailing arms and MacPherson struts at the front. However, when the second-generation 80 made its debut in 1978, no Audis and Volkswagens would again share any outside similarity.

The 80 did make a significant contribution to one particularly iconic VW model: the Golf GTi. The grandfather of all hot hatchbacks gained its motive power from the fuel-injected, 1,558cc engine in the Audi 80GTE, only twisted round into an 'east/west' position in the more compact hatchback body. Audi's short-lived two-door hot-rod was, when introduced to the UK in 976, the fastest accelerating 1.6-litre saloon you could buy, hitting 60mph in 9sec and powering on to a top speed of 112mph.

AUSTIN/MORRIS 1100 & 1300

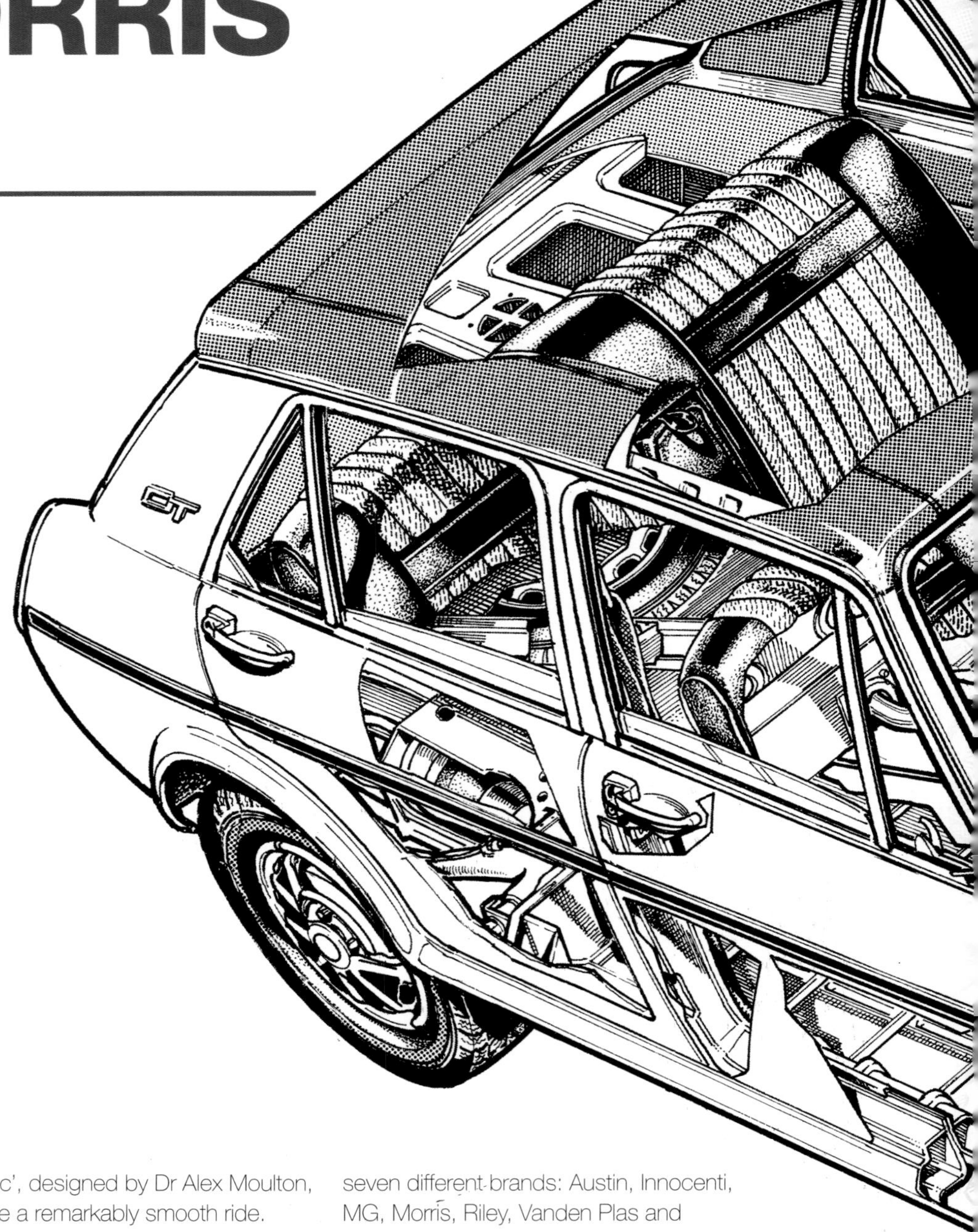

YEARS MADE
1962–74

NUMBER MADE
2,151,007

ORIGINAL PRICE
£611 (Austin 1100 deluxe four-door in 1963)

MECHANICAL LAYOUT
Front engine, front-wheel drive

RANGE OF ENGINES
1,098–1,275cc, four-cylinder

MOST POWERFUL ENGINE
70bhp (1300GT, 1,275cc)

FASTEST VERSION
95mph (1300GT, 1,275cc)

BEST FUEL ECONOMY
28mpg (1,098cc)

WHEELBASE
2,375mm

LENGTH
3,700–3,730mm

NUMBER OF SEATS
4

Following the acclaim garlanded on the Mini in 1959, the British Motor Corporation had absolute faith in its technical director Alec Issigonis to equal the achievement with a bigger family car three years later.

The new BMC saloon borrowed many of the Mini's strengths: transverse engine, front-wheel drive, subframe construction and an extremely spacious interior. But it was actually more sophisticated. In addition to front disc brakes, the new car boasted interconnected fluid suspension called 'Hydrolastic', designed by Dr Alex Moulton, which gave a remarkably smooth ride.

Under the bonnet sat a 1,098cc version of the BMC 'A' series engine, and automatic transmission was available, while detail styling was handled by Italy's Pininfarina studios.

The first version appeared in August 1962, and was entitled the Morris 1100, but other derivatives followed rapidly. In fact, this BMC car became the second most 'badge-engineered' (after General Motors' J platform range) ever, sold under seven different brands: Austin, Innocenti, MG, Morris, Riley, Vanden Plas and Wolseley. Each had its own unique grille and trim, while the more upmarket models boasted twin carburettors. The original four-door saloon was joined by a two-door estate and, later, saloon.

MkII models arrived in 1967, bringing a 1,300cc engine option, and these small saloons continued to prove spectacularly successful in Britain; in 1965/6 and again from 1968–71 this was the nation's best-selling model range.

BLMC
1100 & 1300 Mk I, II & III
1962 to 1974 □ 1098cc & 1275cc
Austin □ Morris □ Wolseley □ Riley □ MG
Owners Workshop Manual
OWM 260

AUSTIN/MORRIS 1800

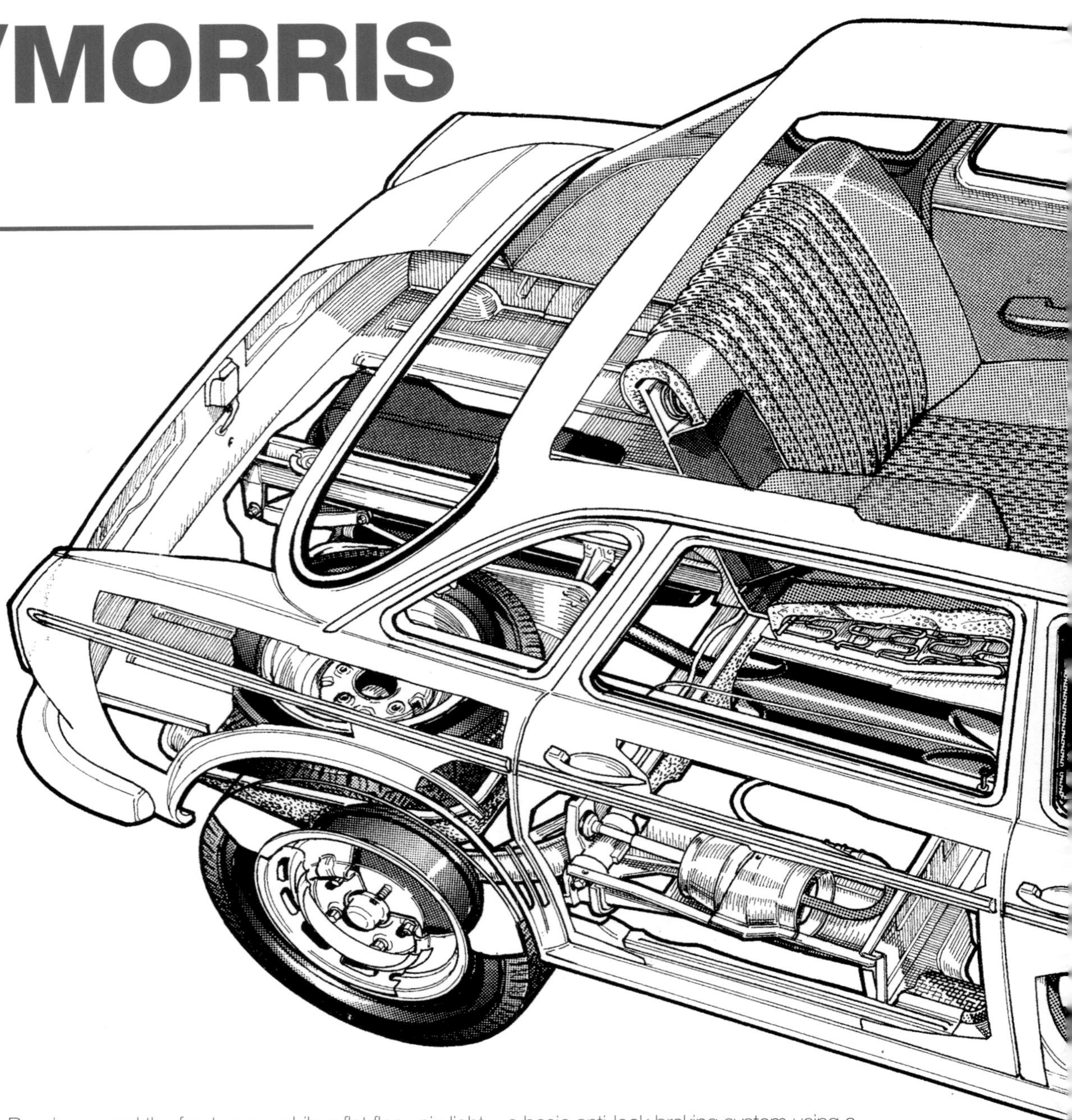

YEARS MADE
1964–75

NUMBER MADE
305,607

ORIGINAL PRICE
£808 (Austin 1800 deluxe in 1964)

MECHANICAL LAYOUT
Front engine, front-wheel drive

RANGE OF ENGINES
1,798cc, four-cylinder

MOST POWERFUL ENGINE
96bhp (1800 Mk2 S, 1,798cc)

FASTEST VERSION
99mph (1800 Mk2 S)

BEST FUEL ECONOMY
22.5mpg (1800)

WHEELBASE
2,689mm

LENGTH
4,221mm

NUMBER OF SEATS
5

Rather like putting together Russian dolls, here was the third size up of front-wheel-drive, transverse-engined family car from the British Motor Corporation. The Austin version was first off the stocks in 1964, joined within three years by the Morris 1800 and luxurious Wolseley 18/85 editions.

The inspired packaging, thanks to its transverse engine, and unusually long wheelbase cradled an extraordinarily roomy interior. The rear seat had an almost stretch-limo amount of space between itself and the front ones, while a flat floor, six-light windows and an austere dashboard – the ribbon-style speedo and umbrella-handle handbrake were oddities – boosted the feeling of space.

The configuration did endow the 1800 with ungainly looks, leading to its 'Landcrab' nickname. Even the master stylists at Pininfarina couldn't add much pizzazz to Issigonis's ruthlessly enforced design hard points. But under the skin it was an interesting concept, featuring the engineer's favoured hydrolastic suspension and even a basic anti-lock braking system using a special valve to automatically distribute braking force between front and rear.

One strong suit on these cars was their extremely rigid body structure. This was just one factor contributing towards lively performance and excellent road manners, even if the very necessary power steering should have been standard rather than an extra-cash option. And consumers proved resistant to the car's engineering purity: BMC's aim to make 4,000 a week was a costly miscalculation.

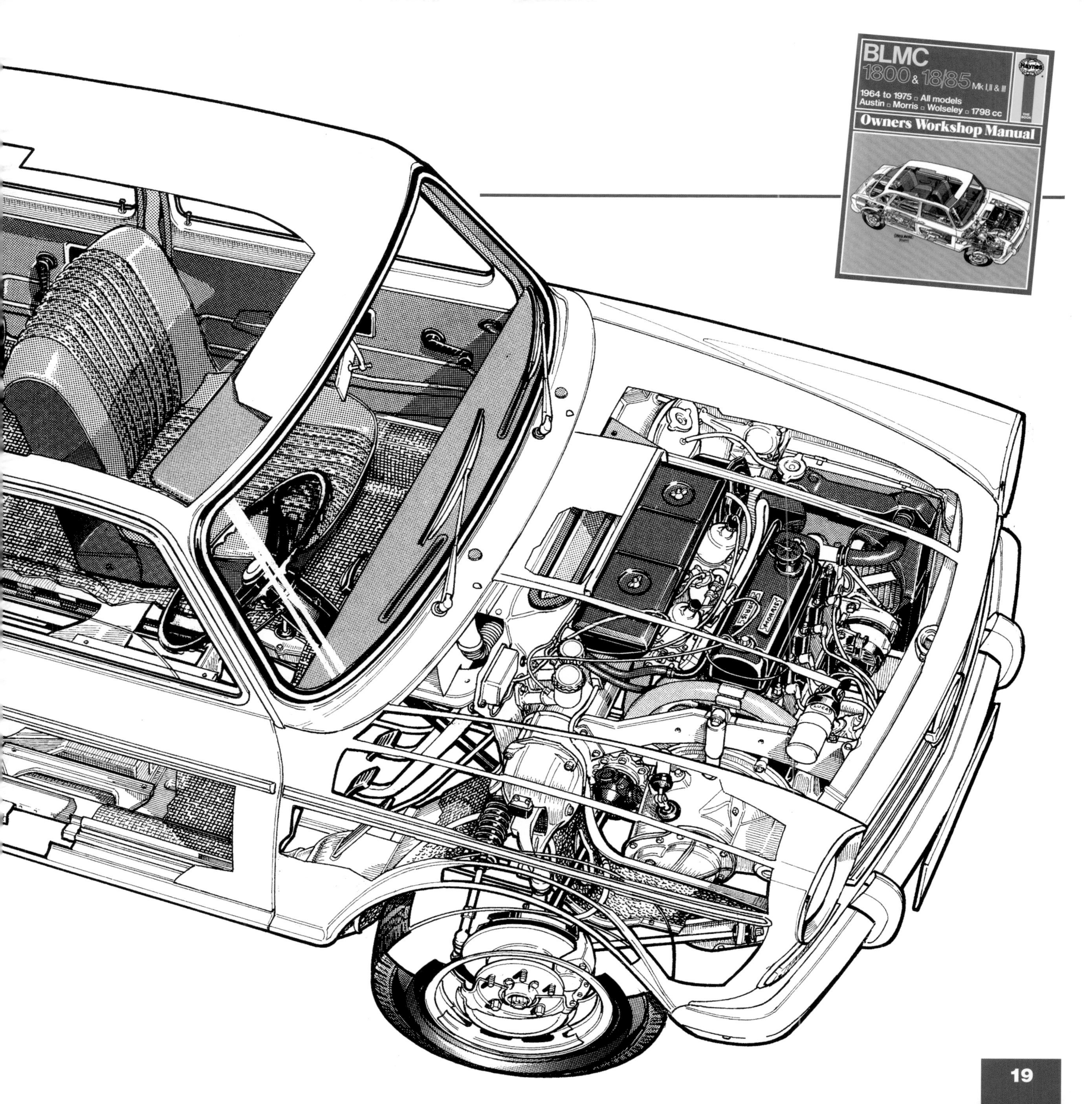
BLMC
1800 & 18/85 Mk I, II & III
1964 to 1975 □ All models
Austin □ Morris □ Wolseley □ 1798 cc
Owners Workshop Manual
Haynes
MORRIS
LUCAS

AUSTIN
A40 FARINA

YEARS MADE
1958–67

NUMBER MADE
364,064

ORIGINAL PRICE
£676 (A40 standard in 1958)

MECHANICAL LAYOUT
Front engine, rear-wheel drive

RANGE OF ENGINES
998–1,098cc, four-cylinder

MOST POWERFUL ENGINE
37bhp (1,098cc)

FASTEST VERSION
75mph (1,098cc)

BEST FUEL ECONOMY
37mpg (1,098cc)

WHEELBASE
2,121–2,210mm

LENGTH
3,664–3,683mm

NUMBER OF SEATS
4

The Austin A40 introduced something novel to the British motoring scene in 1958: Italian styling. A few expensive one-off sports and luxury cars emanating from Britain had boasted bodywork built or designed in Italy – cars like the Bristol 401 and Nash-Healey. In 1958, too, the boring old Standard Vanguard had received a facelift from Turin's Michelotti/Vignale partnership.

But the fact remained that you could buy an A40 at an Austin dealer in just about every town across the country, so it really brought a new Pininfarina-penned crispness and design purity to Britain's roads.

The A40 displaced the dependable A35 in the Austin range, carrying over the trusty A Series engine and most of the rear-wheel-drive drivetrain, but with a wider track to dispel the A35's sit-up-and-beg stance and tottery handling.

The svelte lines also concealed something of an innovation. In its Countryman version, the A40 had real hatchback practicality. Admittedly, there wasn't a tailgate third door – the lower boot lid dropped down while the rear window hinged upwards – but the rear seats could be folded flat, and the whole set-up turned the A40 into a useful load carrier.

There was an engine power upgrade with the Mk2 version launched in 1962, along with an increase in wheelbase and overall length to give extra space to rear seat passengers.

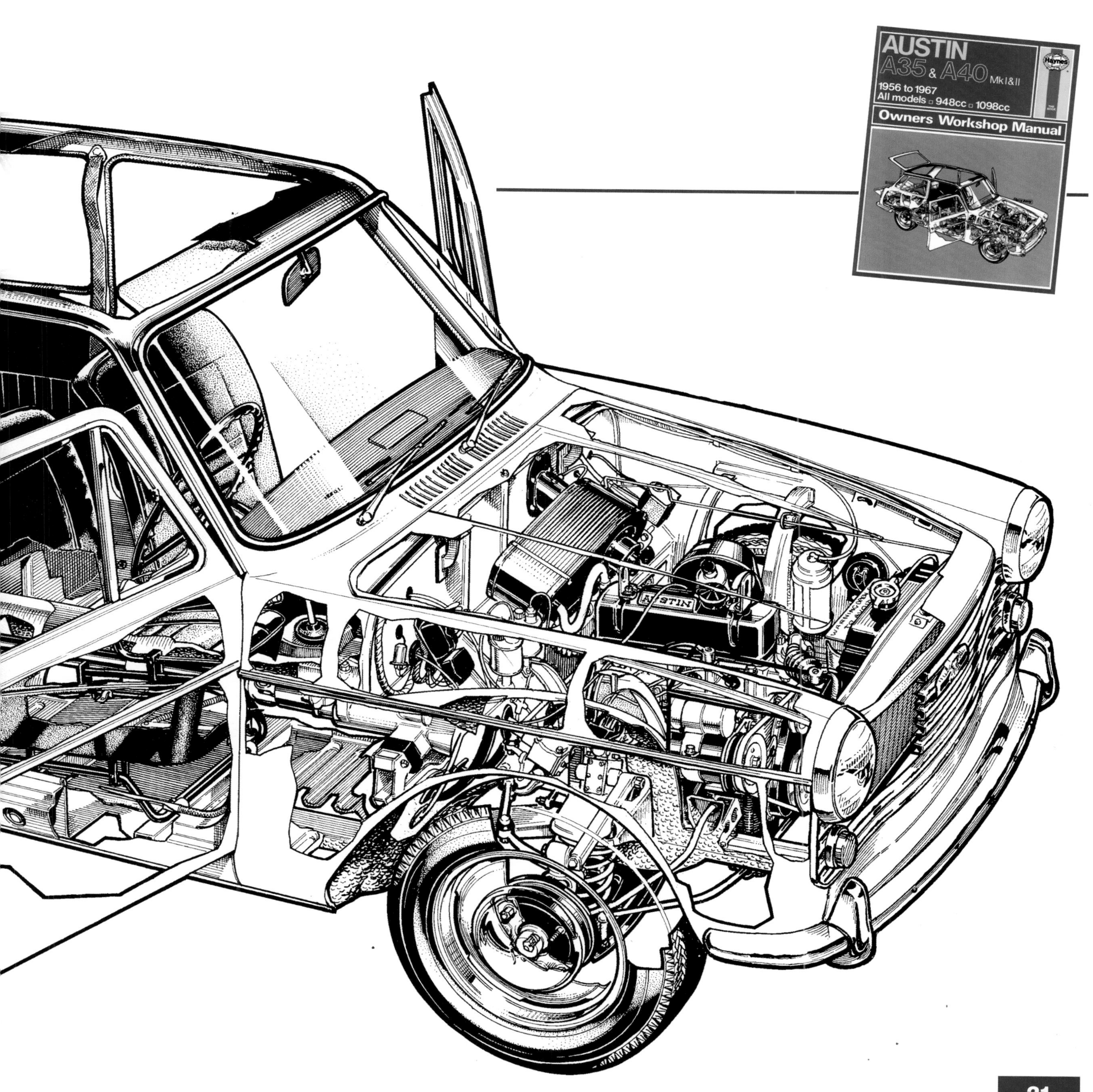
AUSTIN
A35 & A40 Mk I & II
1956 to 1967
All models 948cc 1098cc
Haynes
Owners Workshop Manual
AUSTIN

AUSTIN/MORRIS/ROVER
MINI

YEARS MADE
1959–2000

NUMBER MADE
5,387,862

ORIGINAL PRICE
£497 (Austin Se7en/Morris Mini-Minor in 1959)

MECHANICAL LAYOUT
Front engine, front-wheel drive

RANGE OF ENGINES
848–1,275cc, four-cylinder

MOST POWERFUL ENGINE
94bhp (ERA Turbo)

FASTEST VERSION
101mph (ERA Turbo)

BEST FUEL ECONOMY
40mpg (Austin Mini Se7en/Morris Mini Minor Mk1)

WHEELBASE
2,036mm

LENGTH
3,054mm

NUMBER OF SEATS
4

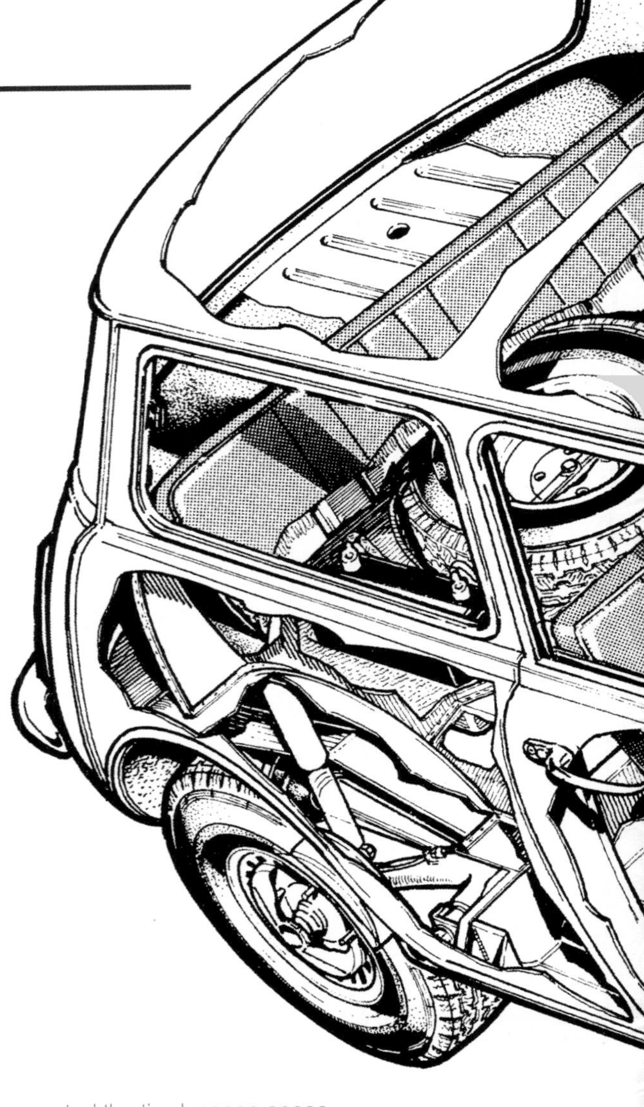

The Mini not only provided cheap transport for everyone, it was a technical masterpiece, a dominant rally car and, as Britain's best-selling car ever, a runaway sales success. Remarkably, it was conceived by one man, Alec Issigonis, the brilliant engineer hired by the British Motor Corporation in 1956…just as the Suez crisis erupted. British drivers were rationed to 10 gallons of petrol monthly and so, suddenly, a new economy car became paramount.

Other cars had used front-wheel drive and transverse engines before, but none within such compact dimensions – the Mini was just 12ft long. Issigonis mounted the gearbox under the engine instead of behind it, specified unique 10in diameter, space-saving wheels, and co-invented a compact rubber cone suspension system with Dr Alex Moulton.

Interior space usage was astoundingly clever. There were door storage bins, the dashboard was pretty much a shelf with a speedo on it, and the bootlid dropped down flat to form a platform that augmented the tiny luggage space.

At £497, the first Minis were pretty much the cheapest cars on sale. Costs had been pared to the bone by fitting sliding windows and cable-pull door releases. The buying public was initially suspicious, but soon grasped what a remarkable car this was. Its go-kart-like footprint gave joyful handling, its running costs were tiny, it was easy to park, and it looked cute too. Nonetheless, no one expected the Mini would endure largely unaltered for 41 years.

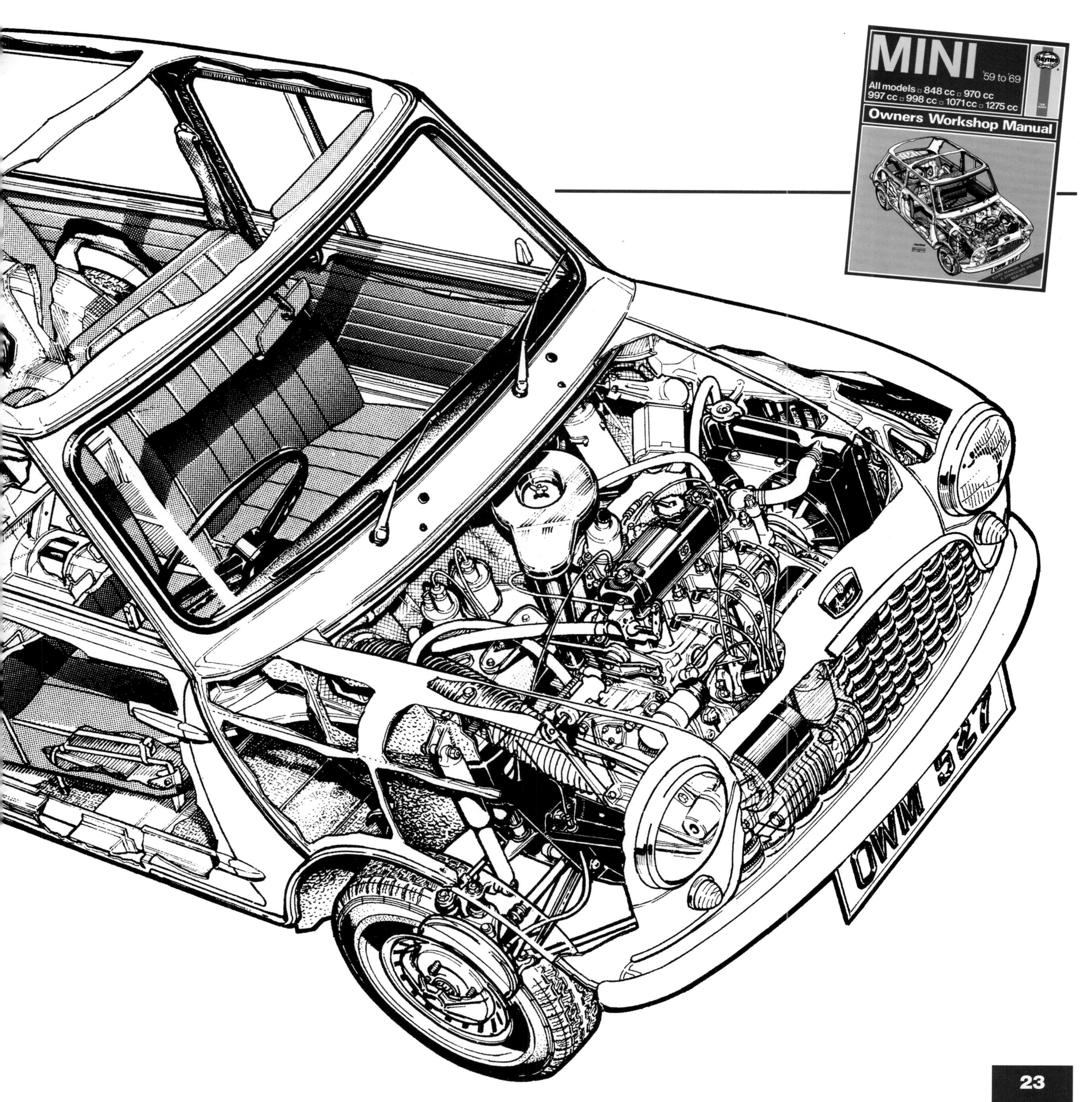
MINI
'59 to '69
All models □ 848 cc □ 970 cc
997 cc □ 998 cc □ 1071cc □ 1275 cc
Owners Workshop Manual
OWM 527

AUSTIN/MORRIS PRINCESS

YEARS MADE
1975–82

NUMBER MADE
224,942

ORIGINAL PRICE
£2,117 (Austin 1800 in 1975)

MECHANICAL LAYOUT
Front engine, front-wheel drive

RANGE OF ENGINES
1,695–2,227cc, four- and six-cylinder

MOST POWERFUL ENGINE
110bhp (2,227cc)

FASTEST VERSION
105mph (2,227cc)

BEST FUEL ECONOMY
29mpg (Princess 2, 1,695cc)

WHEELBASE
2,672mm

LENGTH
4,455mm

NUMBER OF SEATS
5

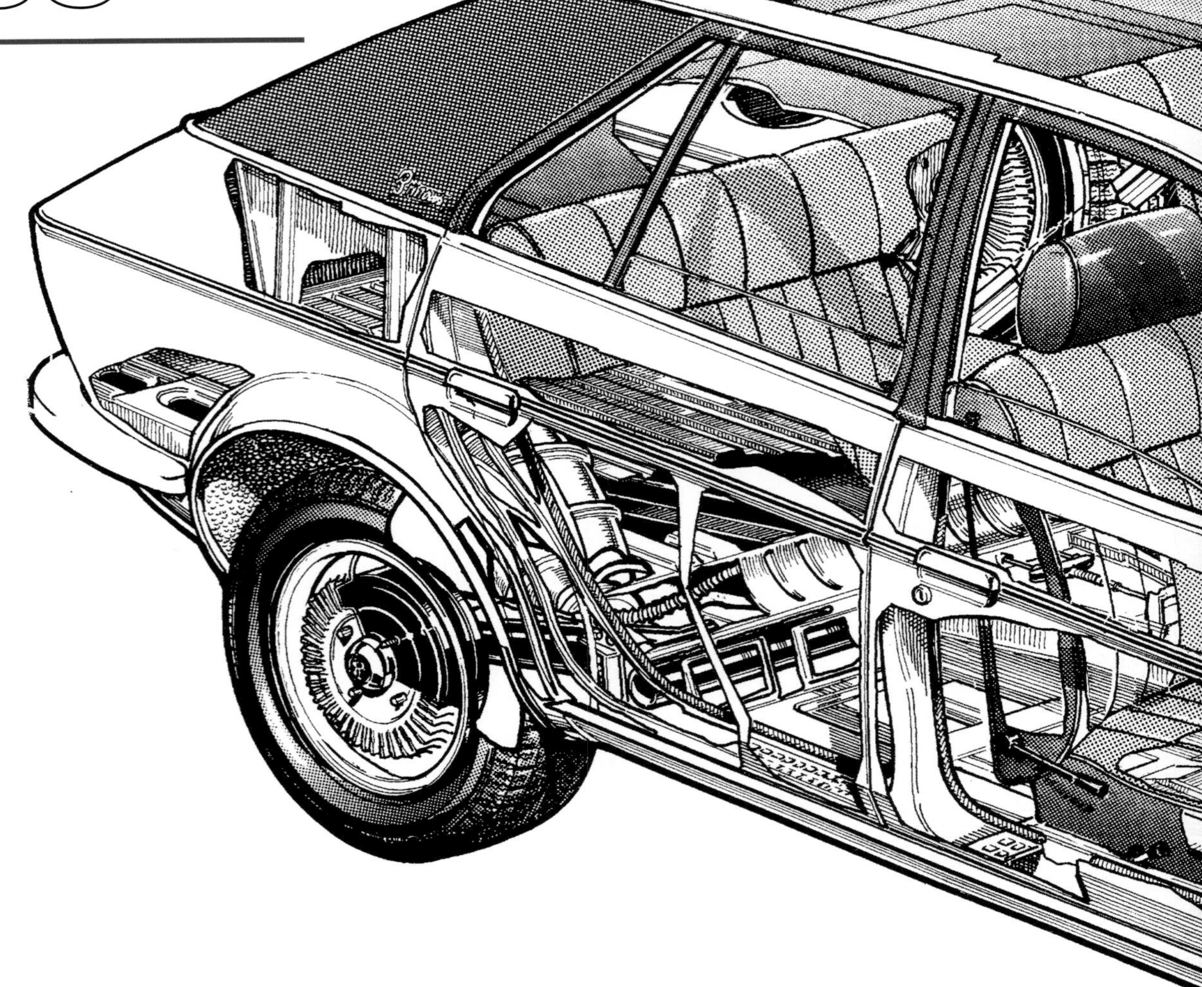

British Leyland's replacement for the old 'Landcrab' series bucked the trend once again with its distinctive styling.

The work of its leading designer Harris Mann, it followed his Allegro and TR7 in employing a wedge-shaped profile, an elongated nose and prominent wheelarches. It looked dynamic but flattered to deceive: the car's very shape seemed to suggest a versatile hatchback; instead, it had a conventional boot.

Under the bodywork was a new suspension system employing Hydragas units to give the car a soft and cosseting – not to say spongy – ride; the interior, typical of cars from the BMC/BL stable, was vastly roomy. Here was a comfortable and practical large family car.

At its launch in 1975, it was offered in Austin, Morris or Wolseley guises with either a 1.8-litre four-cylinder engine or a 2.2-litre straight-six. Within a year, however, British Leyland determined that these cars' slow sales were partly down to a weak identity. So the old brands were dropped (Wolseley was axed for good) and the cars were sold under the newly-created Princess marque. It was an extraordinary about-turn.

In 1978, the Princess 2 ushered in new 1.7- and 2-litre O Series engines along with several improvements aimed at boosting the cars' quality. Somehow, though, the briefly-trendy Princess never made the inroads into Ford's market domination that BL wanted.

BL
1700 & 2000
PRINCESS 2
July 1978 to 1979
All models □ 1695 cc □ 1993 cc
Owners Workshop Manual
Haynes
OWM 452

AUSTIN ALLEGRO

YEARS MADE
1973–82

NUMBER MADE
667,192

ORIGINAL PRICE
£1,009 (Allegro 1100 deluxe four-door in 1973)

MECHANICAL LAYOUT
Front engine, front-wheel drive

RANGE OF ENGINES
998–1,748cc, four-cylinder

MOST POWERFUL ENGINE
90bhp (Allegro 3, 1,748cc)

FASTEST VERSION
100mph (Allegro 3, 1,748cc)

BEST FUEL ECONOMY
36mpg (Allegro 3, 1,275cc)

WHEELBASE
2,430mm

LENGTH
3,920mm

NUMBER OF SEATS
4

When new the Allegro was rather unloved, but then, it did have a very tough act to follow as it tried to take the place of the BMC 1100/1300 in the hearts of the British car-buying public. And, to be fair, British Leyland tried to come up with an advanced replacement: the Allegro featured innovative Hydragas suspension, and went for an unusual rounded profile where the 1100 had been almost brutally straight-laced.

Nevertheless, the flaws were glaring. The rotund Allegro looked like it should feature a versatile hatchback, but it didn't. The car's 'quartic' steering wheel was a much-derided gimmick replaced after just two years by a normal round one. And whereas the 1100 had pin-sharp handling, the gas-sprung Allegro was somewhat bouncy on the move.

All of which wouldn't, perhaps, have been so bad if the car's quality was first-rate. But it was cursed by the rock-bottom morale of the British Leyland workforce of the day. The car quickly gained the unwelcome nickname of 'All-Aggro', and hastened many buyers towards showrooms selling rival Japanese cars for the first time.

Still, after the initial bugbears had been chased away the Allegro was found to be actually a fairly competent family runabout, one that was reliable and particularly resistant to corrosion. It was regularly the fifth or sixth best-selling British car in the late 1970s.

AUSTIN/ROVER METRO

YEARS MADE
1980–90

NUMBER MADE
840,088

ORIGINAL PRICE
£3,095 (miniMetro 1.0 in 1981)

MECHANICAL LAYOUT
Front engine, front-wheel drive

RANGE OF ENGINES
998–1,275cc, four-cylinder

MOST POWERFUL ENGINE
72bhp (Metro Vanden Plas, 1,275cc)

FASTEST VERSION
103mph (Metro Vanden Plas, 1,275cc)

BEST FUEL ECONOMY
46mpg (1.0HLE, 998cc)

WHEELBASE
2,250mm

LENGTH
3,405mm

NUMBER OF SEATS
4

British Leyland's engineers called it LC8 while developing it in secret, but a 1979 poll of BL employees saw the 'Metro' name picked for the company's crucial new supermini. Birmingham's train manufacturer Metro-Cammell then insisted BL could only use the Metro name if prefixed with 'mini'. Still, both sides soon forgot about the agreement and the newcomer became the Austin Metro we now all recall. It was then retitled Rover Metro from 1987 until a comprehensive mechanical refit in 1990.

The little car made a huge impact on its launch date of 8 October 1980 because it was a rare bright spot among the prevailing talk of strikes and factory closures.

Some aspects of the Metro were the equal – if not better – of the Ford Fiesta, Renault 5 and Volkswagen Polo, particularly its interior space and nimble road manners. Several elements, though, were poor because the entire drivetrain was borrowed from the 21-year-old Mini, giving an uncomfortable, milkfloat-like driving position, a four-speed gearbox and a distinct mechanical coarseness.

But the British public seemed oblivious to the Metro's drawbacks because it was also great fun to drive, thrifty to run and maintain, and genuinely versatile with a cavernous hatchback and the novelty of an asymmetrically-split folding rear seat. Orders cascaded in, and by June 1981 a newly-minted Metro trundled out of the Longbridge factory every minute.

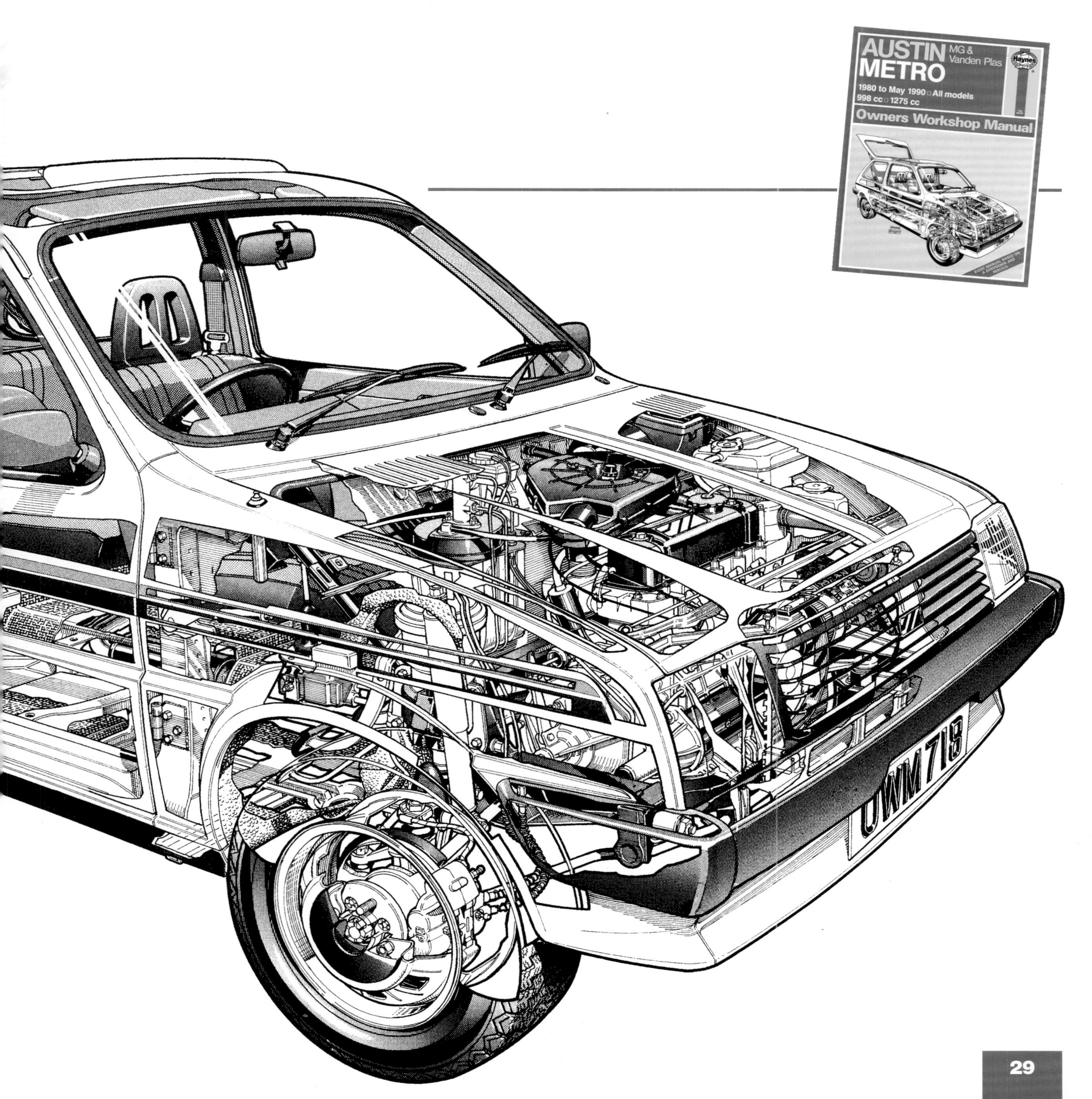
AUSTIN
MG & Vanden Plas
METRO
1980 to May 1990 □ All models
998 cc □ 1275 cc
Owners Workshop Manual
Haynes
UWM 718

AUSTIN/MG/ROVER MAESTRO

YEARS MADE
1983–94

NUMBER MADE
605,411

ORIGINAL PRICE
£4,749 (Maestro 1.3L in 1983)

MECHANICAL LAYOUT
Front engine, front-wheel drive

RANGE OF ENGINES
1,275–1,994cc petrol & 1,994cc diesel, four-cylinder

MOST POWERFUL ENGINE
152bhp (MG Maestro Turbo)

FASTEST VERSION
128mph (MG Maestro Turbo)

BEST FUEL ECONOMY
42mpg (Maestro 1.3HLE)

WHEELBASE
2,510mm

LENGTH
4,000–4,050mm

NUMBER OF SEATS
5

The Maestro was far from being a bad car. This was a roomy and practical family chariot, midway between a Ford Escort and a Ford Sierra in size. Thanks to well-sorted, all-round coil-spring suspension, road manners were good, and there was a wide choice of engine and trim options.

Under its LC10 codename, the car was championed by Sir Michael Edwardes as he struggled between 1977 and 1982 to haul BL back to viability. It was conceived as a simple, conventional front-wheel-drive model, avoiding the costly and weird rubber and gas suspensions used in the Mini, Metro, Maxi and Allegro.

Trouble was, by the mid-1980s the benchmarks were hurtling skywards. The Maestro may, in truth, have been no worse than some French, Italian and South Korean offerings, but it was still nowhere near its Japanese rivals for build quality. And then there was the second generation Volkswagen Golf, a brilliant all-rounder with no obvious downsides except its entirely justifiable higher price. Even the Maestro's digital dashboard and synthesised voice alerts were pilloried rather than admired.

The Maestro suffered mediocre engines, especially the new 1.6-litre R Series fitted to early MG Maestros, which was plagued by problems from its twin Weber carburettors. Indeed, the best Maestros were among the final ones, including the gutsy MG Maestro EFi 2-litre with fuel-injection, and the excellent 2-litre Diesel.

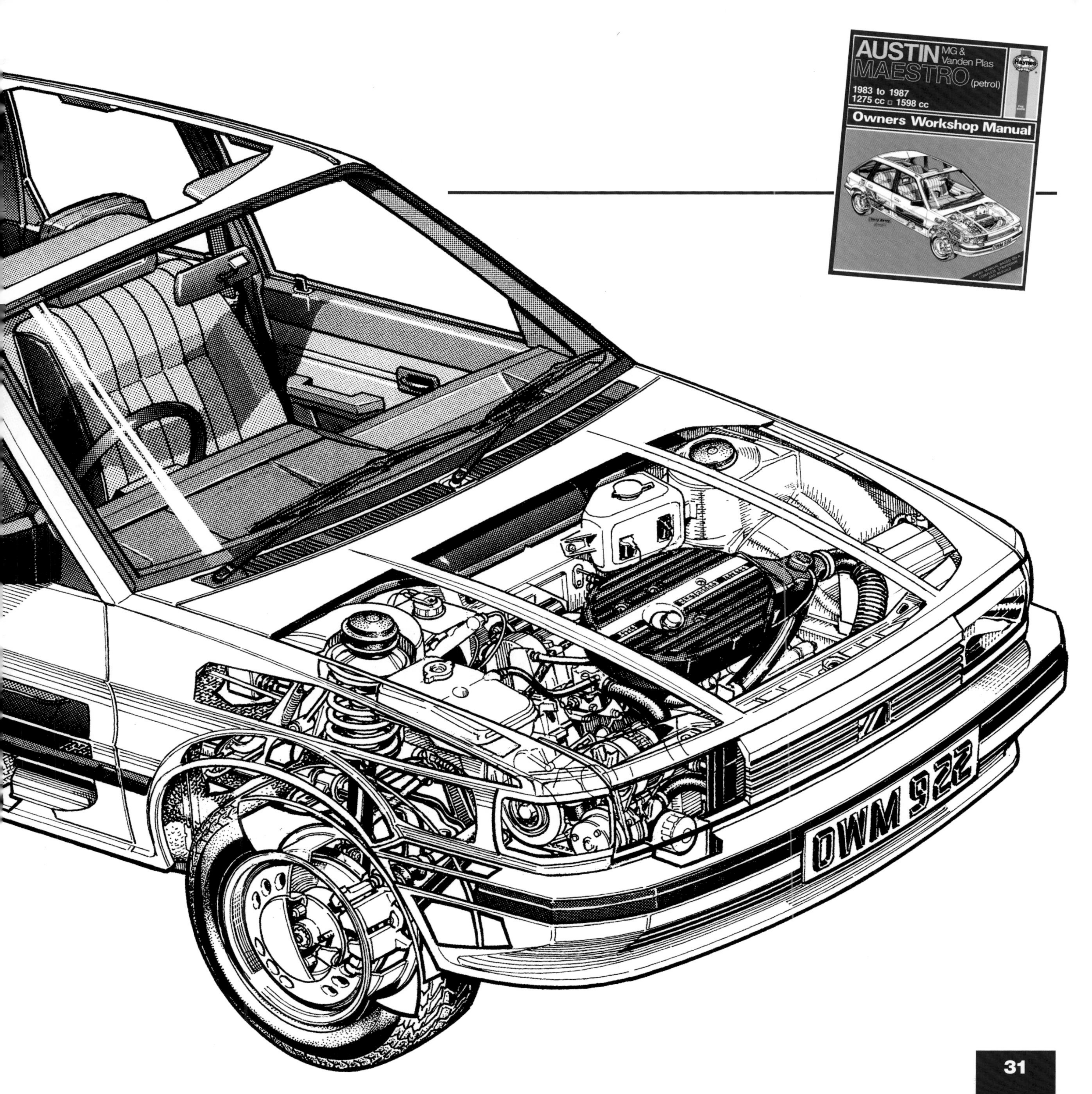
AUSTIN MG & Vanden Plas
MAESTRO (petrol)
1983 to 1987
1275 cc □ 1598 cc
Owners Workshop Manual
OWM 922

AUSTIN/MG/ROVER MONTEGO

YEARS MADE
1984–94

NUMBER MADE
571,460

ORIGINAL PRICE
£5,281 (Montego 1.3L in 1984)

MECHANICAL LAYOUT
Front engine, front-wheel drive

RANGE OF ENGINES
1,275–1,994cc petrol & 1,994cc diesel, four-cylinder

MOST POWERFUL ENGINE
152bhp (MG Montego Turbo)

FASTEST VERSION
124mph (MG Montego Turbo)

BEST FUEL ECONOMY
30mpg (1,275cc)

WHEELBASE
2,570mm

LENGTH
4,468mm

NUMBER OF SEATS
5

The Montego was the conventional four-door saloon alternative to the Maestro, the car being developed from the same British Leyland-instigated platform. While the Maestro had been known as the LC10 or LM10 during its development phase, the Montego was codenamed LM11. The cars had actually been on the drawing board since 1975, but only got the go-ahead after protracted negotiations with the British government, Prime Minister Margaret Thatcher being notably reluctant to bankroll the project.

As it turned out, the Montego was well received, with only a few teething problems at the start of production. For once, it was exactly the right size to compete with the Vauxhall Cavalier in the all-important fleet market, and probably benefited from shifting sentiments among Ford Cortina owners and users who didn't like the new Sierra.

Innovations on the Montego were few, although the body-colour bumpers and windscreen wipers that parked out of sight were neat touches. Obviously, the entire front and rear sections were markedly different to the Maestro. The Montego estate was a notably handsome load-carrier that put a BL-sourced car back on many gravel drives in moneyed suburbia, but the MG Montego Turbo proved an unruly handful with its 150-plus brake-horsepower scrabbling for traction through the front wheels. Like the Maestro, all Montegos bar the MGs were sold as Rovers rather than Austins from 1987.

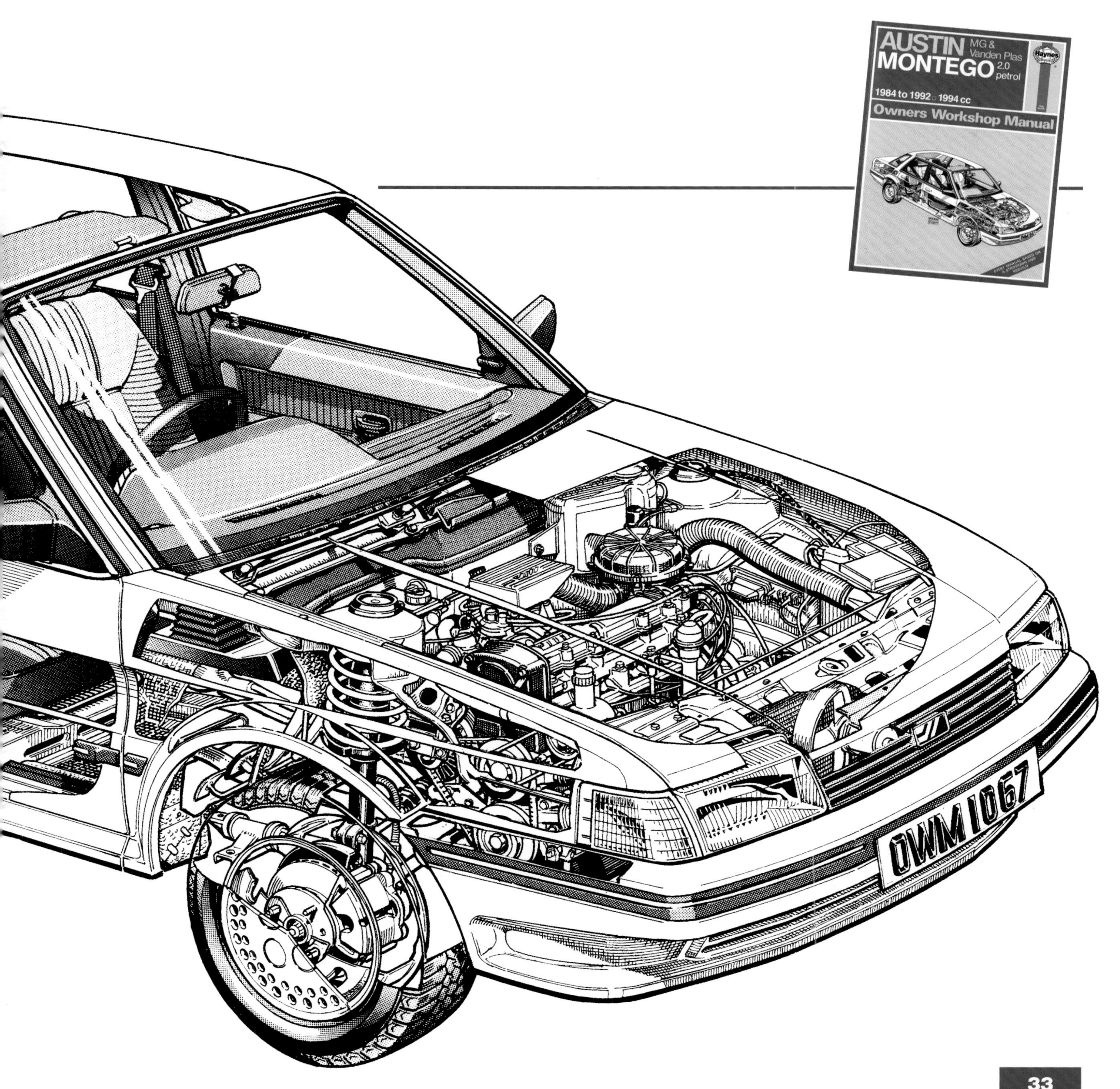
AUSTIN
MG &
Vanden Plas
MONTEGO
2.0
petrol
1984 to 1992
1994 cc
Owners Workshop Manual
OWM 1067

BMW 3.0Si

YEARS MADE
1971–7

NUMBER MADE
20,310

ORIGINAL PRICE
£5,399 (in 1974)

MECHANICAL LAYOUT
Front engine, rear-wheel drive

RANGE OF ENGINES
2,985cc, six-cylinder

MOST POWERFUL ENGINE
200bhp

FASTEST VERSION
133mph

BEST FUEL ECONOMY
15mpg

WHEELBASE
2,692mm

LENGTH
4,700mm

NUMBER OF SEATS
5

Impressive executive saloons with straight-six engines have become a BMW staple today, with one generation after another of the 5 and 7 Series winning fulsome praise from critics and customers alike. But it was this car that catapulted the German manufacturer firmly into Mercedes-Benz and Jaguar territory for the first time.

Well, not quite the 3.0 Si version shown here, it's true. It was actually the 2500 and 2800 models, first seen in 1968, which made company directors suddenly realise that BMW was a player in the executive car park stakes. These were impressive and roomy saloons boasting the first straight-six engines seen in BMWs for decades, along with all-round independent suspension and four-wheel disc brakes. Power steering and automatic transmission were options that most buyers went for.

Three years on and the fuel-injected 3-litre engine first seen in the gorgeous CSi coupé was installed in the saloon. A power unit of exceptional smoothness that remained in production for many years, its 200bhp made this a 130mph car that would eat up the autobahns all day long and still deliver its occupants unruffled.

Build quality was exacting, but the high price asked for the 3.0 Si – a V12-engined Daimler Double Six was £3,794 in 1973, well over a grand less than the BMW – tended to make it an unusual find on British streets in the 1970s.

BMW Saloons
2500, 2800, 3.0 & 3.3
1969 to 1977 □ 2494 cc □ 2788 cc
2986 cc □ 3210 cc □ 3299 cc
Owners Workshop Manual

BMW
320i

YEARS MADE
1975–9

NUMBER MADE
420,184 (all 3 Series Mk1 in four-cylinder form)

ORIGINAL PRICE
£4,749 (in 1976)

MECHANICAL LAYOUT
Front engine, rear-wheel drive

RANGE OF ENGINES
1,990cc, four-cylinder

MOST POWERFUL ENGINE
125bhp (1,990cc)

FASTEST VERSION
113mph (320i)

BEST FUEL ECONOMY
26mpg (approx)

WHEELBASE
2,570mm

LENGTH
4,325mm

NUMBER OF SEATS
4

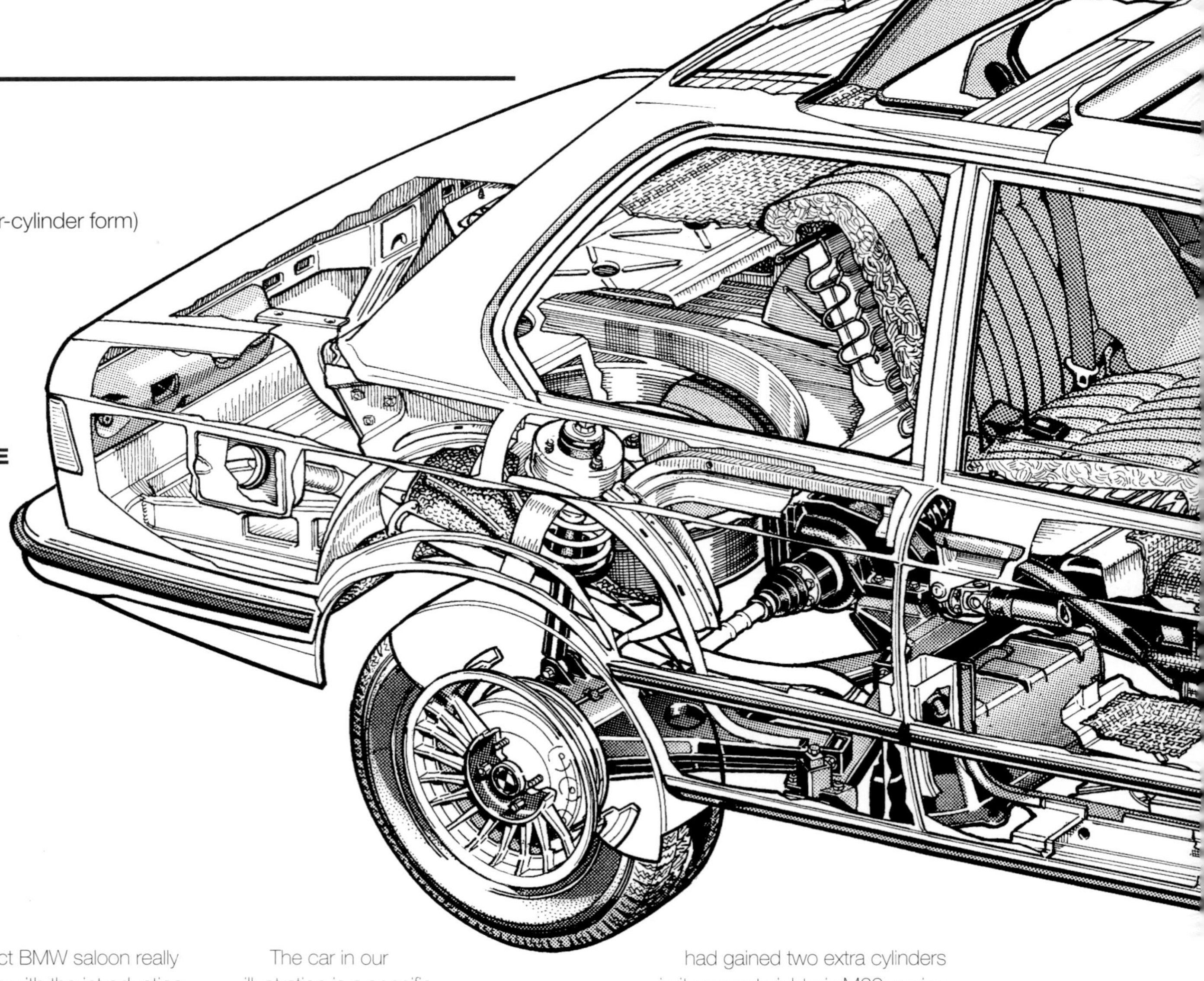

The compact BMW saloon really came of age with the introduction of the first 3 Series cars in 1975. Despite carrying over much of the hardware of the previous generation '02' cars, there was now a wheelbase extended by 2.5in to make the cabin less cramped, there was excellent rack-and-pinion steering, and there was a fastidiously-detailed new body style – with two doors only, for the whole of this car's life in showrooms – that was sleek and tasteful.

The car in our illustration is a specific model: the 320i. In 1975 this was the range-topper with its fuel-injected 2-litre, four-cylinder engine. Other options were the 1.6-litre 316, the 1.8-litre 318 and a 2-litre 320 with carburettor. Both the 2-litre cars featured four round headlamps, the others just a pair.

However, the 320i was to have but a short stint in the UK price lists. In 1977 it was ousted by the 320, which had lost its injection and 3bhp of power but had gained two extra cylinders in its new straight-six M60 engine, which made for a new-found silkiness in everyday driving. There was, in addition, the first 143bhp 323i. Some said this one was rather too spirited and tail-happy for its own good, making the new 320 the connoisseur's pick.

Costly though these cars were in comparison with British equivalents, they laid the cornerstones for BMW's widespread success today.

BMW
316, 320 & 320i
1975 to Feb 1983 □ All 4-cyl models
1573 cc □ 1766 cc □ 1990 cc
Owners Workshop Manual

BMW 2002

YEARS MADE
1968–77

NUMBER MADE
420,184

ORIGINAL PRICE
£1,597 (in 1968)

MECHANICAL LAYOUT
Front engine, rear-wheel drive

RANGE OF ENGINES
1,990cc, four-cylinder

MOST POWERFUL ENGINE
170bhp (2002 Turbo)

FASTEST VERSION
130mph (2002 Turbo)

BEST FUEL ECONOMY
24mpg (2002)

WHEELBASE
2,500mm

LENGTH
4,230mm

NUMBER OF SEATS
4

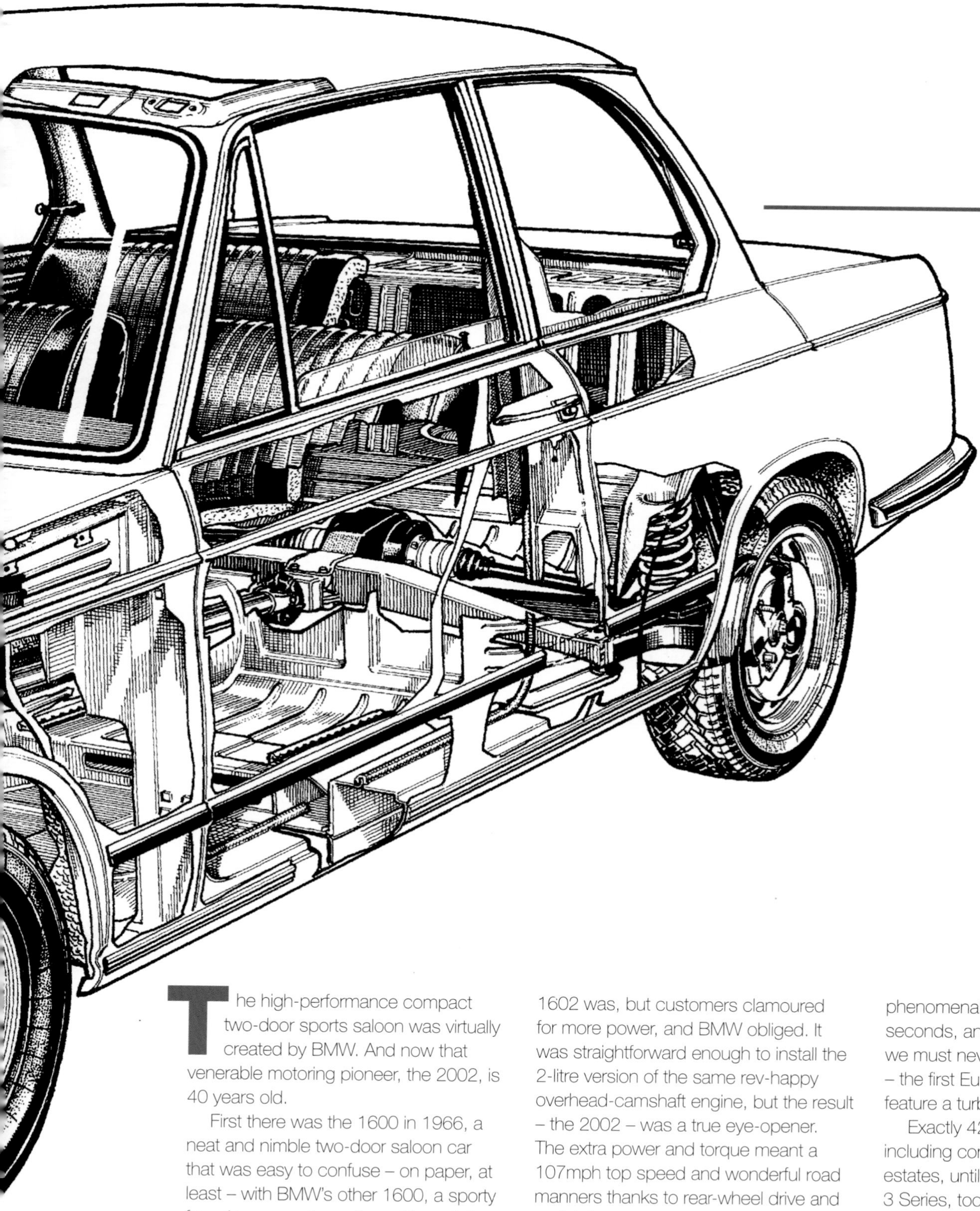

The high-performance compact two-door sports saloon was virtually created by BMW. And now that venerable motoring pioneer, the 2002, is 40 years old.

First there was the 1600 in 1966, a neat and nimble two-door saloon car that was easy to confuse – on paper, at least – with BMW's other 1600, a sporty four-door executive saloon. The solution was to add a distinctive '2' to its name, and a new BMW speciality was born.

Fine-handling and beautifully built the 1602 was, but customers clamoured for more power, and BMW obliged. It was straightforward enough to install the 2-litre version of the same rev-happy overhead-camshaft engine, but the result – the 2002 – was a true eye-opener. The extra power and torque meant a 107mph top speed and wonderful road manners thanks to rear-wheel drive and a slick five-speed gearbox.

But that wasn't all: the subsequent 2002Tii featured a fiery, fuel-injected twin-carburettor engine giving it the then phenomenal 0–60mph time of eight seconds, and 110mph top speed. And we must never forget the 2002 Turbo – the first European production car to feature a turbocharger.

Exactly 420,184 2002s were made, including convertibles and Touring estates, until its 1977 replacement, the 3 Series, took its marque into the 1980s era. The basic layout, spirit, and high quality of the 2002, however, lives on undiluted in today's fifth-generation 3 Series.

CHRYSLER ALPINE

YEARS MADE
1975–9

NUMBER MADE
108,405

ORIGINAL PRICE
£2,164 (in 1976)

MECHANICAL LAYOUT
Front engine, front-wheel drive

RANGE OF ENGINES
1,294–1,442cc, four-cylinder

MOST POWERFUL ENGINE
85bhp (1,442cc)

FASTEST VERSION
100mph (1,442cc)

BEST FUEL ECONOMY
34mpg (1,294cc)

WHEELBASE
2,603mm

LENGTH
4,242mm

NUMBER OF SEATS
5

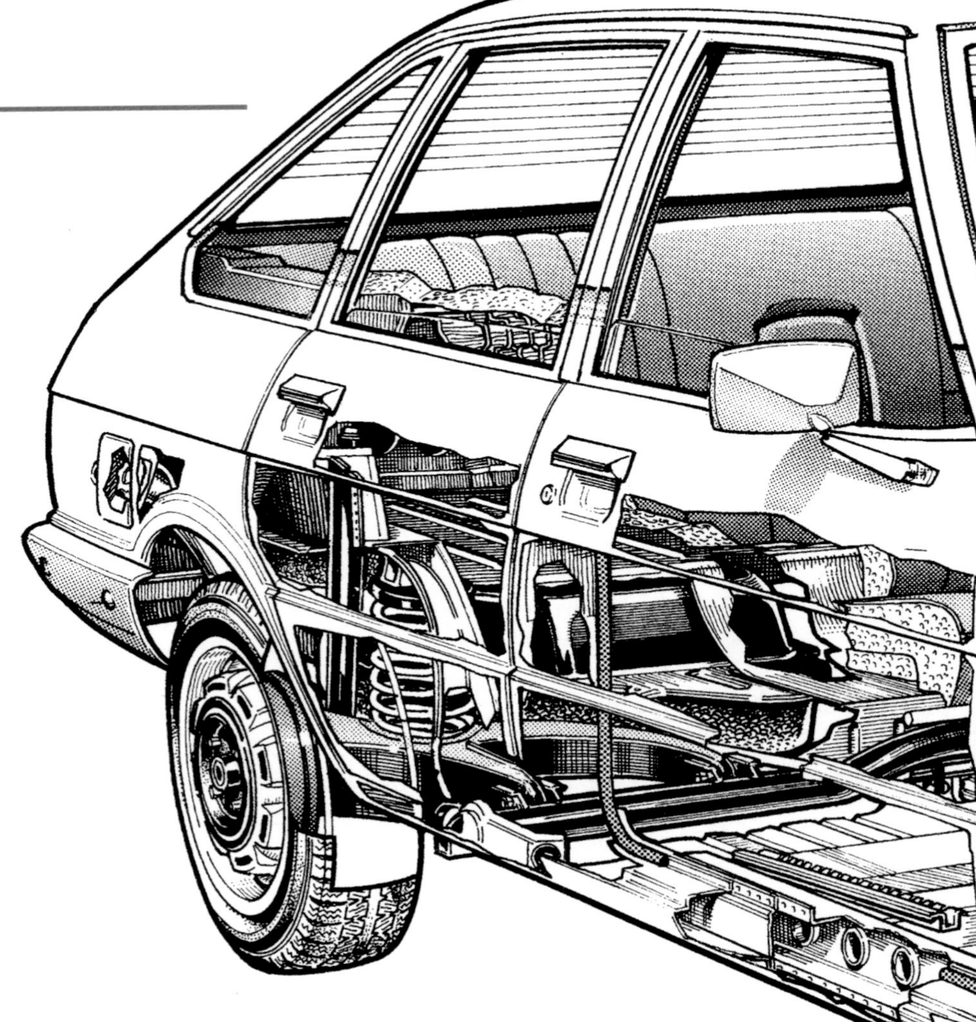

This five-door family hatchback was a genuine Anglo-French co-production. As America's Chrysler owned both Simca in Paris and the former Rootes Group in the West Midlands, it insisted the two divisions co-operate. Their first effort, the Chrysler 180 of 1970, was something of a lemon, but the Alpine of 1975 was bang on – such a well-resolved package, in fact, that it scooped the coveted European Car Of The Year award in 1976.

The French side looked after the engineering, specifying the dependable if noisy four-cylinder engines and four-speed transmission from the Simca 1100. Meanwhile, British stylists carried off an excellent job with the five-door body style and spacious interior.

There were differences between the two sides, though. For one thing, the French decided they were not ready to sell Chryslers, instead naming the car the Simca 1307, while for the British market the sporty Alpine name was dusted off and reused. Also, as manufacture got under way in Simca's Paris plant in 1975 Chrysler UK was staving off insolvency, and the cars didn't start rolling off the Coventry production lines until mid-1976.

The Alpine struggled against opposition from the Ford Cortina and even the Morris Marina, perhaps because British buyers preferred the convention of four-door saloons and a separate boot. All Chrysler UK cars were renamed Talbots in autumn 1979, after Chrysler's troubled European operations were acquired by Peugeot.

CHRYSLER
ALPINE
1975 to 1978
All models □ 1294 cc □ 1442 cc
Owners Workshop Manual
Haynes
CHRYSLER
OWM 337

CHRYSLER SUNBEAM

YEARS MADE
1977–9

NUMBER MADE
104,547

ORIGINAL PRICE
£2,324 (1.0 in 1977)

MECHANICAL LAYOUT
Front engine, rear-wheel drive

RANGE OF ENGINES
928–1,598cc, four-cylinder

MOST POWERFUL ENGINE
100bhp (1,598cc)

FASTEST VERSION
100mph (Ti, 1,598cc)

BEST FUEL ECONOMY
40mpg (1.0LS, 928cc)

WHEELBASE
2,413mm

LENGTH
3,828mm

NUMBER OF SEATS
4

The Sunbeam was born of a political storm and ended up a rallying hero. The rallying bit occurred after Henri Toivonen took it to victory in the 1980 Lombard RAC Rally, and Sunbeam Lotus subsequently clinched the 1981 Manufacturers' Championship for its builder. The rear-wheel-drive balance may have been good for the circuits, but it had its roots in the Hillman/Chrysler Avenger.

The Sunbeam was created, in a mere 19 months, as Chrysler UK's side of a bargain struck with the British government. In return for state aid to bolster the ailing company, Chrysler agreed to design a new small car to build at its Linwood, Scotland, plant, using as many British-made components as possible.

So the Avenger was shortened, given a neat two-box body with an opening glass tailgate (engineering a proper hatchback into the existing structure was too costly), and an engine line-up that included 1.3- and 1.6-litre Avenger units and the 1-litre aluminium engine formerly used in the Hillman Imp.

A lash-up? Actually, the Sunbeam was a decent enough small car with a simple mechanical layout. It was certainly capable of spawning two 'hot' versions: a twin-carburettor Ti, and the beefed-up Lotus-built special with its 16-valve, 150bhp 2.2-litre engine and ZF five-speed gearbox. Only…this ultimate Sunbeam hit the market in 1980, by when all European-built Chryslers had been renamed Talbots.

CHRYSLER
SUNBEAM
1977 to 1979 LS, GL, S & GLS
928 cc 1295 cc 1598 cc
Haynes
Owners Workshop Manual

CITROËN

YEARS MADE
1970–9

NUMBER MADE
1,874,754

ORIGINAL PRICE
£1,088 (GS Club in 1971)

MECHANICAL LAYOUT
Front engine, front-wheel drive

RANGE OF ENGINES
1,015–1,299cc, flat-four-cylinder

MOST POWERFUL ENGINE
65bhp (1,299cc)

FASTEST VERSION
98mph (1,299cc)

BEST FUEL ECONOMY
29mpg (X2, 1,222cc)

WHEELBASE
3,125mm

LENGTH
4,120mm

NUMBER OF SEATS
5

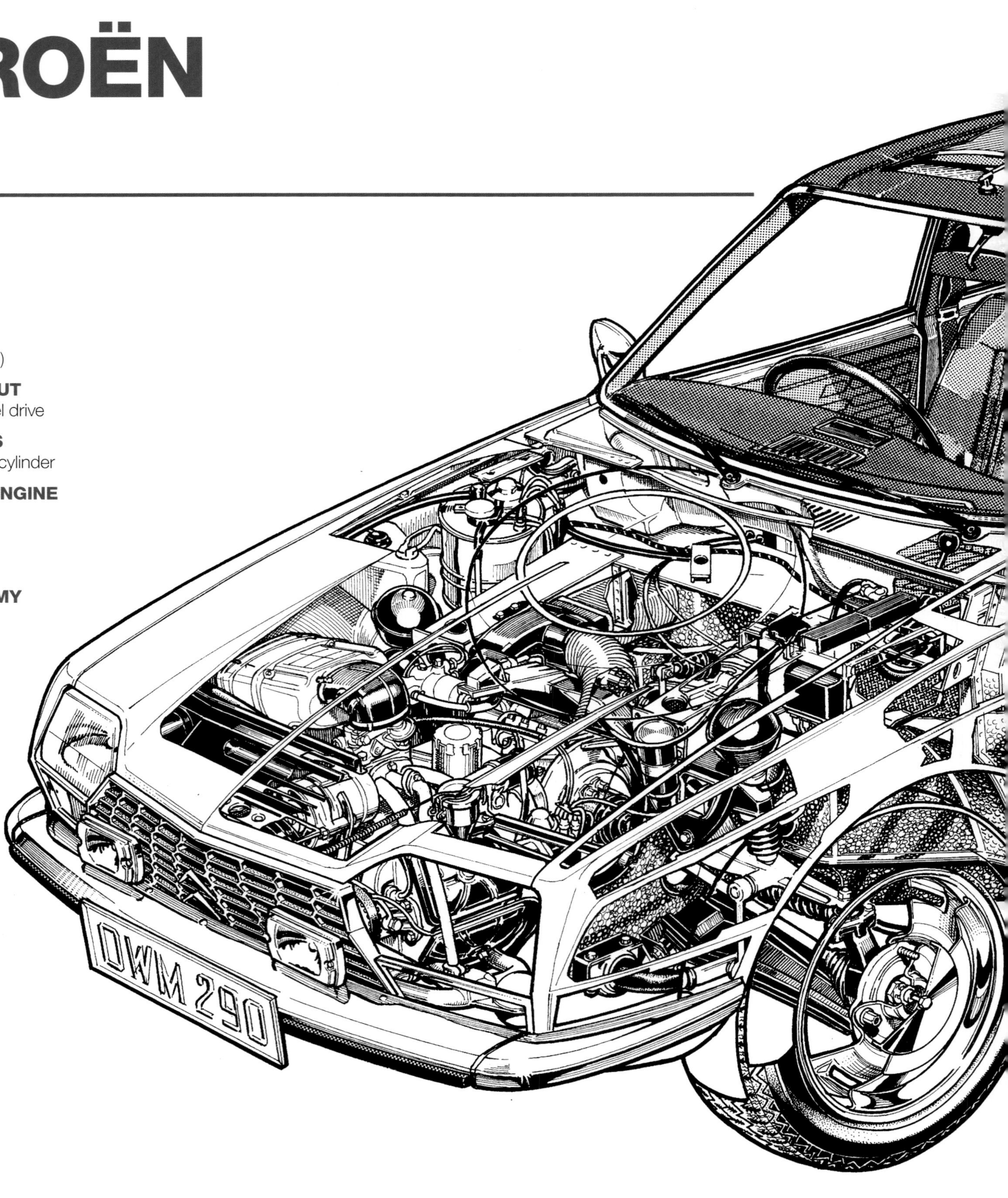

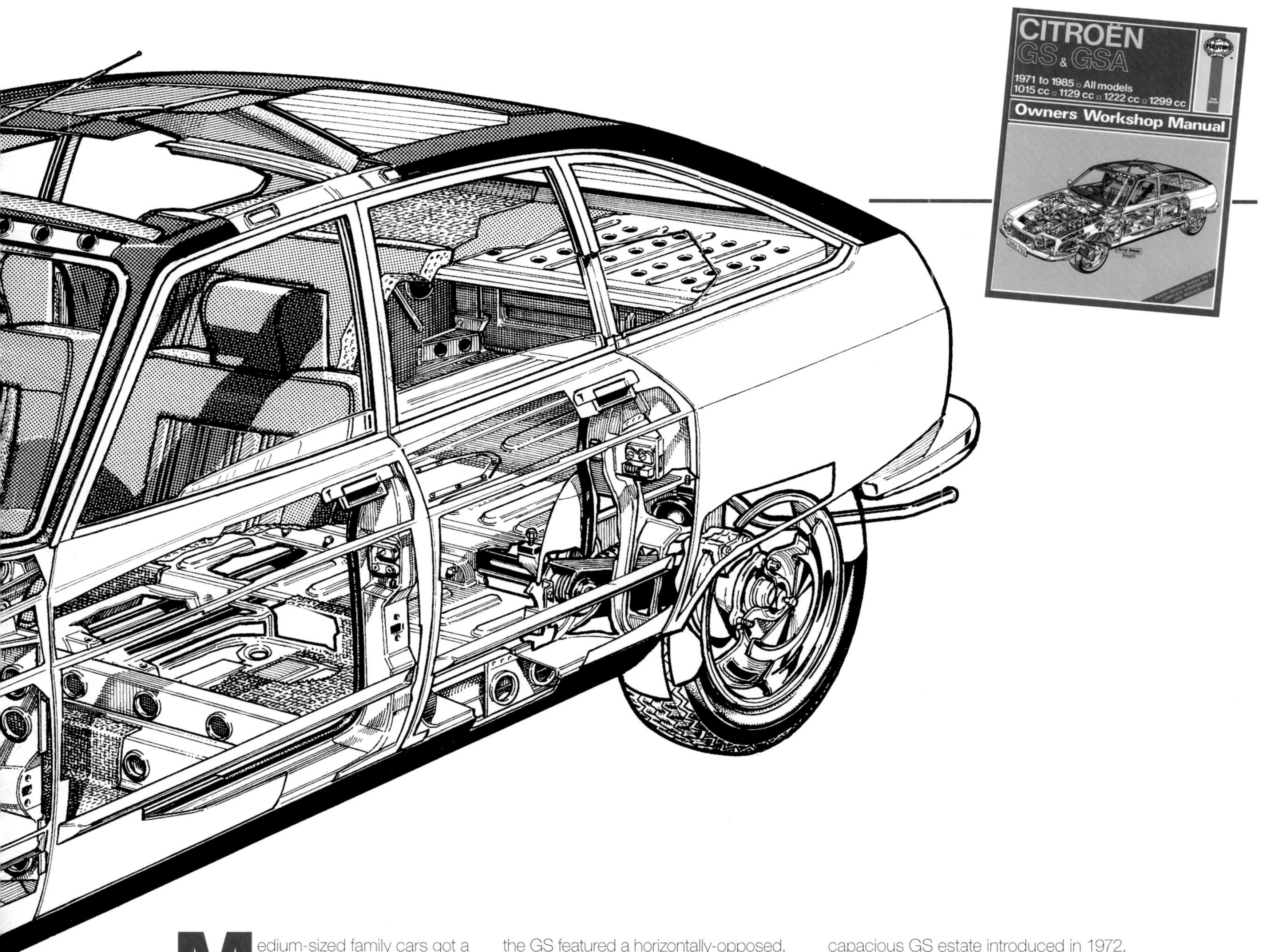

Medium-sized family cars got a whole lot more adventurous in 1970 after Citroën took the wraps off its aerodynamic GS. It was very much the Toyota Prius of its time, bristling with interesting technological features yet aimed at those who perhaps valued comfort and economy above ultimate performance.

The GS, in fact, filled the yawning chasm between the little Dyane and Ami models and the shark-like DS, and mixed the iconic features of both. Like the Dyane, the GS featured a horizontally-opposed, air-cooled engine, albeit an all-new unit with four cylinders instead of two.

But like the DS, its sleek lines concealed hydropneumatic suspension with adjustable ride height, and all round disc brakes. Also like its older brother, the GS had a wacky, single-spoke steering wheel.

Relatively meagre luggage accommodation (there was no hatchback until the replacement GSA arrived in 1979) was made up for by the capacious GS estate introduced in 1972, and levels of trim ranged from the plain Confort to the leather-rich Pallas.

With its exceptionally smooth ride, fine roadholding and roomy cabin, the GS was a multi-faceted car bound to inspire pride in any technologically-minded owner. For more conventional British buyers, though, it was largely viewed with suspicion, and wasn't a popular choice as a used car, leading to a rapid dwindling of GSs on UK roads during the 1980s.

CITROËN BX

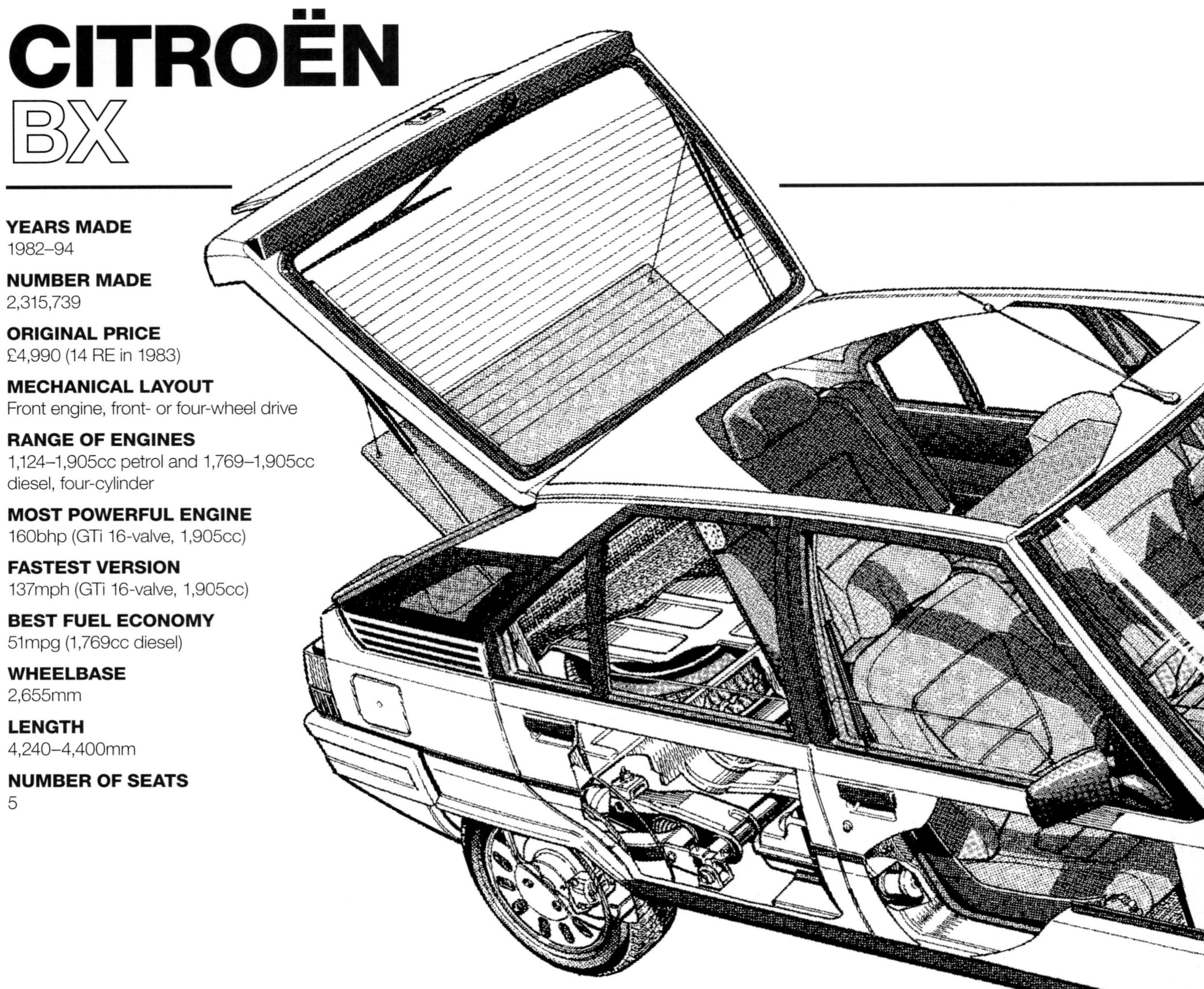

YEARS MADE
1982–94

NUMBER MADE
2,315,739

ORIGINAL PRICE
£4,990 (14 RE in 1983)

MECHANICAL LAYOUT
Front engine, front- or four-wheel drive

RANGE OF ENGINES
1,124–1,905cc petrol and 1,769–1,905cc diesel, four-cylinder

MOST POWERFUL ENGINE
160bhp (GTi 16-valve, 1,905cc)

FASTEST VERSION
137mph (GTi 16-valve, 1,905cc)

BEST FUEL ECONOMY
51mpg (1,769cc diesel)

WHEELBASE
2,655mm

LENGTH
4,240–4,400mm

NUMBER OF SEATS
5

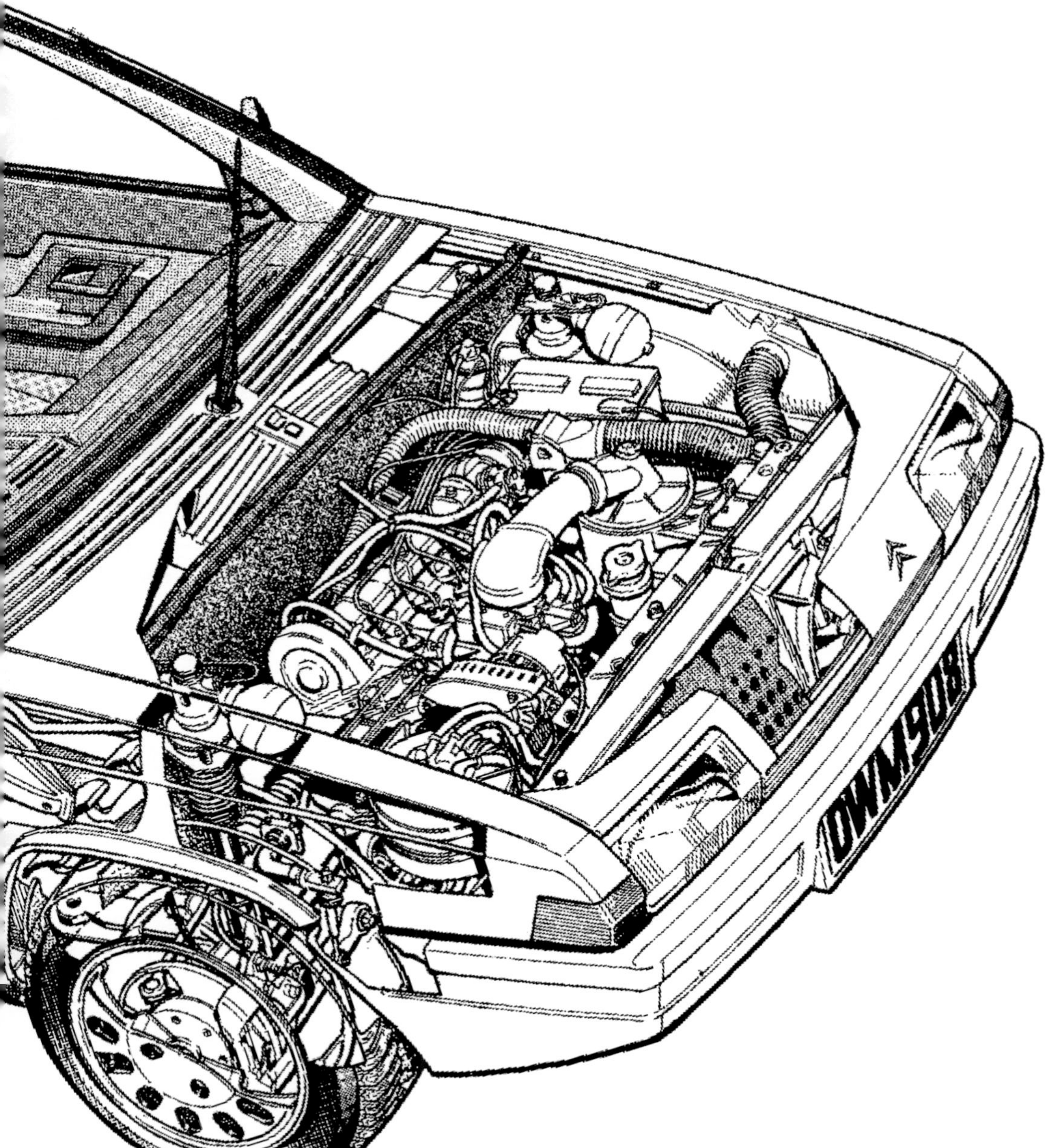

Citroën's history is peppered with landmark models like the Traction Avant, 2CV and DS but, although often overlooked these days, the BX is also a very significant model. It took the best of the eccentricities for which the French company had become renowned – some might say notorious – and packaged them into a 'normal' family car offering space and performance that could equal and better anything from Ford or Volkswagen.

The BX had an all-new platform that incorporated hydropneumatic suspension and powered disc brakes; marque traditionalists might also have approved of the single-spoke steering wheel and controls in dash-mounted drums rather than on stalks.

Indeed, this was the first corporate model developed by the Peugeot group which made its debut as a Citroën; the Bertone-styled BX formed the basis of the Pininfarina-penned Peugeot 405 five years later. So, of course, it featured Peugeot 1.3- and 1.6-litre engines from the start, while for certain markets there was a gutless if thrifty 1.1. Beginning in 1984, the company's excellent diesel and later turbodiesel units were offered, while the GTi could boast France's first-ever 16-valve engine.

There were some other innovations, too. The BX was among the first family saloons to offer the option of four-wheel drive, while the car broke new ground in its use of weight-saving plastic, having a glass fibre bonnet, hatchback and bumpers.

DAF
66

YEARS MADE
1972–5

NUMBER MADE
146,297

ORIGINAL PRICE
£1,135 (66SL in 1973)

MECHANICAL LAYOUT
Front engine, rear-wheel drive

RANGE OF ENGINES
1,108–1,289cc, four-cylinder

MOST POWERFUL ENGINE
57bhp (66 Marathon, 1,289cc)

FASTEST VERSION
84mph (66 Marathon, 1,289cc)

BEST FUEL ECONOMY
27mpg (1,108cc)

WHEELBASE
2,250mm

LENGTH
3,875mm

NUMBER OF SEATS
4

It was a real surprise in 1958 when a Dutch manufacturer of trucks and trailers beat the motor industry big guns to produce an automatic city car. Moreover, DAF's crisp-looking Daffodil came only with automatic transmission.

The system was called Variomatic, and was the forerunner of today's CVT (continuously-variable transmission) drivelines found in cars such as the Nissan Micra. In effect there was only one forward and one reverse 'speed', the 'stepless' infinitely-variable drive being taken to the rear wheels via toothed rubber belts in a V-formation. And, of course, no clutch or clutch pedal.

The 66 was developed directly from this first DAF car, although with a longer wheelbase, a de Dion-type rear axle and big-car styling from Italian consultant Michelotti, it was rather more mature. First in the 55 range and then for the 66 that replaced it, air-cooled twins were replaced by Renault-supplied four-cylinder, water-cooled engines more usually found in the Renault 4, 5 and 6.

The compact 66, offered as a tiny estate or coupé as well as a two-door saloon, was neither thrifty nor fast. But it was supremely easy to drive, endearing it to the elderly and those too timid ever to master a manual gearbox. Eventually Volvo acquired the car-making side of DAF, and from 1975 to 1980 these little runabouts were sold under the Volvo 66 banner.

VOLVO 66 & 343
DAF 55 & 66
1968 to 1979 □ 1108 cc □ 1289 cc □ 1397 cc
All models with Variomatic transmission
Owners Workshop Manual

DATSUN
CHERRY 100A/120A

YEARS MADE
1971–6

NUMBER MADE
389,807

ORIGINAL PRICE
£766 (two-door in 1971)

MECHANICAL LAYOUT
Front engine, front-wheel drive

RANGE OF ENGINES
988–1,171cc, four-cylinder

MOST POWERFUL ENGINE
69bhp (120A coupé, 1,171cc)

FASTEST VERSION
89mph (120A coupé, 1,171cc)

BEST FUEL ECONOMY
32mpg (998cc)

WHEELBASE
2,335mm

LENGTH
3,660–3,690mm

NUMBER OF SEATS
4

DATSUN
CHERRY
1971 to 1976
100A & 120A □ 988 cc □ 1171 cc
Owners Workshop Manual

You're looking at a real piece of Japanese history here, all the more so because our illustration gets right under the skin of the little Datsun. Not quite the first transverse-engined, front-wheel-drive car from Japan (that was Honda's N360/600) but Datsun's first and, as Datsun sales were sky-rocketing in the UK in the early 1970s, a very important car because it really was a credible rival to such upcoming greats as the Fiat 127 and Renault 5.

To the surefootedness of the configuration Datsun brought its typically light clutch and steering, a fairly competent all-independent suspension system and front disc brakes. There was, however, no hatchback despite the slightly tinny-looking styling of the two- and four-door saloons, although there was a small two-door estate, and the Cherry 120A coupé did come with a tailgate (and a very high sill) as well as the added zest of a 1.2-litre motor.

It would be fanciful to describe the little Cherry as an exciting car, but its mechanical excellence, general refinement, and dependability certainly endeared it to anyone who bought one. The Toyota Corolla is often credited with establishing the credentials of Japanese cars outside their home country; but, in Britain at least, Datsun led the charge, and the Cherry was one of its true breakthrough cars. Shame their propensity to rust means that very few of these cars are left.

FIAT
124 COUPÉ

YEARS MADE
1967–75

NUMBER MADE
279,672

ORIGINAL PRICE
£1,298 (1,438cc)

MECHANICAL LAYOUT
Front engine, rear-wheel drive

RANGE OF ENGINES
1,438–1,756cc, four-cylinder

MOST POWERFUL ENGINE
118bhp (1,756cc)

FASTEST VERSION
110mph (1,756cc)

BEST FUEL ECONOMY
21mpg (1,438cc)

WHEELBASE
2,420mm

LENGTH
4,123mm

NUMBER OF SEATS
4

Could the Fiat 124, begetter of the infamously dreary Lada, really be related to this stylish little GT? Well, yes indeed – the 124 Coupé shared the entire Fiat 124 rear-wheel drivetrain, which meant the all-round coil-spring suspension and beam rear axle and four-wheel disc brake set-up.

What never found their way into any Lada but are in all 124 Coupés are the delightful twin-cam engines and five-speed gearboxes that made the cars such an all-Italian joy on the roads of 1970s Britain.

These 124 Coupés were incredibly strong sellers across Europe, with their engine sizes steadily increasing over the eight years they were on offer. At the same time, the nose treatment of the car – unusually, for the time, designed in-house by Fiat and not by one of the august coachbuilders in Turin – was revised three times too, as the car gained four round headlights and differing detail trim.

They were a pretty popular choice in the UK in those far-back days before hot hatchbacks arrived on the scene. There were also 124 Spiders that, by contrast, were virtually never supplied with right-hand drive. Yet little account was taken of the cars' ability to withstand the damp British climate, and 124 Coupés rapidly turned to cornflakes on the second-hand market. Now that was something that could never be levelled at the indestructible Lada…

FIAT
124 Sport
1967 to 1977 Coupe
1438cc 1592cc 1608cc 1756cc
Haynes
Owners Workshop Manual
OWM 094
FIAT
H.172

FIAT 126

YEARS MADE
1972–2000

NUMBER MADE
4,670,000

ORIGINAL PRICE
£698 (in 1973)

MECHANICAL LAYOUT
Rear engine, rear-wheel drive

RANGE OF ENGINES
594–704cc, two- and flat-two-cylinder

MOST POWERFUL ENGINE
26bhp (704cc)

FASTEST VERSION
72mph (704cc)

BEST FUEL ECONOMY
48mpg (704cc)

WHEELBASE
1,840mm

LENGTH
3,054mm

NUMBER OF SEATS
4

The enormously long production run – and vast production total – hint at something special about the 126. Yes, it replaced the much-loved Nuova 500 that put Italy on wheels during the 1950s and '60s. But it proved far more of a 'motor-vator' to car ownership in Eastern Europe.

The Fiat 126 started Polish assembly just one year after its announcement at the 1972 Turin Motor Show; after nearly 1.4 million had been built in Italy, Poland became its exclusive home, for both inside and outside the Iron Curtain. The boxy little city car, with its rear-mounted, air-cooled engine, put millions of people in former Communist countries on the road.

In the West, the 126 never recaptured the charisma of the Nuova 500. As new-generation, front-wheel-drive 'superminis' arrived in the 1970s its cramped cabin, noisy power unit and feeble performance felt truly anachronistic. Even Fiat offered a lot more car in its Panda of 1980.

However, the Poles never stopped improving the 126. It gained its biggest upgrade in 1987 when they unveiled the BIS edition, boasting an all-new, water-cooled engine whose more compact dimensions, thanks to a horizontal configuration, meant a hatchback could finally be included. Yet ever-mindful that the 'Maluch' ('small one'), as it was nicknamed, was usually chosen as a first car, the old air-cooled 126 lived on alongside it right to the end.

FIAT X1/9

YEARS MADE
1972–89

NUMBER MADE
200,000 approx

ORIGINAL PRICE
£2,997 (1,290cc in 1977)

MECHANICAL LAYOUT
Mid engine, rear-wheel drive

RANGE OF ENGINES
1,290–1,498cc, four-cylinder

MOST POWERFUL ENGINE
85bhp (1,498cc)

FASTEST VERSION
110mph (1,498cc)

BEST FUEL ECONOMY
30mpg (1,290cc)

WHEELBASE
2,202mm

LENGTH
3,830–3,970mm

NUMBER OF SEATS
2

If ever there was a proper poor man's Ferrari then the Fiat X1/9 was it. Launched to unanimous praise from the motoring – and design – critics in 1972, Bertone's razor-edged styling, with a neat removable 'targa' roof panel, and the superb mid-engined road manners meant the car was virtually assured success.

It wasn't until the mid-1980s that it had any sort of serious competitor, from Toyota's MR-2. British Leyland critics often cited the X1/9 as the car MG should have been building, rather than the archaic Midget (the two were contemporaries for six years).

Initially fitted with a 1,290cc four-cylinder engine and four-speed gearbox from the breezeblock-shaped Fiat 128 Rallye, the original cars were adequately brisk (100mph and a 0–60mph in 13sec), but hardly fast enough to exploit the X1/9's sensational grip and pin-sharp handling. Even so, novices and seasoned drivers alike took it to their hearts because it was so easy to drive: even Fiat boss Giovanni Agnelli abandoned his limo so he could take himself to work every day in an X1/9.

Extra performance arrived in 1978 with a 1,500 engine and five-speed 'box from the Ritmo/Strada, but big 'impact' bumpers had by then spoilt its once crisp looks. In 1982 production and marketing were taken over entirely by Bertone, which continued to manufacture the car as the Bertone X1/9 until its demise in 1989.

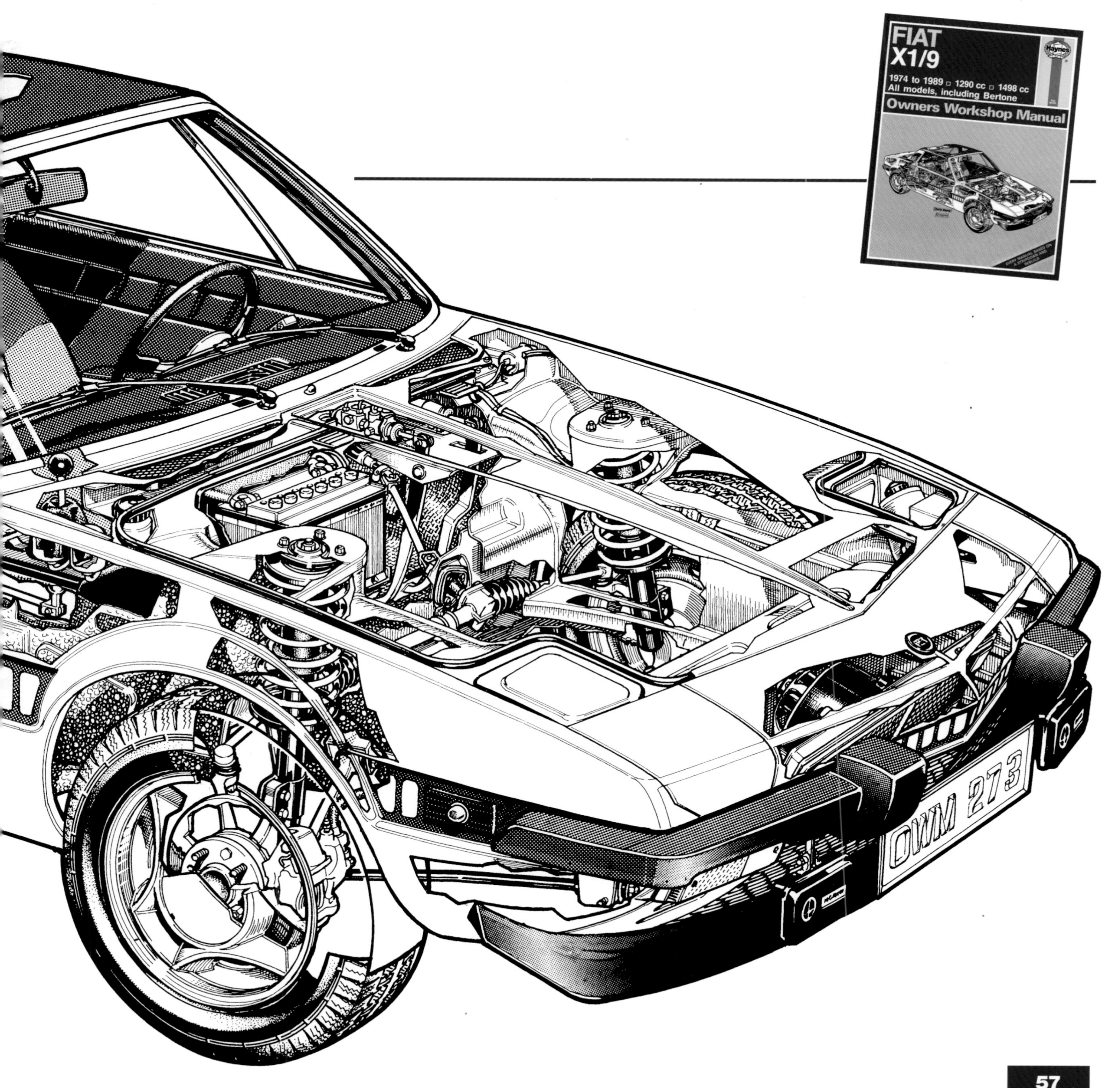
FIAT
X1/9
1974 to 1989 □ 1290 cc □ 1498 cc
All models, including Bertone
Owners Workshop Manual
Haynes
OWM 273

FIAT STRADA

YEARS MADE
1978–88

NUMBER MADE
1,790,000

ORIGINAL PRICE
£3,244 (Strada 60 in 1979)

MECHANICAL LAYOUT
Front engine, front-wheel drive

RANGE OF ENGINES
1,116–1,995cc petrol and 1,714–1,929cc diesel, four-cylinder

MOST POWERFUL ENGINE
130bhp (Abarth 130TC, 1,995cc)

FASTEST VERSION
122mph (Abarth 130TC, 1,995cc)

BEST FUEL ECONOMY
45mpg (60 ES, 1,116cc)

WHEELBASE
2,450mm

LENGTH
3,940mm

NUMBER OF SEATS
5

A very big fuss was made about this car. Revealed in April 1978 and on UK sale in March of the following year, its arrival was heralded by one of the best-remembered TV commercials ever. Entitled 'Handbuilt By Robots', it was shot by Hugh 'Chariots Of Fire' Hudson, and followed the Strada's highly-robotised production process to a stirring arrangement of Rossini's Figaro.

The Strada's almost completely automated assembly did indeed set a new industry benchmark, and the car itself was pretty striking too, with its bug-eyed headlights gazing out from a moulded plastic nose cone that could withstand 4mph impacts, a similar plastic section at the back, circular door handles and weird, styled wheels.

Beneath the chunky exterior of the Golf-sized family hatchback, though, lay the underpinnings of the 128, the very first Fiat-labelled front-drive car from the group, including overhead-camshaft 1.3- and 1.5-litre engines derived from it.

The car was known as the Strada (Italian for 'street') only in the USA and UK; elsewhere it was called the Ritmo (Italian for 'rhythm'). There were plentiful changes throughout its life, including a major bodywork facelift to 'normalise' those looks in 1982; there were sprightly 105TC and roaring 130TC performance models, diesels, turbodiesels, cabriolets and even a four-door saloon spin-off, the Regata. But none of these, somehow, ever managed to cap that great TV ad for iconic status.

FIAT PANDA

YEARS MADE
1980–2003

NUMBER MADE
4,500,000

ORIGINAL PRICE
£2,995 (Panda 45 in 1981)

MECHANICAL LAYOUT
Front engine, front-wheel drive

RANGE OF ENGINES
650cc, two-cylinder, 750–1,108cc four-cylinder petrol and 1,301cc diesel, plus electric-powered model

MOST POWERFUL ENGINE
51bhp (1,108cc)

FASTEST VERSION
88mph (999cc)

BEST FUEL ECONOMY
45mpg (750cc)

WHEELBASE
2,160mm

LENGTH
3,380–3,410mm

NUMBER OF SEATS
4

Fiat had one of its periodic bouts of design brilliance in 1980, when it allowed Giorgetto Giugiaro free rein to reinterpret the basic economy car for the 1980s.

The result was the startlingly straight-lined, upright Panda, with its all-round plastic body-cladding – for fending off city dings – and flat glass, even the windscreen, to cut production costs.

The interior was an industrial designer's dream, with its removable front seats that could form a (pretty uncomfortable) bed and whose upholstery could be detached and bunged in the washing machine. There was a clip-on ashtray for the hammock-like front parcel shelf, while the sun could blaze in through front and rear fabric roofs.

Under the bonnet was a choice of engines, although the early 650cc twin never came to the UK. The standard four-cylinder 903cc unit made the Panda a nippy buzzbox, and a new range of Fiat's FIRE engines in 1986, a five-speed gearbox and improved rear suspension set-up made the already-capacious Panda vastly more pleasant and less harsh to own.

The Panda's utilitarian cred was boosted in 1983 by the arrival of a version equipped with selectable four-wheel drive and raised ride-height, and given another uplift with a tiny diesel engine option three years later.

The original Panda is a design classic that served Europe well, and in Britain precisely 59,397 were sold.

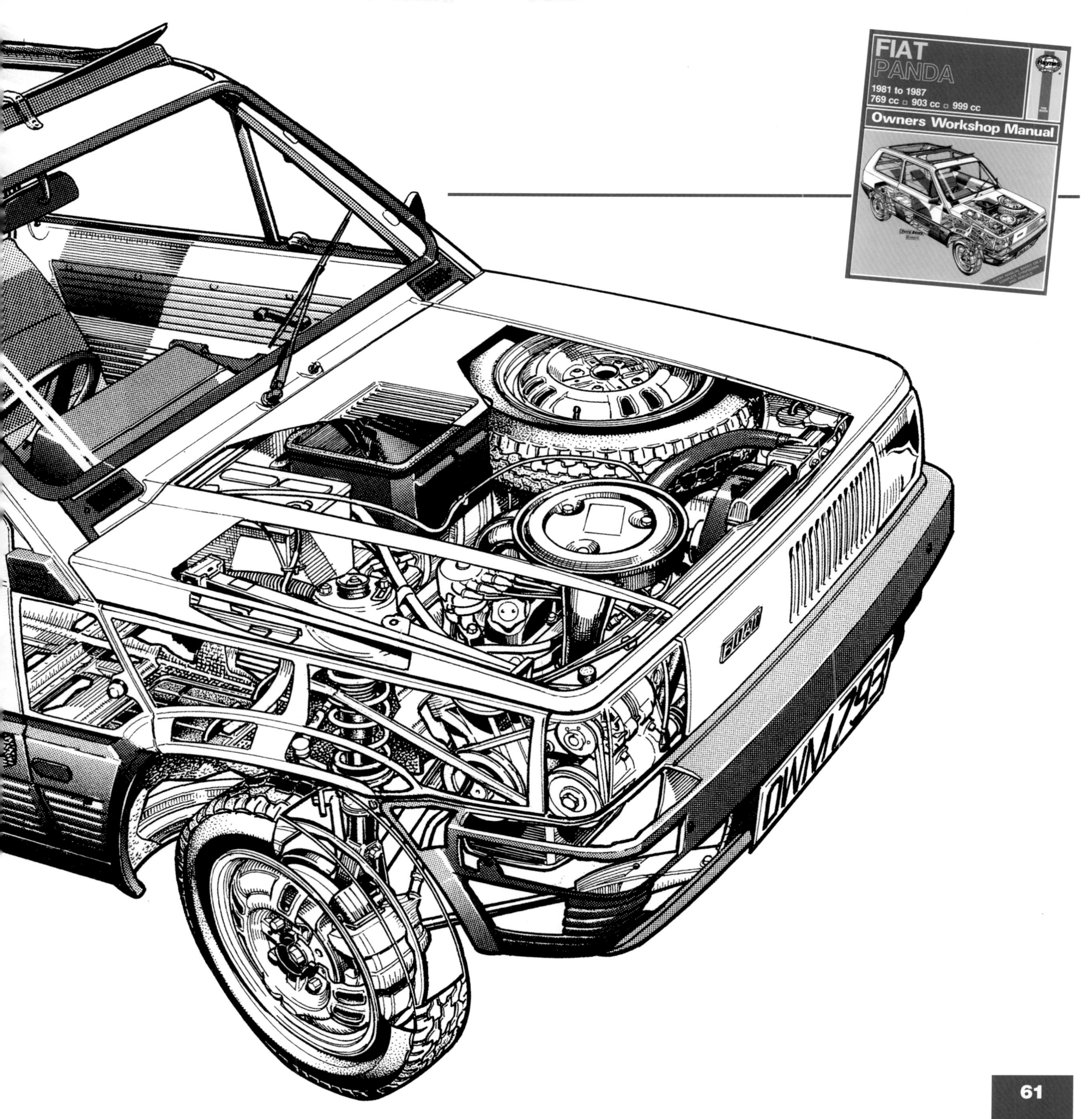
FIAT
PANDA
1981 to 1987
769 cc □ 903 cc □ 999 cc
Owners Workshop Manual
DWM 793

FIAT
131 MIRAFIORI

YEARS MADE
1974–84

NUMBER MADE
1,513,800

ORIGINAL PRICE
£1,619 (1300 in 1975)

MECHANICAL LAYOUT
Front engine, rear-wheel drive

RANGE OF ENGINES
1,297–1,995cc petrol & 1,995–2,445cc diesel, four-cylinder

MOST POWERFUL ENGINE
138bhp (131 Abarth Volumex, 1,995cc)

FASTEST VERSION
112mph (131 Mirafiori Sport, 1,995cc)

BEST FUEL ECONOMY
40mpg (1,995cc diesel)

WHEELBASE
2,490mm

LENGTH
4,260mm

NUMBER OF SEATS
5

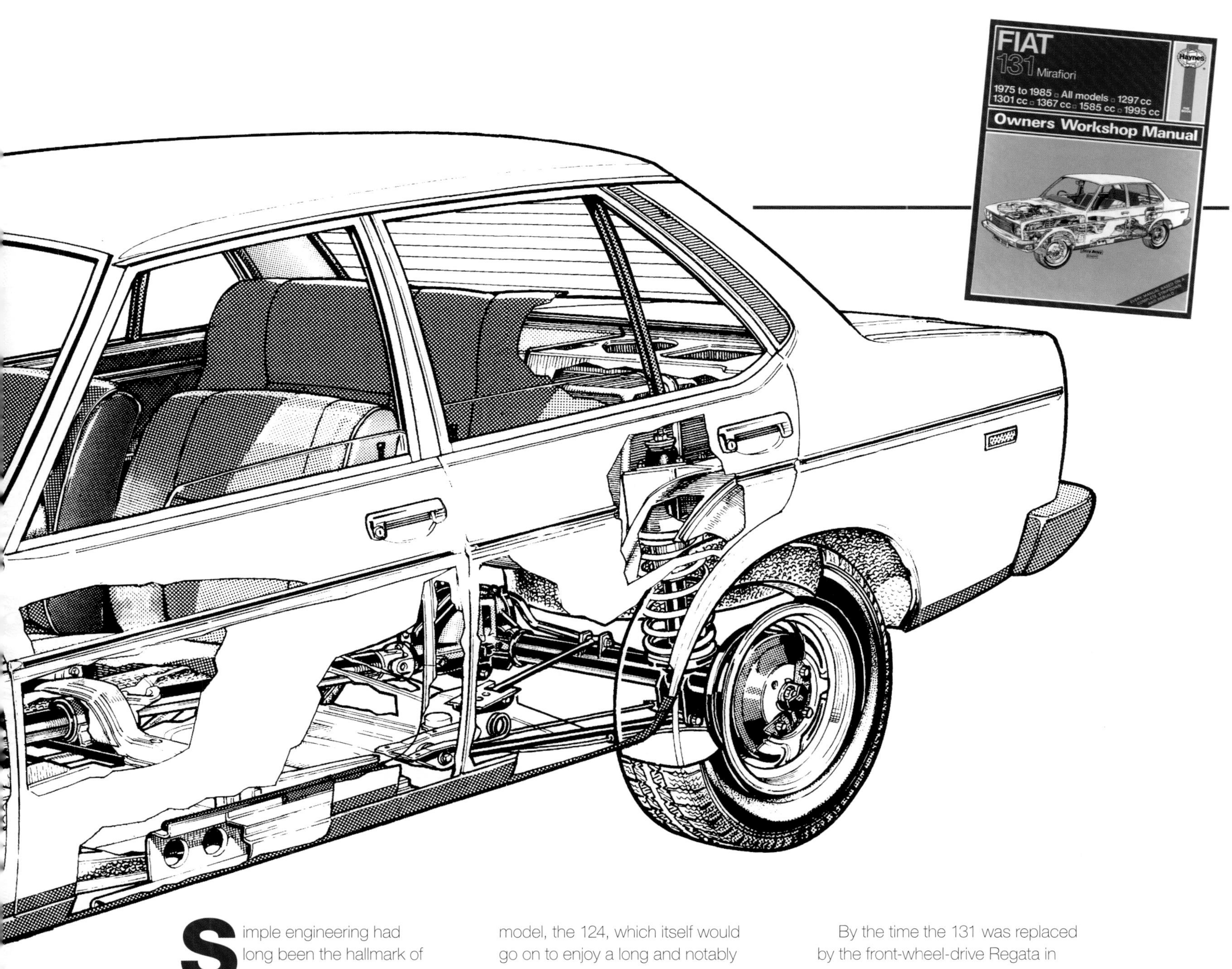

Simple engineering had long been the hallmark of mainstream Fiat family cars. This was typified by the 131 Mirafiori (it was named after the Turin suburb where the factory that made it was situated), which offered a conventional configuration of front engine/rear-wheel drive (with a beam back axle) in a boxy saloon car body.

Launched at the end of 1974 and available in the UK the year after, the 131 replaced a similarly straightforward model, the 124, which itself would go on to enjoy a long and notably popular stint on sale as Russia's Lada – a true testimony to its innate ruggedness.

In 1978 the revised Mirafiori became just that little bit more sparkling, as twin-camshaft engines were introduced. At first there was just a new 1.6-litre twin-cam motor on offer but then came a fiery 2-litre powering the gaudy two-door Mirafiori Sport, a car known as the 131 Racing in Italy.

By the time the 131 was replaced by the front-wheel-drive Regata in 1984 it was a very old-fashioned machine indeed. After all, the class-leading Vauxhall Cavalier had switched to front-wheel drive three years before, so Fiat's British salesmen had a hard job convincing business drivers that a 131 was the car for them. The gutsy estate 2-litre Supermirafiori model, however, had a one-year stay of execution as the reliable load-lugger of the Fiat range.

FORD
PREFECT 100E/107E

YEARS MADE
1953–61

NUMBER MADE
138,708

ORIGINAL PRICE
£560 (100E in 1953)

MECHANICAL LAYOUT
Front engine, rear-wheel drive

RANGE OF ENGINES
997–1,172cc, four-cylinder

MOST POWERFUL ENGINE
39bhp (997cc)

FASTEST VERSION
75mph (997cc)

BEST FUEL ECONOMY
30mpg (1,172cc)

WHEELBASE
2,209mm

LENGTH
3,860mm

NUMBER OF SEATS
4

If you were after typical Ford dependability in compact four-door form during the 1950s then this was the car for you. However, like the bigger Consul and Zephyr models, the Prefect was a modern design with integral monocoque construction and the MacPherson strut front suspension that those bigger Fords had pioneered.

Where the 100E Prefect was a bit dated was in its engine department, where the faithful sidevalve 1,172cc engine held sway. Neither very fuel-efficient nor that lively, this little lump did at least offer technical simplicity and few maintenance headaches. A three-speed gearbox reflected the Prefect's limited aspirations towards vivid acceleration, although the hydraulic brakes were a massive improvement over the feeble mechanical items in the previous 'sit-up-and-beg' Prefect.

The 100E range, of course, also included the two-door Popular and Escort estate. Apart from its four doors, the Prefect was immediately distinguishable from its little brother thanks to its vertical grille bars. Its estate twin the two-door Squire shared the Prefect's convex frontage.

There were major changes in store for the Prefect in 1959. Ford installed the all-new, overhead-valve 997cc engine from the all-new 105E Anglia. Despite its smaller capacity, it transformed the Prefect's performance, which could be fully exploited thanks to an Anglia four-speed gearbox. Known as the 107E series, it survived until 1961 and was sold only in natty two-tone paint schemes.

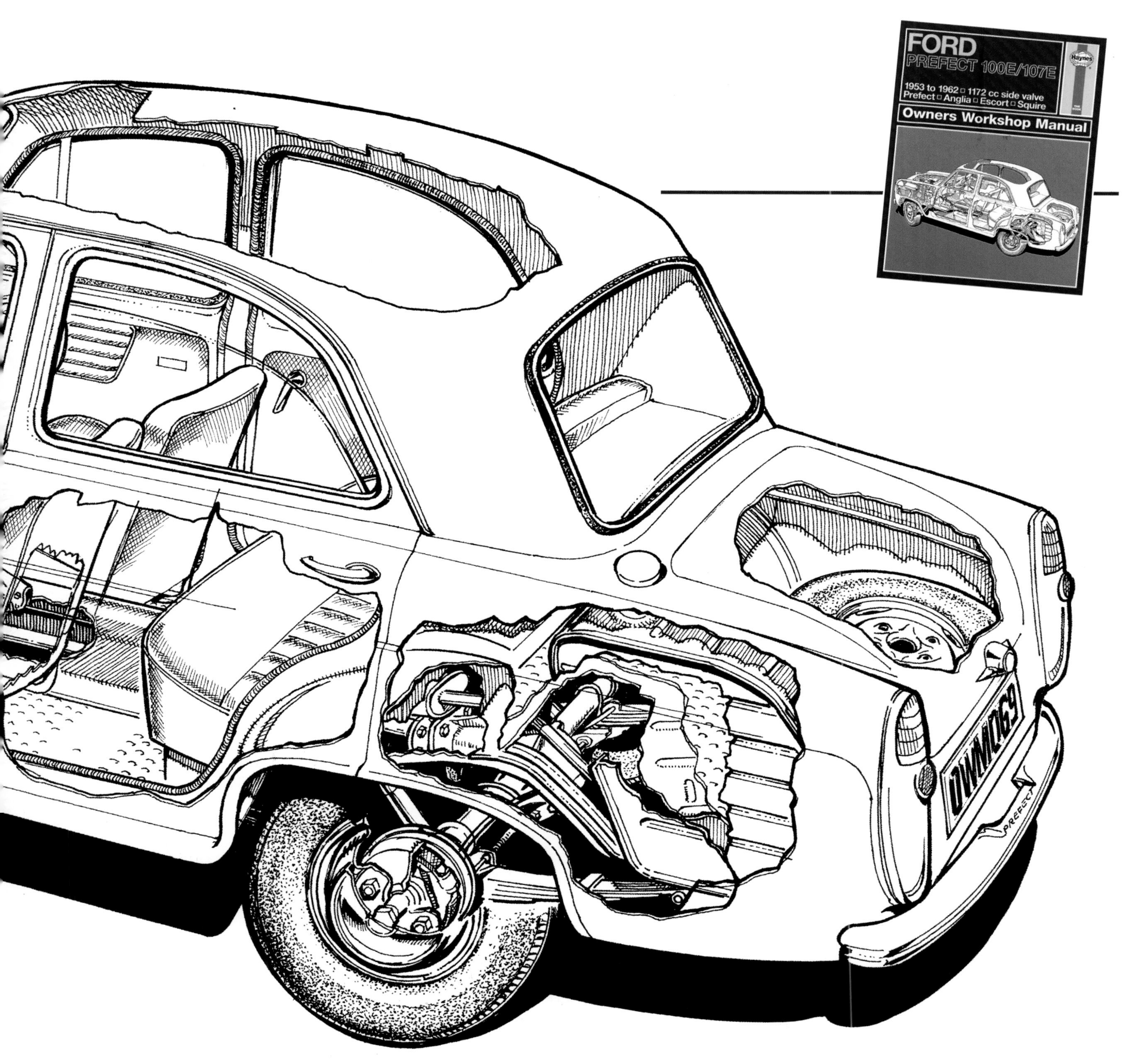
FORD
PREFECT 100E/107E
1953 to 1962 □ 1172 cc side valve
Prefect □ Anglia □ Escort □ Squire
Owners Workshop Manual
Haynes

FORD ANGLIA 105E

YEARS MADE
1959–67

NUMBER MADE
1,083,960

ORIGINAL PRICE
£589 (Anglia standard in 1959)

MECHANICAL LAYOUT
Front engine, rear-wheel drive

RANGE OF ENGINES
997–1,197cc, four-cylinder

MOST POWERFUL ENGINE
48.5bhp (Anglia Super, 1,197cc)

FASTEST VERSION
83mph (Anglia Super, 1,197cc)

BEST FUEL ECONOMY
36mpg (997cc)

WHEELBASE
2,311mm

LENGTH
3,912mm

NUMBER OF SEATS
4

During the 1950s, Ford's Anglia 100E had provided cheap, economical transport to thousands of motorists. Its 1959 replacement, the Anglia 105E, was startlingly different and succeeded in becoming Ford's first million-seller in Britain.

Compared to the tedious old Anglia it replaced, the 105E was astonishingly original. For instance, no one could ignore that angular 'Breezeway' rear window treatment: it was supposed to keep the rear screen clean and offer greater headroom.

Compared to the opposition, the Anglia was some hotshot: a 76mph top speed and 0–60mph in 16.5sec was exceptionally fast for a little saloon. The urgent performance was all thanks to an inspired new overhead-valve engine, the first of the long-running 'Kent' series of which over ten million were eventually made. Although it was compact it had very 'oversquare' dimensions (the bore was almost double the stroke). This allowed tremendous potential for expanding and tuning, and made for a very tough engine.

Another first for Ford was a four-speed gearbox – amazingly, all Ford road cars had had just three forward speeds before then.

Ford offered an enlarged 123E version of the engine in the Anglia Super from 1962, which boasted 13bhp more than the standard Anglia's 53bhp, while the Super spec included chrome flashes, carpets and a heater. There was one other body style for the Anglia, an attractive estate available from 1961.

FORD
ANGLIA
105E & 123E Series: 1959 to 1968
997 cc (61 cu in) □ 1198 cc (73 cu in)
Owners Workshop Manual
OWM 001

FORD
ZODIAC MK3

YEARS MADE
1962–6

NUMBER MADE
77,709

ORIGINAL PRICE
£982 (in 1964)

MECHANICAL LAYOUT
Front engine, rear-wheel drive

RANGE OF ENGINES
2,553cc, six-cylinder

MOST POWERFUL ENGINE
109bhp (2,553cc)

FASTEST VERSION
100mph

BEST FUEL ECONOMY
18mpg

WHEELBASE
2,718mm

LENGTH
4,642mm

NUMBER OF SEATS
5

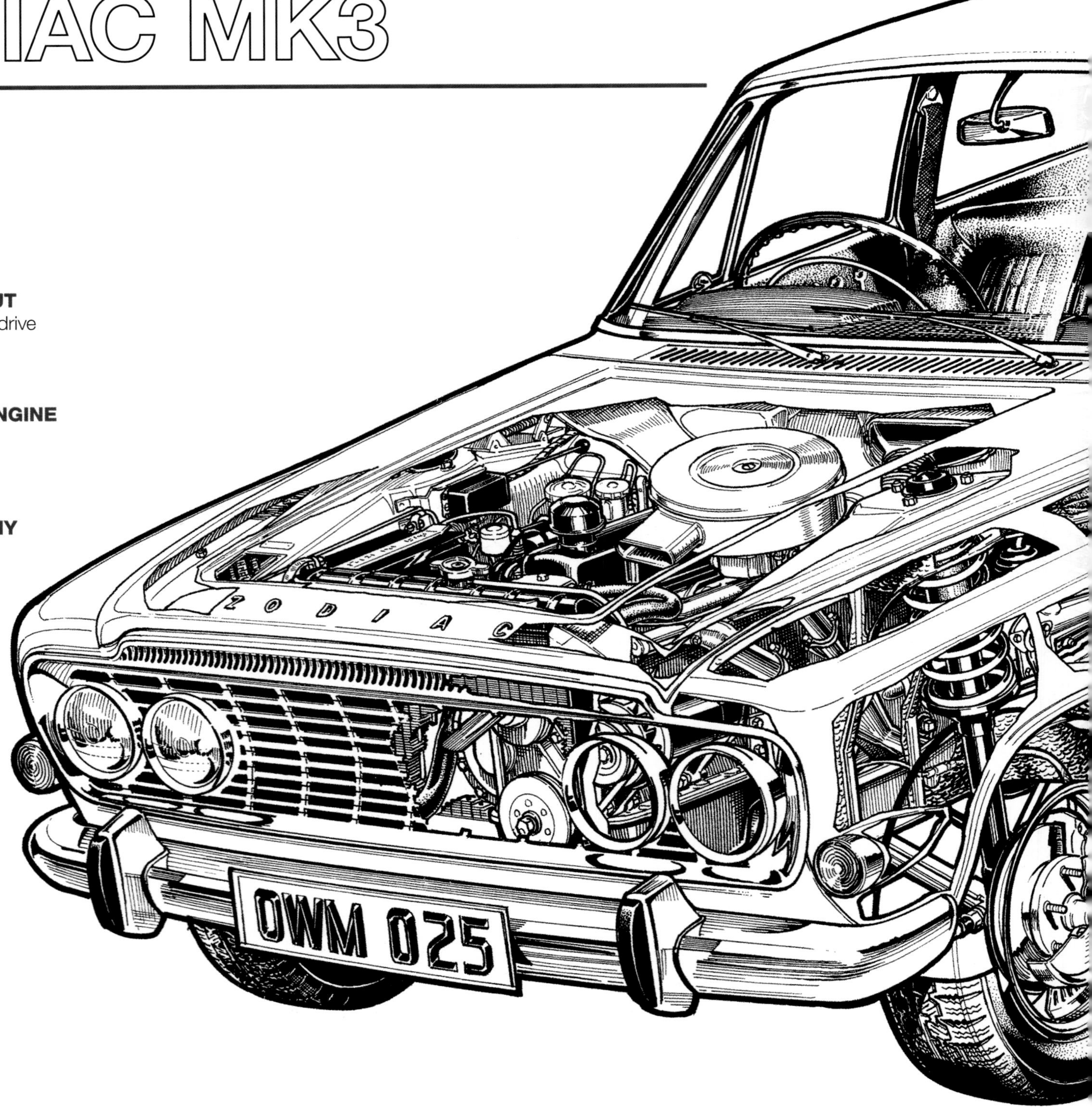

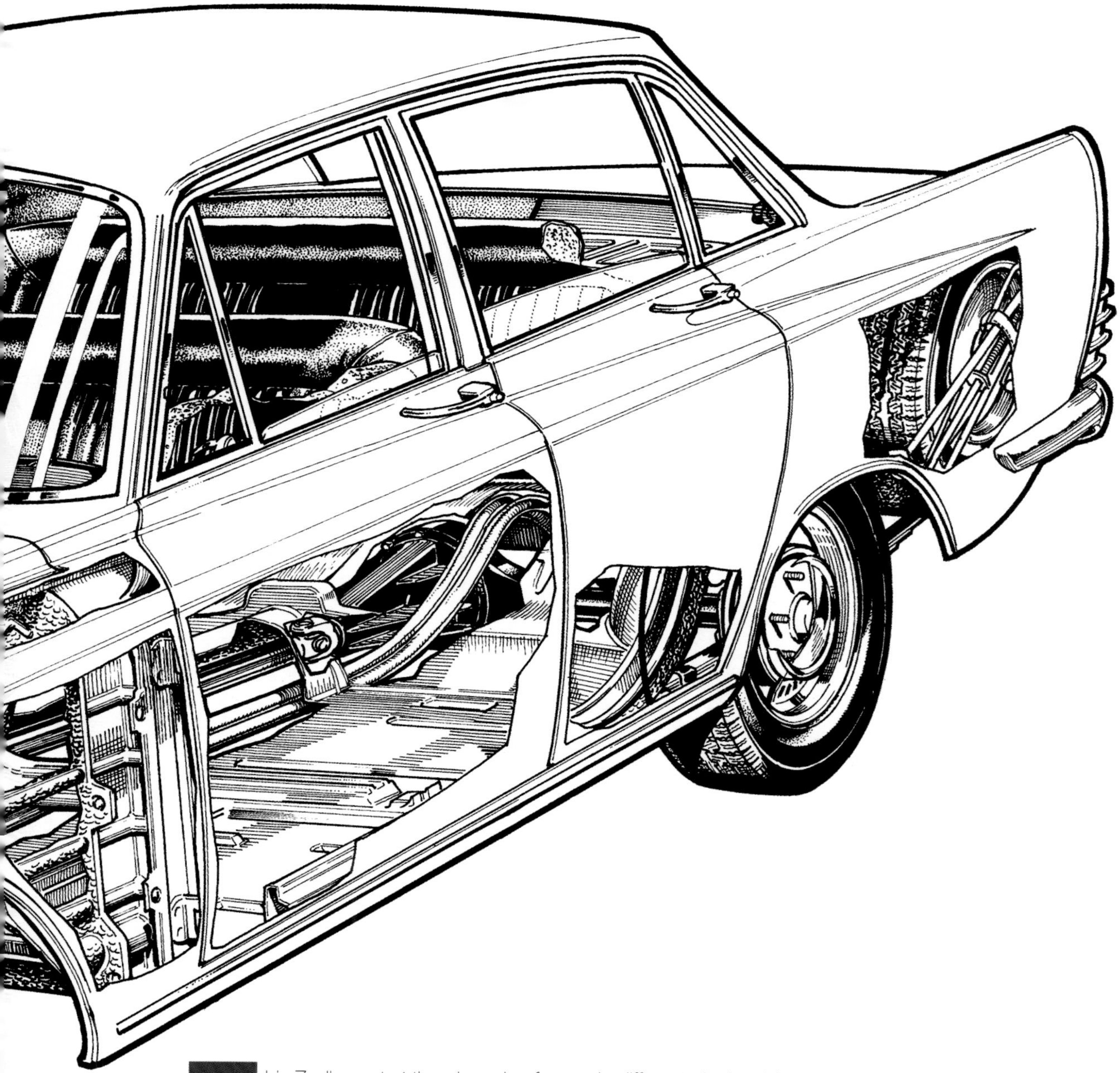

This Zodiac sat at the pinnacle of Ford's British range throughout the early 1960s, a powerful and luxurious businessman's express with, in its befinned styling, more than a hint of early 1960s Detroit. Indeed, the lines were evolved by an American, Roy Brown, who had worked on the first Cortina and also the ill-fated Edsel.

At the heart of the Zodiac was a gruff straight-six engine first encountered in the 1956 Zephyr/Zodiac Mk2 (Zephyrs and Zodiacs were, essentially, the same car in different trim levels) driving the rear wheels through a four-speed gearbox with overdrive, automatic being a popular option.

The Mk3 Zephyr and Zodiac diverged rather more than had been usual for big Fords, the Zodiac having 11bhp more power than the austere Zephyr 6 and a more limousine-like six-light side window arrangement. There was also a very rare Zodiac estate. The company went even further in 1963 with a leather-trimmed Executive edition of the Zodiac that mixed those American looks with appointments to match anything equivalent in size from Daimler or Rover.

Cornering was never a particularly strong suit for these softly-sprung barges, but they still became a firm favourite with motorway police patrols, and on TV Mk3 Zephyrs featured prominently in the gritty Northern police drama *Z-Cars*. The chunky Zodiac, meanwhile, lured ever more British buyers away from the likes of Wolseley and Humber.

FORD ESCORT MK1 MEXICO

YEARS MADE
1970–4

NUMBER MADE
9,382

ORIGINAL PRICE
£1,150 (in 1970)

MECHANICAL LAYOUT
Front engine, rear-wheel drive

RANGE OF ENGINES
1,599cc, four-cylinder

MOST POWERFUL ENGINE
86bhp

FASTEST VERSION
100mph

BEST FUEL ECONOMY
24mpg

WHEELBASE
2,400mm

LENGTH
4,084mm

NUMBER OF SEATS
4

Here's one of the seminal Fords that built the company's reputation for performance and excitement throughout the 1960s and '70s.

Although a two-door sports saloon docile enough for daily commuting, the Mexico was based on Ford's gutsy rally machine, the Escort RS1600, shown here. That one was the ultimate Mk1 Escort, exploiting the design's rear-wheel drive, simple yet supple suspension and rack-and-pinion steering to best competitive effect. It was equipped with a hybrid Ford/Cosworth DBA 16-valve engine used principally in Formula 3 single-seaters, which made the factory rally team virtually unbeatable in the late 1960s and early '70s. One of its most awe-inspiring victories was in the 1970 Mexico World Cup Rally, driven by Hannu Mikkola.

That's how the Mexico got its name, of course, and it also shared the RS1600's sports-biased suspension, stiffened body structure, wider wheels and tyres, purposeful cabin and weight-saving front quarter bumpers.

Unlike the RS1600, it was garish, with bold 'MEXICO' stripes and four-spoke alloy wheels. Yet – and also unlike the rallying icon – it had a sensible engine: the 1.6-litre straight-four Kent first seen in the Cortina Mk2 GT. So owners got hot Escort image and great road manners with a motor that was easy to service on any Sunday morning! Nonetheless, many Mexicos were tuned up and modified for use in amateur motor sport events by hundreds of wannabe Mikkolas…

FORD Escort
MEXICO & RS models
1970 to 1974
1598 cc 1601 cc 1993 cc
Owners Workshop Manual
Haynes
OWM 139
CIBIE

FORD CORTINA MK1 GT

YEARS MADE
1963–6

NUMBER MADE
76,947

ORIGINAL PRICE
£766 (in 1963)

MECHANICAL LAYOUT
Front engine, rear-wheel drive

RANGE OF ENGINES
1,498cc, four-cylinder

MOST POWERFUL ENGINE
83bhp

FASTEST VERSION
95mph

BEST FUEL ECONOMY
26mpg

WHEELBASE
2,489mm

LENGTH
4,274mm

NUMBER OF SEATS
5

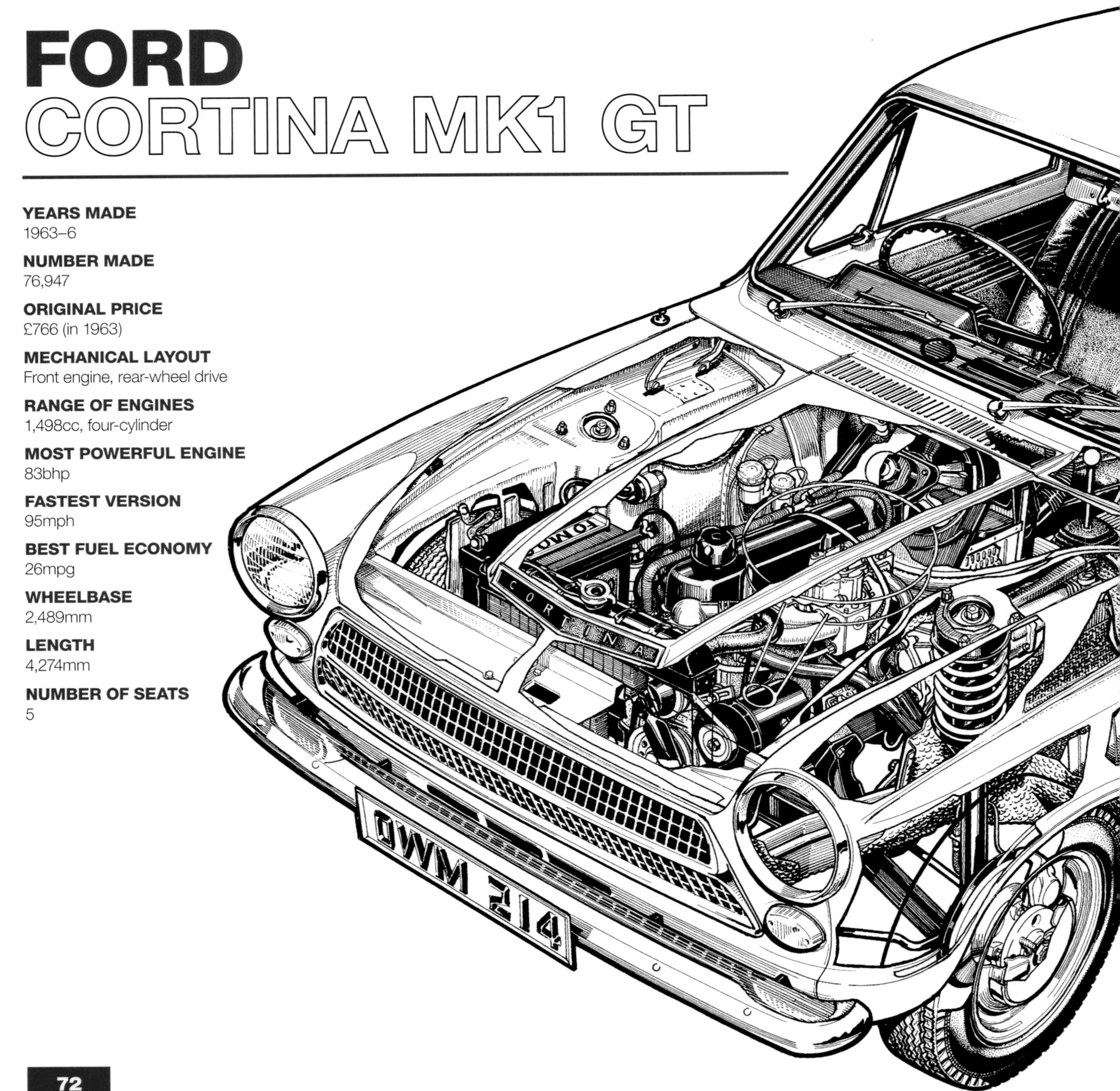

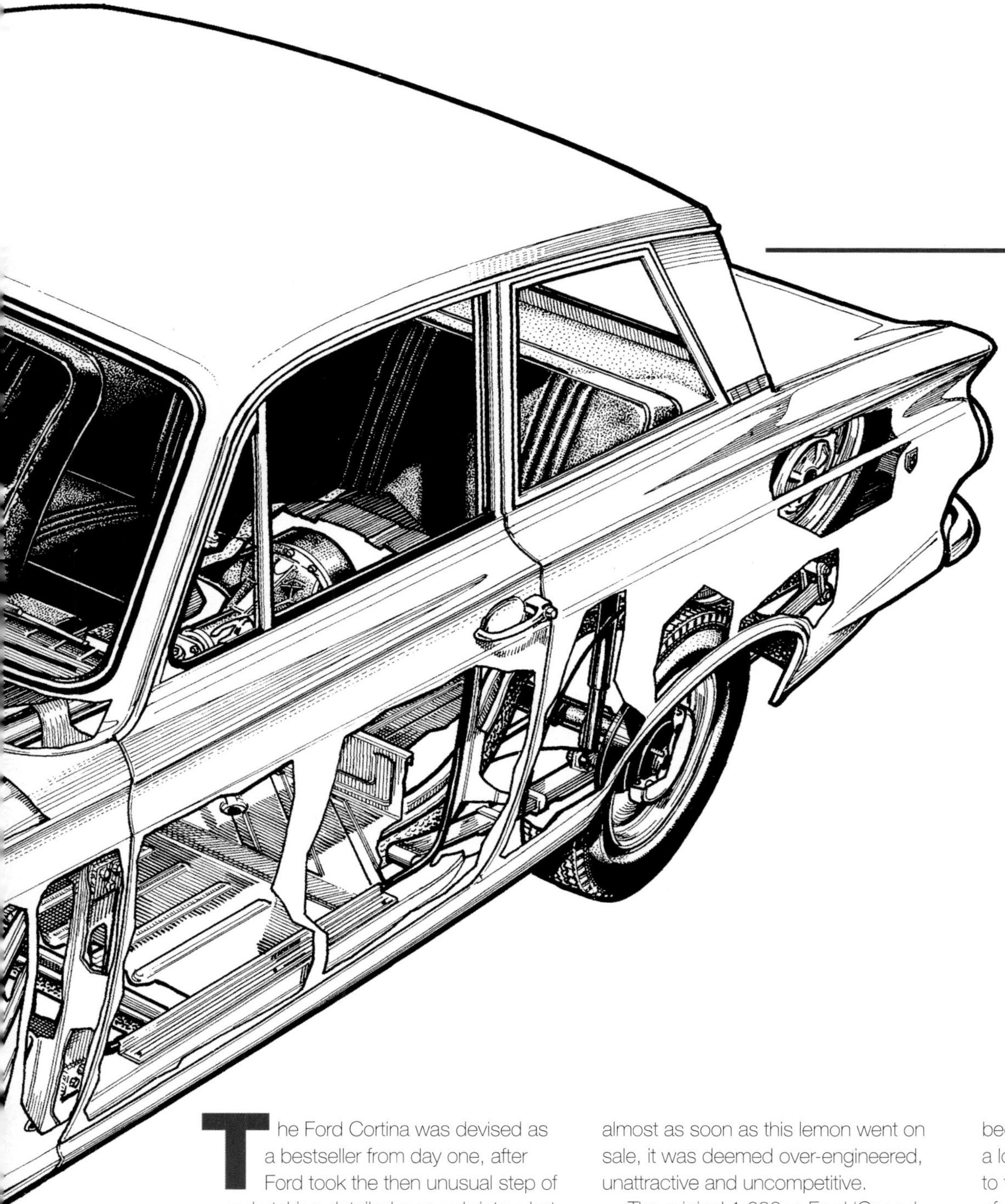

The Ford Cortina was devised as a bestseller from day one, after Ford took the then unusual step of undertaking detailed research into what buyers actually wanted. The answer was a simple, light, economical, roomy and rapid family saloon – the recipe, in fact, for the typical 'company car' of the unfolding motorway age.

Ironically, Ford had already launched a near-identically sized saloon in 1961, just one year before the Cortina hit the showrooms: the Consul Classic. But almost as soon as this lemon went on sale, it was deemed over-engineered, unattractive and uncompetitive.

The original 1,200cc Ford 'Consul Cortina' offered an all-synchromesh four-speed gearbox, just as the Classic had but, once the Super was added in 1963, with a 1,500cc five-bearing engine, the Classic was utterly overshadowed. And the next Cortina debut was the GT.

It was the first time those magical initials, standing for 'Gran Turismo', had been applied to a saloon car rather than a low-slung coupé, and the tag alluded to the car's peppy performance, courtesy of a larger Weber carburettor, tauter suspension for sharper handling, and front disc brakes (added to all Cortinas in 1965) to rein it all in. Surprisingly, automatic transmission was an option.

Although the Mk1 Lotus-Cortina soon grabbed the headlines as the ultimate performance car of the range, the GT still matters as Ford's first souped-up family car.

FORD CORTINA MK3

YEARS MADE
1970–6

NUMBER MADE
1,126,559

ORIGINAL PRICE
£1,338 (2000 GXL in 1971)

MECHANICAL LAYOUT
Front engine, rear-wheel drive

RANGE OF ENGINES
1,297–1,993cc, four-cylinder

MOST POWERFUL ENGINE
98bhp (1,993cc)

FASTEST VERSION
105mph (1,993cc)

BEST FUEL ECONOMY
30mpg (1,297cc)

WHEELBASE
2,184mm

LENGTH
3,760mm

NUMBER OF SEATS
5

If you want to analyse the formula for a bestseller in 1970s Britain then you can do no better than look at the Ford Cortina in Mk3 form. For four years, from 1972 to 1975 inclusive, the Mk3 dominated the new car sales league; and if you were eligible for a company car during this period, then this is invariably what you were issued with.

Ford created an all-new car in the Mk3, with its supple wishbone suspension at the front and coil springs all round to see it safely over Britain's none-too-impressive tarmac. It was mechanically conventional, sticking to rear-wheel drive, and an array of different engines in 1.3-, 1.6- and 2.0-litre sizes was only outdone by a bewildering choice of trim. That started with the sticky plastic interior of the base Cortina and rose to the velour-lined splendour of the top 2000E versions that also boasted a wooden facia, sporty wheels and a contrasting vinyl roof.

The car's swoopy styling reflected trends from Detroit, where designers attempted to add a little voluptuous to otherwise slab-sided saloons. It looked, to be frank, a bit tacky even at the time, but the Cortina's sterling attributes of specification choice, non-nonsense technology, toughness, dependability and – with larger engines, at any rate – gutsy performance kept Ford showrooms buzzing.

FORD
1300 & 1600 ohv
CORTINA III
1970 to 1976 (1300) ▫ 1970 to 1973 (1600)
1298 cc ▫ 1599 cc ▫ Saloon & Estate
Owners Workshop Manual
Haynes

FORD CORSAIR

YEARS MADE
1964–70

NUMBER MADE
331,095

ORIGINAL PRICE
£701 (deluxe four-door in 1963)

MECHANICAL LAYOUT
Front engine, rear-wheel drive

RANGE OF ENGINES
1,498–1,996cc, four-cylinder

MOST POWERFUL ENGINE
106bhp (1,996cc)

FASTEST VERSION
97mph (V4 GT, 1,996cc)

BEST FUEL ECONOMY
29mpg (1,498cc)

WHEELBASE
2,565mm

LENGTH
4,489mm

NUMBER OF SEATS
5

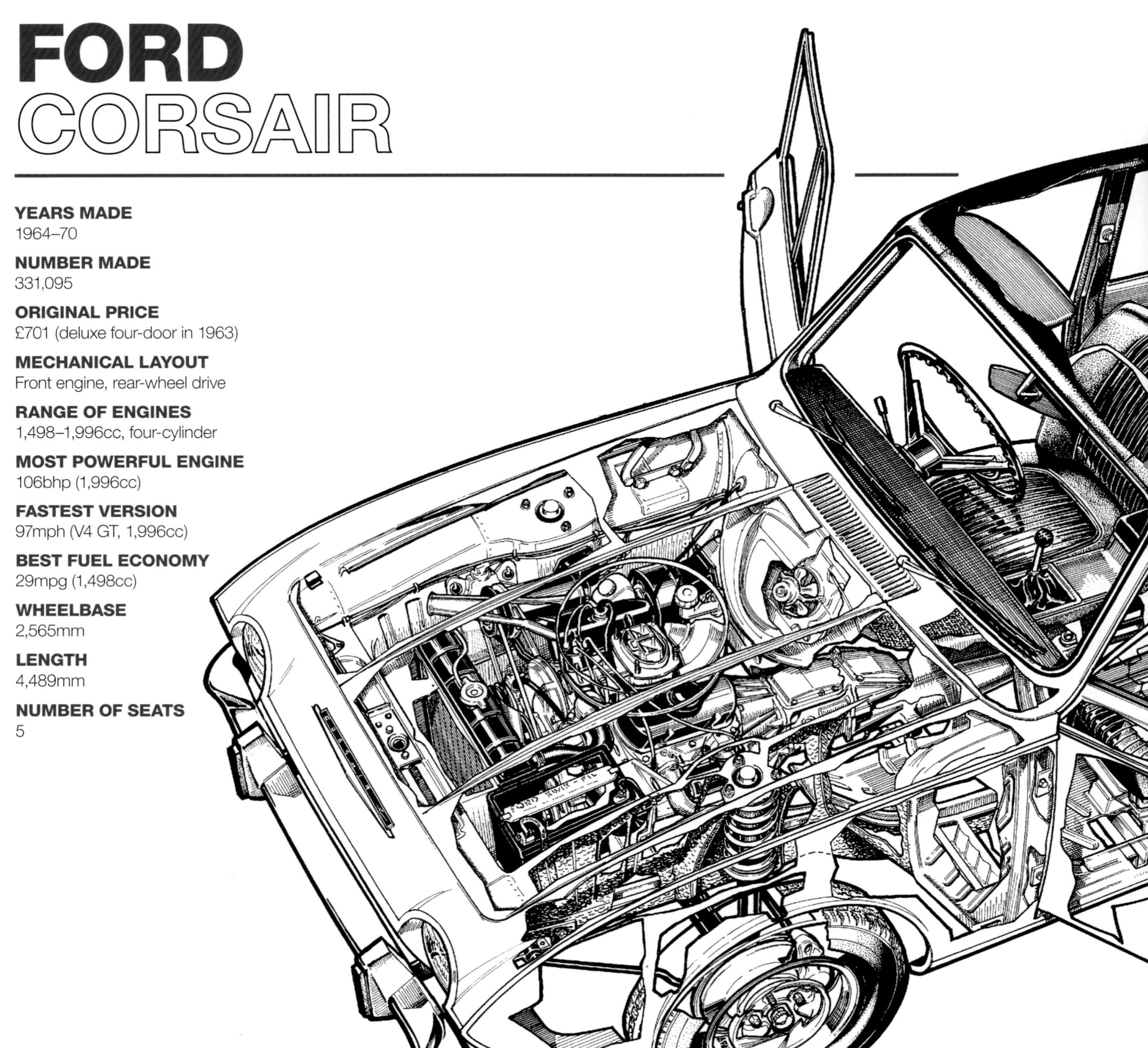

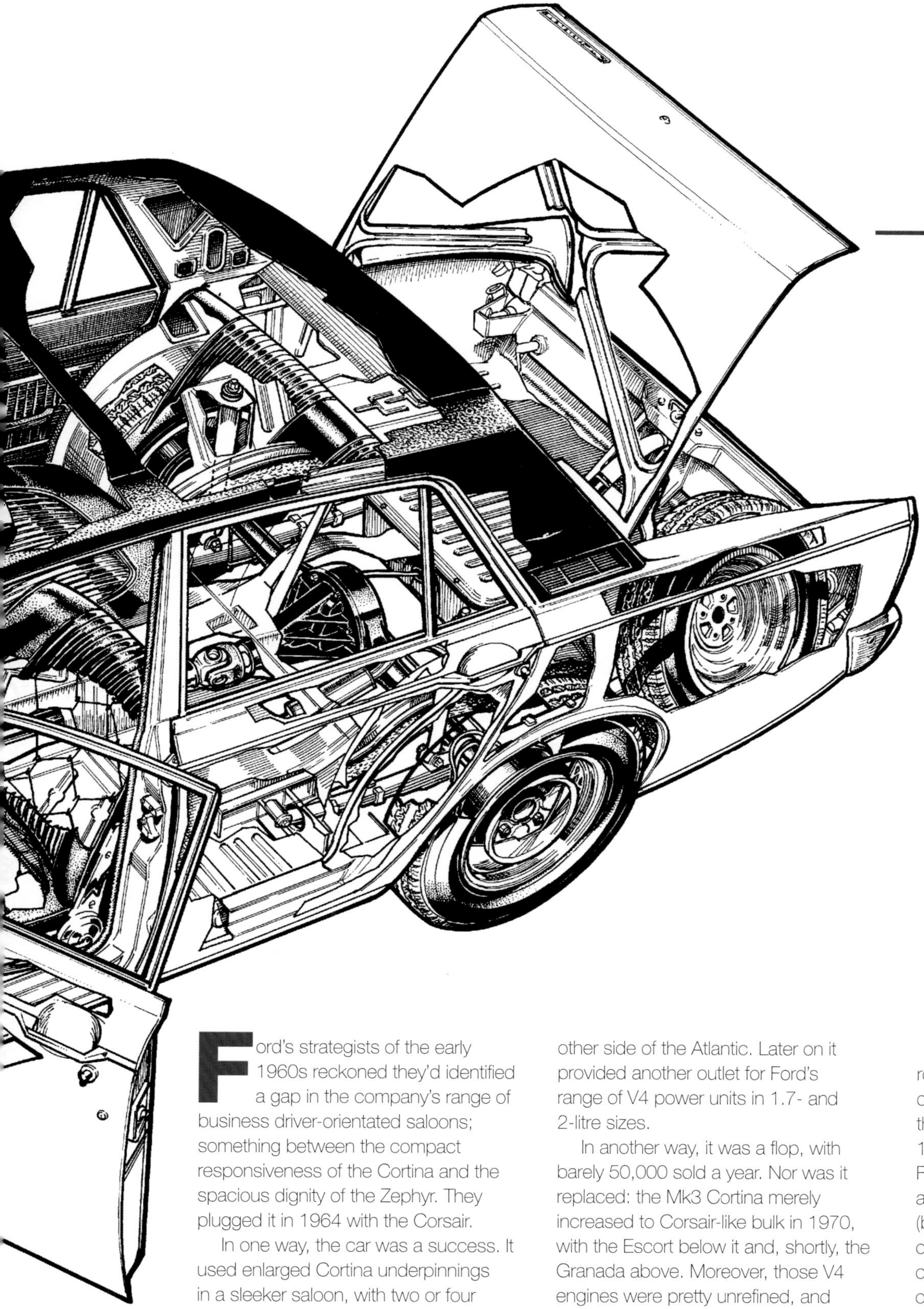

Ford's strategists of the early 1960s reckoned they'd identified a gap in the company's range of business driver-orientated saloons; something between the compact responsiveness of the Cortina and the spacious dignity of the Zephyr. They plugged it in 1964 with the Corsair.

In one way, the car was a success. It used enlarged Cortina underpinnings in a sleeker saloon, with two or four doors, and styling that mimicked the desirable Ford Thunderbird made on the other side of the Atlantic. Later on it provided another outlet for Ford's range of V4 power units in 1.7- and 2-litre sizes.

In another way, it was a flop, with barely 50,000 sold a year. Nor was it replaced: the Mk3 Cortina merely increased to Corsair-like bulk in 1970, with the Escort below it and, shortly, the Granada above. Moreover, those V4 engines were pretty unrefined, and hardly endowed any Corsair with sparkling urge.

Nonetheless, the car was attractive, roomy and well suited to long-distance driving on a mixture of trunk roads and the occasional motorway – the norm in 1960s Britain. In addition to the saloon, Ford-approved conversions were available to turn a Corsair into an estate (by Surrey-based coachbuilder Abbott) or a convertible (by Kent-based coachbuilder Crayford). And it did have one small innovation: the Corsair 2000E was the first British car with a vinyl roof as standard!

FORD
CAPRI MK1 3000

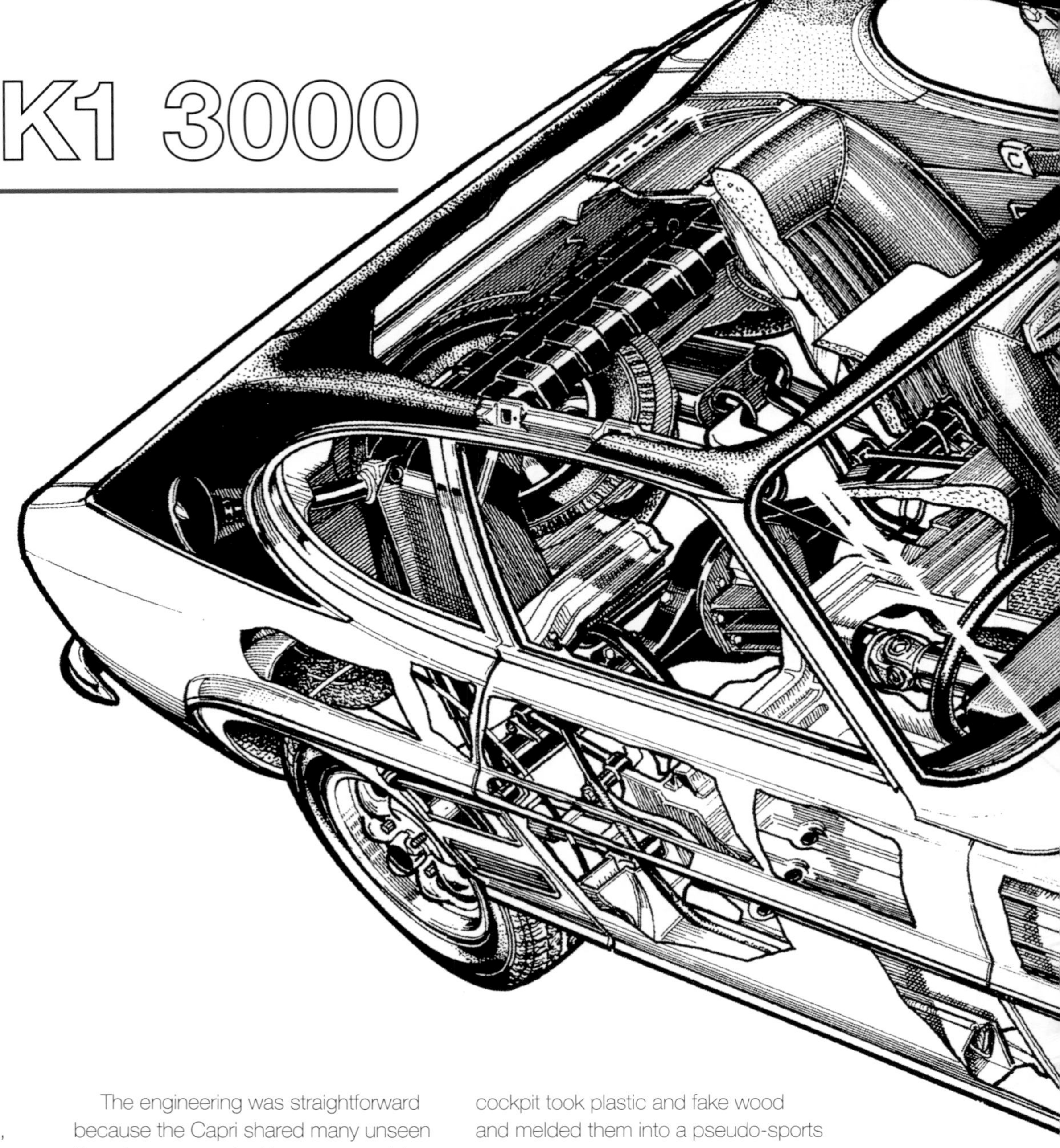

YEARS MADE
1969–74

NUMBER MADE
1,172,900 (all Capri Mk1s)

ORIGINAL PRICE
£1,291 (3000GT in 1969)

MECHANICAL LAYOUT
Front engine, rear-wheel drive

RANGE OF ENGINES
2,994cc, V6-cylinder

MOST POWERFUL ENGINE
128bhp (2,994cc)

FASTEST VERSION
110mph (2,994cc)

BEST FUEL ECONOMY
20mpg (2994cc)

WHEELBASE
2,560mm

LENGTH
4,262mm

NUMBER OF SEATS
4

The Capri wasn't developed on a hunch; it was coldly calculated, its sporty persona precisely cut to the millimetre. And yet from this clinical process a car emerged which the public adored. In 1970, one in every four European Fords sold was a Capri, and the car gave hard-up family motorists (only children, after all, were suited to the cramped rear quarters) a sporty coupé resembling the same cars dominating the contemporary European Touring Car Championships.

The engineering was straightforward because the Capri shared many unseen Escort components. However, provision was made for 2-litre V4 and 3-litre V6 engines never offered in the Escort, so bigger-engined Capris would always be light but powerful. Front disc brakes and rack-and-pinion steering were standard.

The fastback styling was an artful mixture of everyday practicality, a low roofline and groovy touches, including those characteristic fake air intakes just in front of the rear wheelarches. The cockpit took plastic and fake wood and melded them into a pseudo-sports car cocoon.

Retrospectively, much is made by devotees of the 3-litre Capri, as showcased here – a potent and fine-handling car. Yet the typical Capri sold in Britain was actually a 1600 with L, GL or XL trim and a four-speed gearbox, and this couldn't even manage 100mph. The base 1300, a car for the timid or frugal, cost just £890, while even a peppy 2000GT was a mere £1,088.

FORD
2000 & 3000
CAPRI
Mk 1
1969 to 1974
All models 1996 cc V4 2994 cc V6
Owners Workshop Manual
OWM 035

FORD
CAPRI MK2 1600GT

YEARS MADE
1974–7

NUMBER MADE
403,612 (all Capri Mk2s)

ORIGINAL PRICE
£1,633 (in 1974)

MECHANICAL LAYOUT
Front engine, rear-wheel drive

RANGE OF ENGINES
1,593cc, four-cylinder

MOST POWERFUL ENGINE
88bhp (1,593cc)

FASTEST VERSION
105mph (1,593cc)

BEST FUEL ECONOMY
24mpg (1,593cc)

WHEELBASE
2,553mm

LENGTH
4,356mm

NUMBER OF SEATS
4

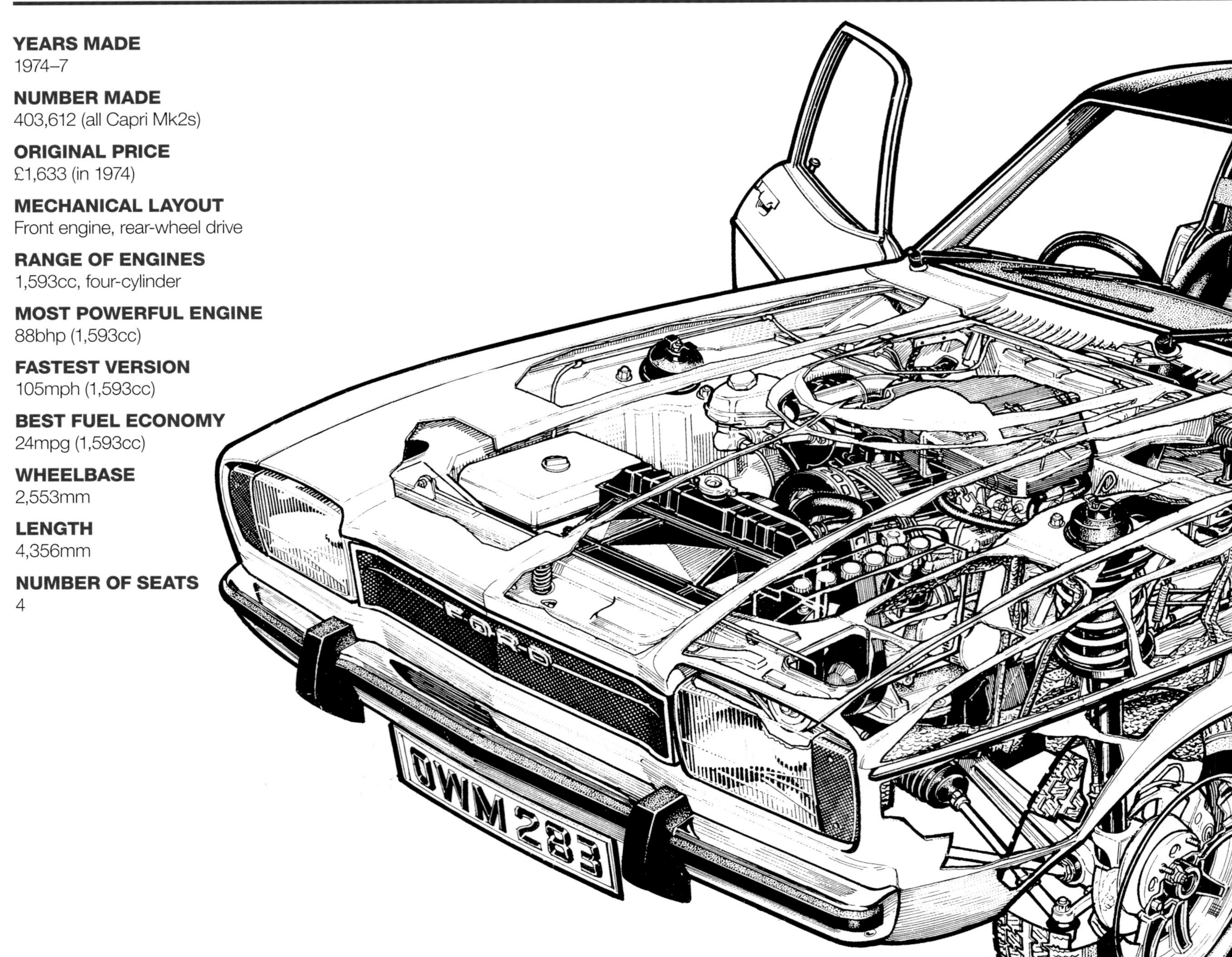

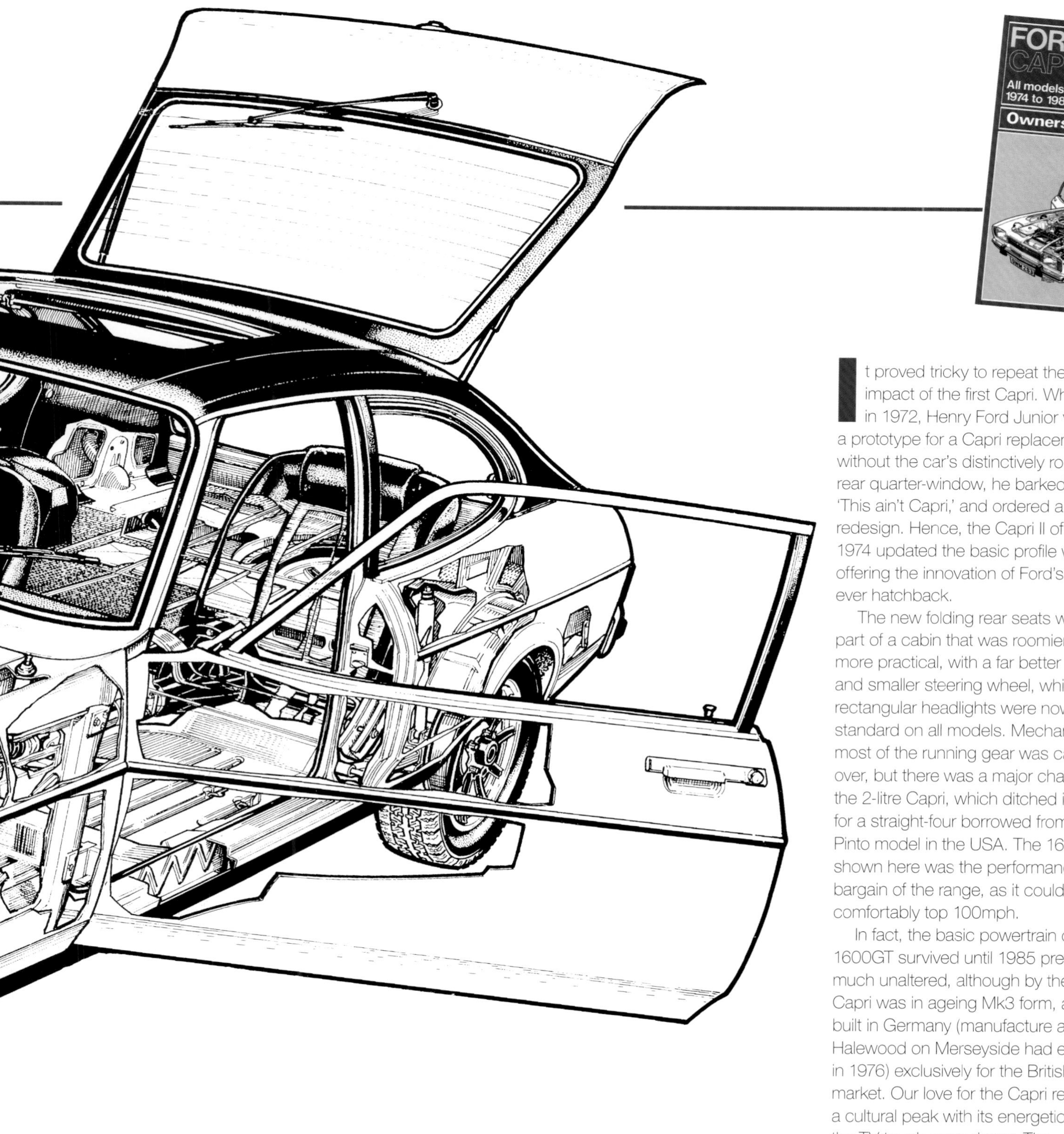

It proved tricky to repeat the impact of the first Capri. When, in 1972, Henry Ford Junior viewed a prototype for a Capri replacement without the car's distinctively rounded rear quarter-window, he barked 'This ain't Capri,' and ordered a redesign. Hence, the Capri II of 1974 updated the basic profile while offering the innovation of Ford's first ever hatchback.

The new folding rear seats were part of a cabin that was roomier and more practical, with a far better dash and smaller steering wheel, while rectangular headlights were now standard on all models. Mechanically, most of the running gear was carried over, but there was a major change for the 2-litre Capri, which ditched its V4 for a straight-four borrowed from the Pinto model in the USA. The 1600GT shown here was the performance bargain of the range, as it could comfortably top 100mph.

In fact, the basic powertrain of the 1600GT survived until 1985 pretty much unaltered, although by then the Capri was in ageing Mk3 form, and built in Germany (manufacture at Halewood on Merseyside had ended in 1976) exclusively for the British market. Our love for the Capri reached a cultural peak with its energetic role in the TV tough guys drama *The Professionals* of the late 1970s, and the final-run, fuel-injected 280i was still well liked by enthusiasts when the last Capri was built on 19 December 1986.

FORD
CONSUL/GRANADA MK1

YEARS MADE
1972–7

NUMBER MADE
846,609

ORIGINAL PRICE
£2,031 (Granada GXL, 2,994cc in 1972)

MECHANICAL LAYOUT
Front engine, rear-wheel drive

RANGE OF ENGINES
1,993–2,994cc, V4-, four- and V6-cylinder

MOST POWERFUL ENGINE
138bhp (2,994cc)

FASTEST VERSION
113mph (Consul GT, 2,994cc)

BEST FUEL ECONOMY
22mpg (1,993cc)

WHEELBASE
2,769mm

LENGTH
4,572–4,673mm

NUMBER OF SEATS
5

This excellent large saloon and estate range had an important job to do for Ford in Europe: its task was to replace the Zephyr/Zodiac in Britain and the Taunus 20M/26M in Germany – two big cars that were losing out to rivals due to their mediocre performance and unattractive looks.

This it certainly did in style. The Consul (with smaller engines) and the Granada (V6 only) offered a totally new structure with all-round independent suspension featuring coil springs and wishbones at the front, plus the slightly surprising reversion to front disc brakes only. The styling, meanwhile, was a skilful blend of chunky, US-inspired lines with European finesse, and the sumptuously trimmed Granada range-topper became the first European Ford to carry the insignia of the Italian Ghia design house.

The delineation between Consul and Granada was scrapped in 1975, when all the cars, including the truly capacious estates, became Granadas. At the same time, Ford took the opportunity to dump the unlovely V4 2-litre engine and replace it with the 1993 Pinto unit.

The Granada was built in both the UK and Germany, but the latter was the sole source of the desirable coupé version. This came in two styles, pre- and post-'75, but only the latter was sold in the UK, and even then only in opulent Ghia-liveried form.

The production total attests to the enormous popularity of these stylish, comfortable and rapid cars.

FORD CONSUL
& GRANADA 2.0, 2.5 & 3.0
1972 to August 1977 ▫ All models
1993cc ▫ 1996cc ▫ 2494cc ▫ 2994cc
Haynes
Owners Workshop Manual
FoMoCo
FORD
H.165

FORD ESCORT MK2 RS MEXICO/2000

YEARS MADE
1975–80

NUMBER MADE
27,080

ORIGINAL PRICE
£2,444 (RS Mexico in 1976)

MECHANICAL LAYOUT
Front engine, rear-wheel drive

RANGE OF ENGINES
1,593–1,993cc, four-cylinder

MOST POWERFUL ENGINE
110bhp (1,993cc)

FASTEST VERSION
109mph (RS 2000, 1,993cc)

BEST FUEL ECONOMY
27mpg (RS Mexico, 1,593cc)

WHEELBASE
2,405mm

LENGTH
3,978–4,150mm

NUMBER OF SEATS
4

In the 1970s, the object of desire for every young blade on Britain's roads was an RS Escort, that user-friendly hot-rod based on Ford's top-seller.

The fiery RS (it stands for Rallye Sport) derivatives of the Mk2 Escort arrived more than a year after the rest of the range, which already included mildly peppery 1300 and 1600 Sport models. The Mexico was similar to Ford's RS1800 Escort rally car, except its engine was an eminently sensible 1.6-litre Pinto unit that provided a useful 10bhp extra over the 1600 Sport. The interior was basic and workmanlike, and there were spoilers front and back.

The car offered excellent performance for most keen drivers but was dropped in 1978, after less than 1,500 had been sold. This was because the RS 2000, its bigger brother with a 2-litre engine and depicted in our illustration, had really grabbed the limelight thanks to an eye-catching and supposedly 16 per cent more aerodynamic plastic nose cone, with four round headlamps and modified front wings and bonnet. As well as its swifter acceleration and higher cruising speeds, it was considerably more luxurious and included touches like bronze-tinted glass and reclining Recaro seats.

With the Mexico deleted, Ford opted to offer the RS 2000 in 'base' and Custom form, the former having such penny-pinchers as steel wheels instead of alloys. In either form, though, this ultimate Mk2 Escort oozed driver appeal.

FORD FIESTA MK1

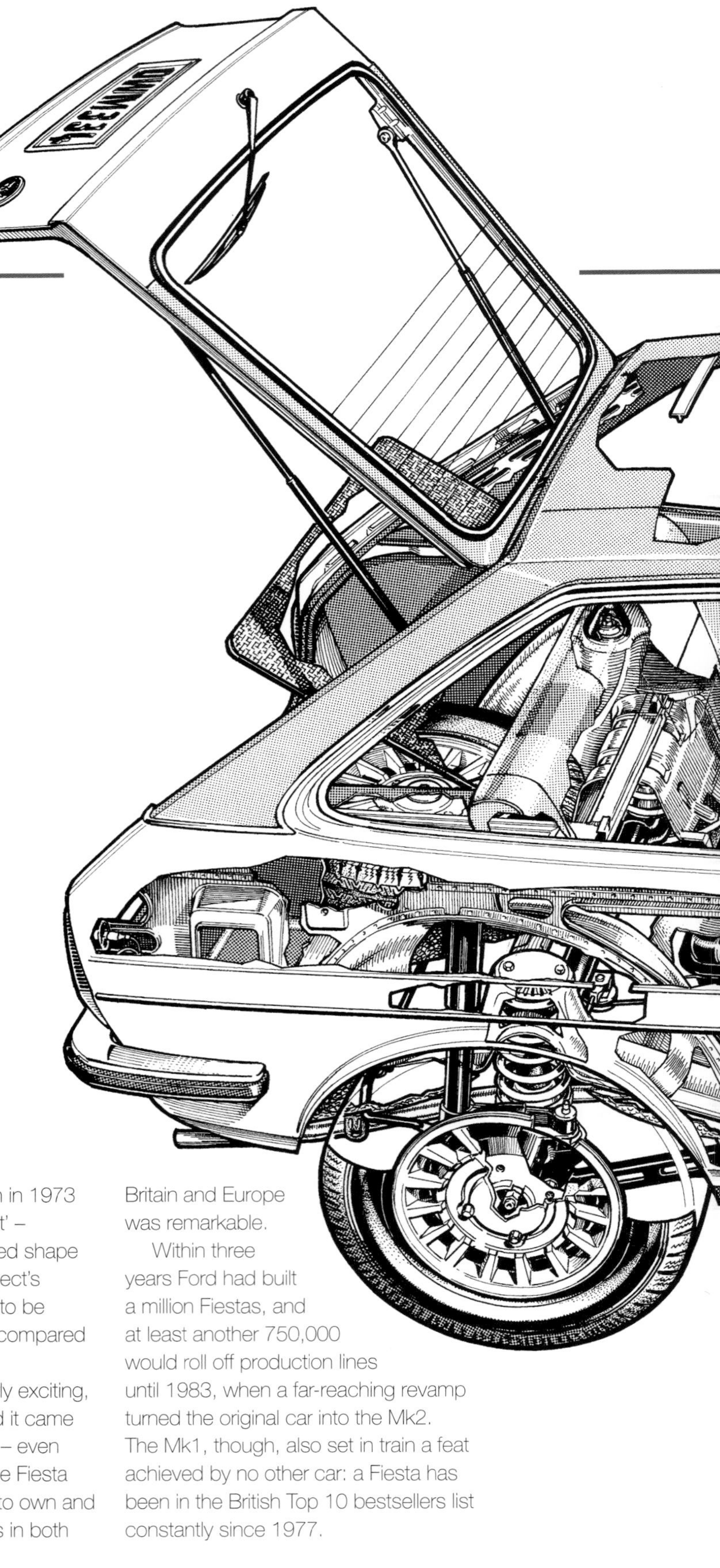

YEARS MADE
1976–83

NUMBER MADE
1,750,000 approx

ORIGINAL PRICE
£1,856 (950 in 1976)

MECHANICAL LAYOUT
Front engine, front-wheel drive

RANGE OF ENGINES
957–1,598cc, four-cylinder

MOST POWERFUL ENGINE
84bhp (1,598cc)

FASTEST VERSION
104mph (XR2, 1,598cc)

BEST FUEL ECONOMY
43mpg (957cc)

WHEELBASE
2,286mm

LENGTH
3,565mm

NUMBER OF SEATS
4

Ford was something of a latecomer to the 'supermini' sector but when it arrived, in 1976 with the first Fiesta, it certainly made a huge impact.

For the American-owned company, it broke new ground on several fronts. Not only was it the first small Ford hatchback in the compact style established by the Renault 5 five years earlier, it was also the company's first front-wheel-drive car with a transverse engine, and also the first manufactured in Spain, in a new, purpose-built plant in Valencia.

Design of the car had begun in 1973 under the codename of 'Bobcat' – signifying both its short, truncated shape and the fact that one of the project's stipulations was that $100 had to be docked from production costs compared to the contemporary Escort!

Its engines weren't particularly exciting, four economical OHV units, and it came only with a four-speed gearbox – even in the early XR2 of 1981. But the Fiesta immediately proved itself good to own and drive. Indeed, the car's success in both Britain and Europe was remarkable.

Within three years Ford had built a million Fiestas, and at least another 750,000 would roll off production lines until 1983, when a far-reaching revamp turned the original car into the Mk2. The Mk1, though, also set in train a feat achieved by no other car: a Fiesta has been in the British Top 10 bestsellers list constantly since 1977.

FORD
FIESTA
Haynes
1976 to 1983 □ All models
957 cc □ 1117 cc □ 1298 cc □ 1598 cc
Owners Workshop Manual

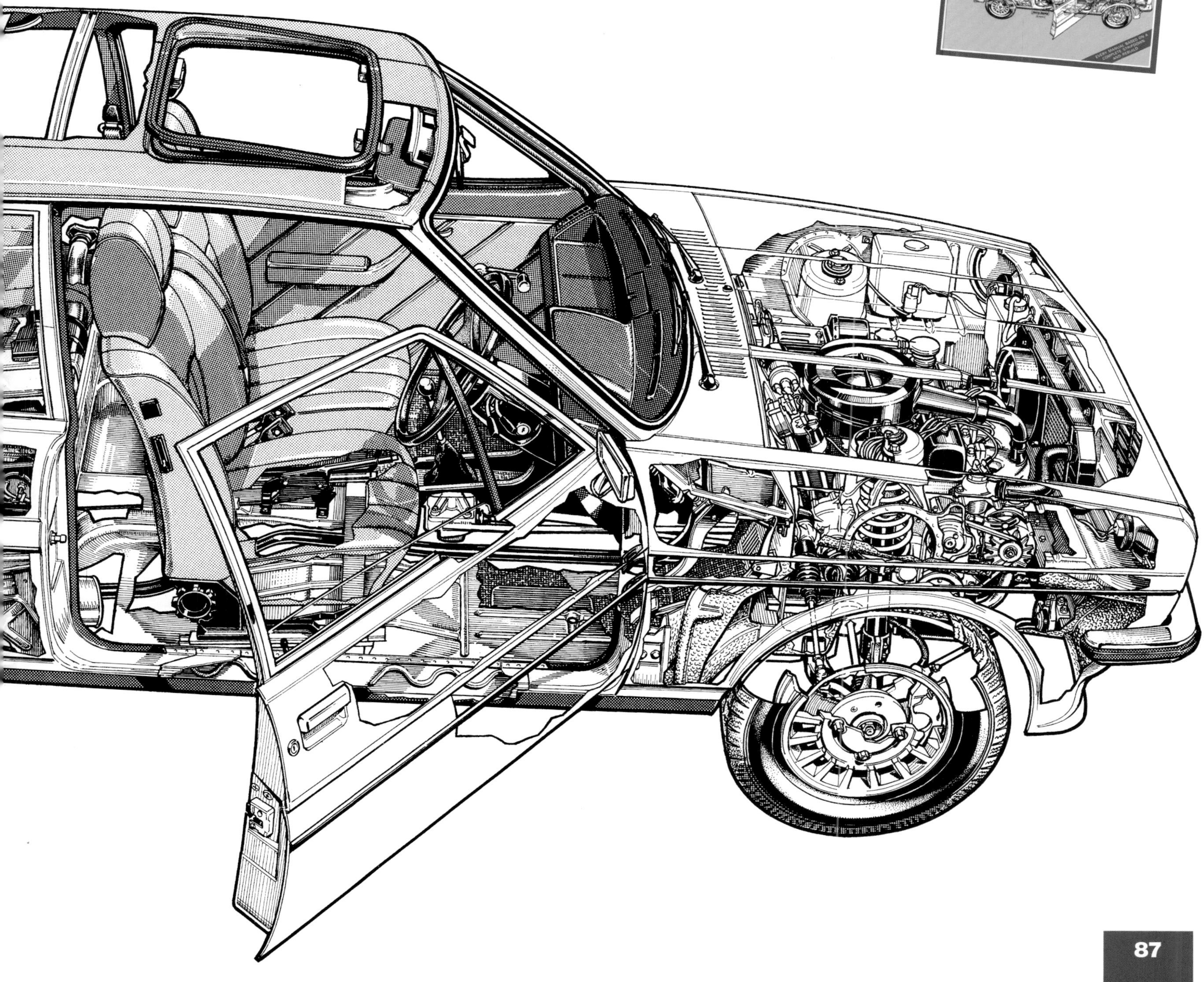

FORD
ESCORT MK3 XR3

YEARS MADE
1981–3

NUMBER MADE
Unknown

ORIGINAL PRICE
£5,123 (in 1980)

MECHANICAL LAYOUT
Front engine, front-wheel drive

RANGE OF ENGINES
1,596cc, four-cylinder

MOST POWERFUL ENGINE
96bhp (1,596cc)

FASTEST VERSION
113mph (1,596cc)

BEST FUEL ECONOMY
32mpg approx (1,596cc)

WHEELBASE
2,398mm

LENGTH
4,059mm

NUMBER OF SEATS
4

While the RS sub-brand had ruled the Ford performance car roost during the 1970s, as the 1980s dawned Ford replaced it with the XR moniker, and the Escort XR3 unveiled in the autumn of 1980 was the standard-bearer.

It was part of an all-new Escort range that transferred drive from the back to the front, and introduced an entirely new range of CVH four-cylinder engines. There would ultimately be seven body variations, including three- and five-door hatchbacks, three- and five-door estates, a van, a cabriolet and the Orion four-door saloon derivative.

The XR3 shared the three-door hatch structure with the humblest Escorts, but was easily distinguishable from them thanks to the stylish cloverleaf-style alloy wheels, rear spoiler and matt-black window surrounds.

Under the bonnet lurked the biggest 1.6-litre CVH unit, equipped with two twin-choke Weber carburettors, which gave a lively 96bhp; enough for the 0–60mph dash to be completed in 9.2sec and a top speed of 113mph.

The car was supposed to take the hot hatch battle to the VW Golf GTi, but, although selling very strongly, against that benchmark it was left slightly wanting. Ford opted to partly remedy this by offering, in late 1982, a five-speed gearbox to replace the four-speeder. But the car really came of age in 1983 when it was replaced by the XR3i. With its fuel injection and tweaked handling, this could at last give the German master a run for its money.

FORD
ESCORT (petrol)
Sept 1980 to 1987 1117 cc 1296 cc
1297 cc 1392 cc 1597 cc
Owners Workshop Manual
1·6

FORD SIERRA

YEARS MADE
1982–93

NUMBER MADE
3,444,229

ORIGINAL PRICE
£4,783 (1300 in 1982)

MECHANICAL LAYOUT
Front engine, rear- and four-wheel drive

RANGE OF ENGINES
1,294–1,998cc petrol and 1,753–2,304cc diesel, four-cylinder, 2,294–2,933cc V6-cylinder

MOST POWERFUL ENGINE
224bhp (Cosworth RS500, 1,993cc)

FASTEST VERSION
149mph (Cosworth RS500, 1,993cc)

BEST FUEL ECONOMY
40mpg (Sapphire 1.6E, 1,593cc, and Turbodiesel, 1,753cc)

WHEELBASE
2,610mm

LENGTH
4,465–4,510mm

NUMBER OF SEATS
5

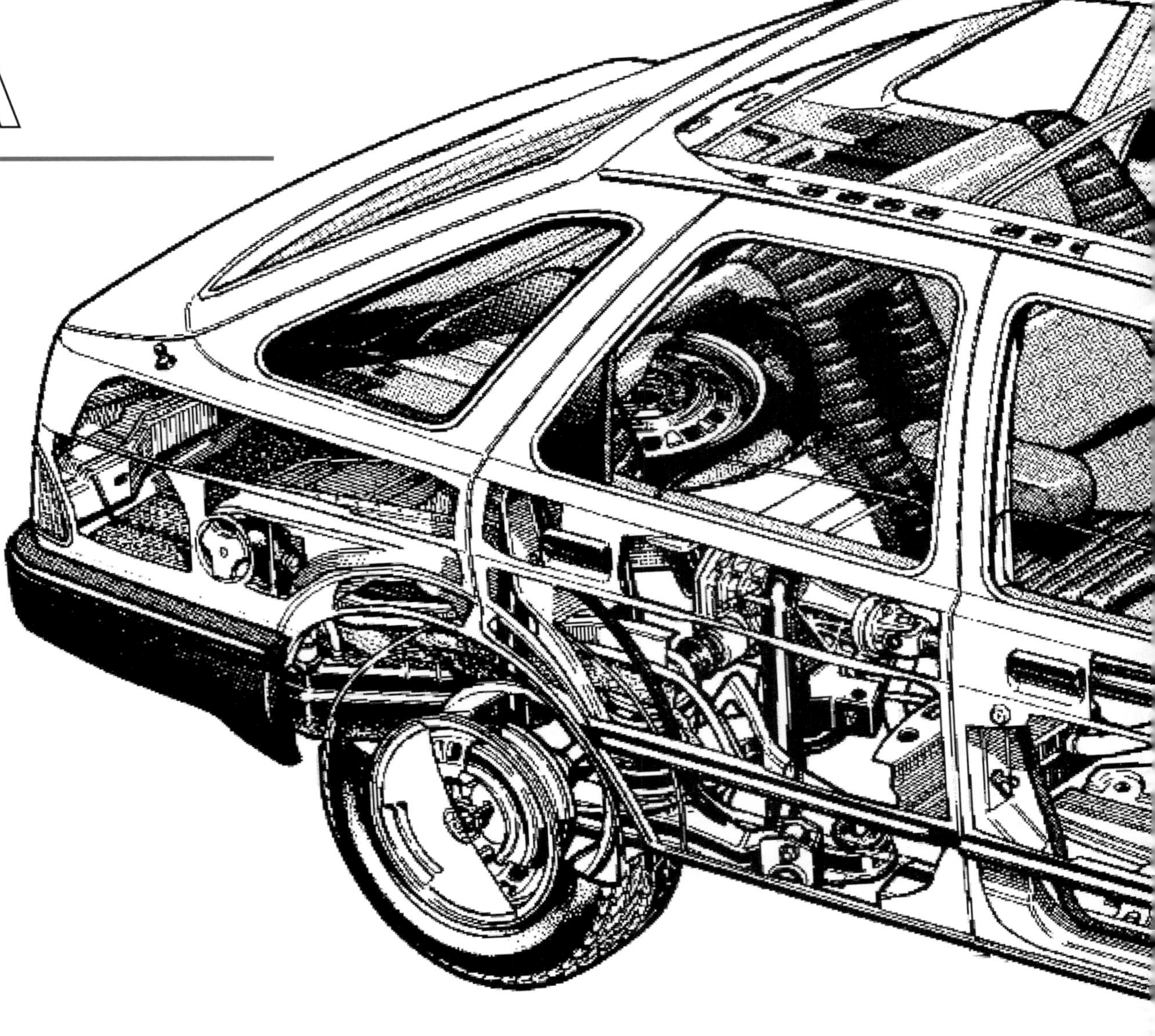

If the shattering performance of the Cosworth RS500 in our data panel leaps out at you, you may be thinking the Sierra was principally an out-and-out racing car.

Yet the Cosworth-engined models, with their turbochargers and, latterly, four-wheel drive, represent but a drop in the Sierra ocean; the same goes for the XR4x4, a four-wheel-drive, V6-engined luxury spin-off. The overwhelming majority of Sierras were 1.6- or 1.8-litre models providing trusty service to business users across Europe, but especially in the UK.

The Sierra caused a storm in 1982, with its curvaceous, wind-cheating shape, large plastic bumpers and ergonomic interior, leading to its derogatory 'jelly mould' nickname. Under the skin, though, the car wasn't so far removed from the boxy Ford Cortina it was replacing.

Although there was a new independent suspension system at the back, the driveline and engine choice was Cortina through and through. At a time when rivals, such as Vauxhall, were switching wholesale to front-wheel drive, this caused just as much controversy as the styling itself.

And yet the Sierra did innovate, as self-levelling suspension featured on the 2.3-litre Ghia estate, and the aforementioned XR4x4 helped popularise all-wheel drive for conventional road cars. As for sporty versions, the initial XR4i, despite its 150bhp, stiffer suspension and bi-plane rear spoiler received a lukewarm reception. On the other hand, those Cosworths made sensational competition (and getaway) cars…

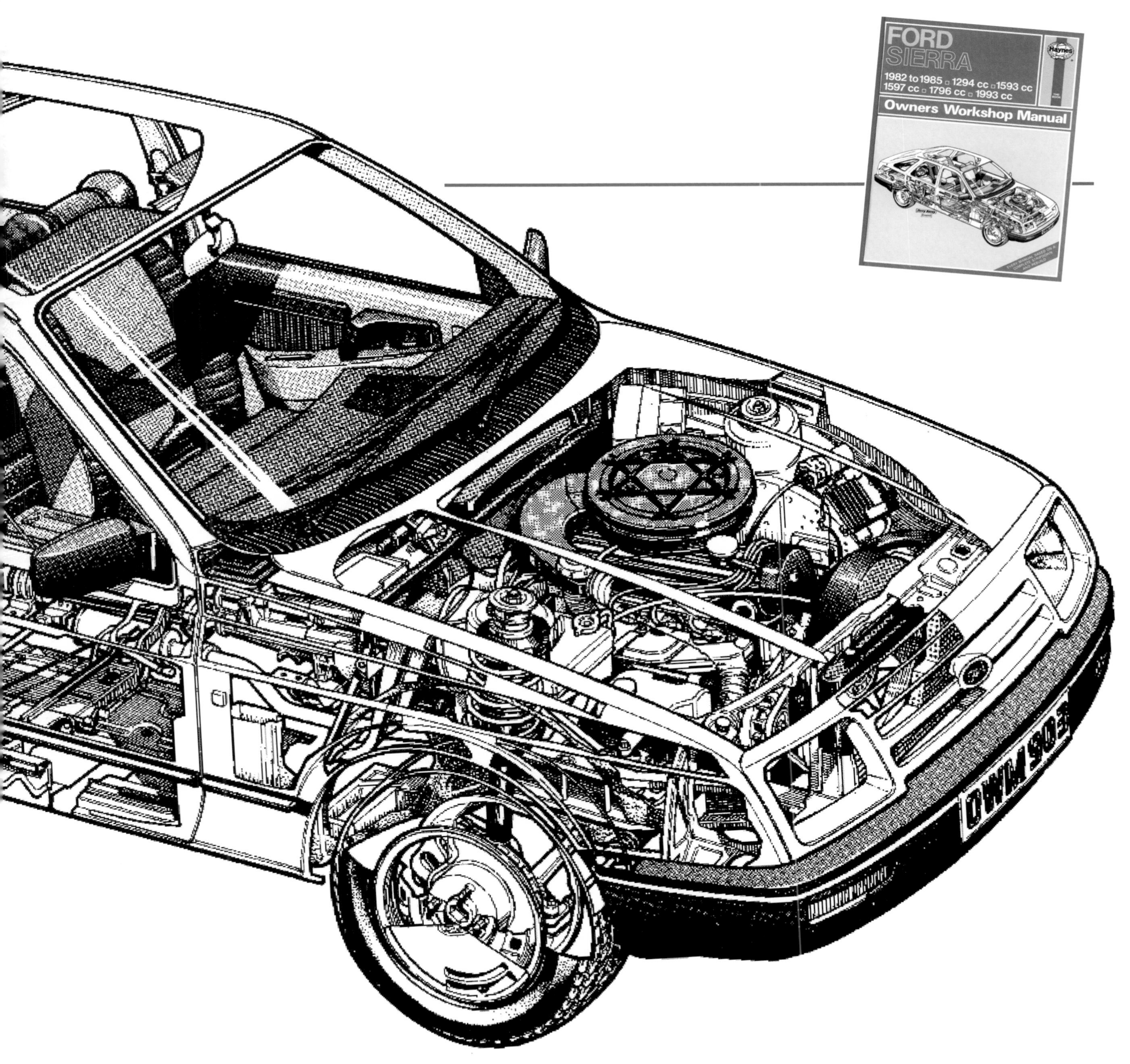
FORD
SIERRA
1982 to 1985 □ 1294 cc □ 1593 cc
1597 cc □ 1796 cc □ 1993 cc
Owners Workshop Manual
Haynes

HILLMAN

YEARS MADE
1963–76

NUMBER MADE
440,032 (all Imp models)

ORIGINAL PRICE
£508 (standard Imp in 1963)

MECHANICAL LAYOUT
Rear engine, rear-wheel drive

RANGE OF ENGINES
875cc, four-cylinder

MOST POWERFUL ENGINE
39bhp (875cc)

FASTEST VERSION
80mph (875cc)

BEST FUEL ECONOMY
40mpg (875cc)

WHEELBASE
2,082mm

LENGTH
3,581mm

NUMBER OF SEATS
5

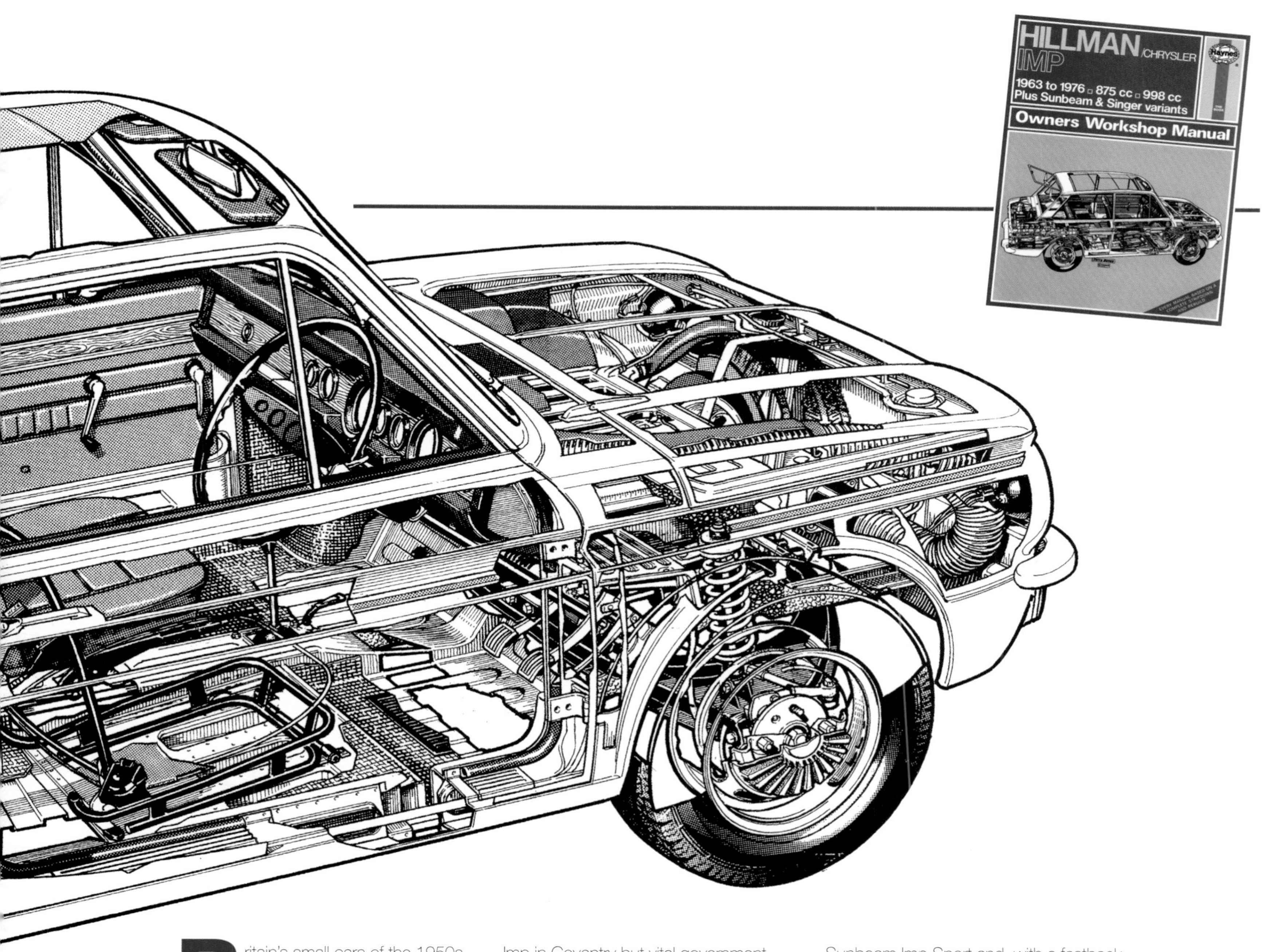

Britain's small cars of the 1950s were uniformly dreary but in 1959 the Mini, Anglia and Herald broke new ground. The Rootes Group was without a rival product for another four years. And when it came in 1963 it, too, was very different. Rootes had shunned the space-saving Mini and instead followed VW, Fiat and Renault by putting the engine in the back of its Hillman Imp.

That certainly allowed decent cabin space but also made for tail-heavy weight distribution. Rootes wanted to build the Imp in Coventry but vital government grants were only available if a new factory was erected in an unemployment black spot. A plant was duly constructed at Linwood, near Glasgow.

Technically, the Hillman Imp was choc-full of interest. The 875cc engine was a light-alloy overhead camshaft unit derived from a Coventry Climax racing engine. That made it nippy and versatile, and tuned Imps were very successful on the track. Rootes offered its own tuned 50bhp engine in versions called the Sunbeam Imp Sport and, with a fastback roof, Sunbeam Stiletto. Other Imp derivatives were the fastback Imp Californian, Commer van, Husky estate and plush Singer Chamois.

Sadly the Imp gained a reputation for unreliability. Its quirky pneumatic throttle was troublesome and was quickly changed; Imps further suffered water leaks, gasket failures and overheating engines. The practical lifting rear window and folding rear seats were some recompense.

HILLMAN AVENGER

YEARS MADE
1970–6

NUMBER MADE
638,631

ORIGINAL PRICE
£850 (1250 Super in 1970)

MECHANICAL LAYOUT
Front engine, rear-wheel drive

RANGE OF ENGINES
1,248–1,598cc, four-cylinder

MOST POWERFUL ENGINE
107bhp (Tiger II, 1,498cc)

FASTEST VERSION
105mph (Tiger II, 1,498cc)

BEST FUEL ECONOMY
28mpg (1,248cc)

WHEELBASE
2,489mm

LENGTH
4,100–4,204mm

NUMBER OF SEATS
5

In 1970, the Hillman Avenger was something that's actually quite rare in the car industry – brand new from nose to tail.

A range of two- and four-door saloons and estates, it was pitched straight at mainstream Escort, Viva and Marina competitors, with rear-wheel drive and newly-developed 1,250 and 1,500cc (uprated to 1,300cc and 1,600cc in 1974) overhead-valve engines. Conventional engineering still produced a tough, simple workhorse, with MacPherson strut front suspension, coil springs at the back and rack-and-pinion steering, and its Americanised styling was neat and modern. It sold well, and deserved to, because it was well executed and pretty much spot-on for the British market – which couldn't always be said of contemporaries like the Austin Allegro and Morris Marina.

The only pulse-raiser was the rare and short-lived 1972–3 Avenger Tiger, with twin carbs, brash boy-racer war paint and tail spoiler.

The Avenger, incredibly, had six personalities over its long production run. In 1976 all Hillmans, Avenger included, were rechristened Chryslers, and in 1980 the car, now looking fairly ancient, was turned into a Talbot. It had been sold in the USA as the Plymouth Cricket and in mainland Europe as a Sunbeam Avenger. And, when UK production stopped in 1981, the car lived on for 11 more years in Argentina, first as the Dodge 1500 and then, due to curious industry moves, as the Volkswagen 1500.

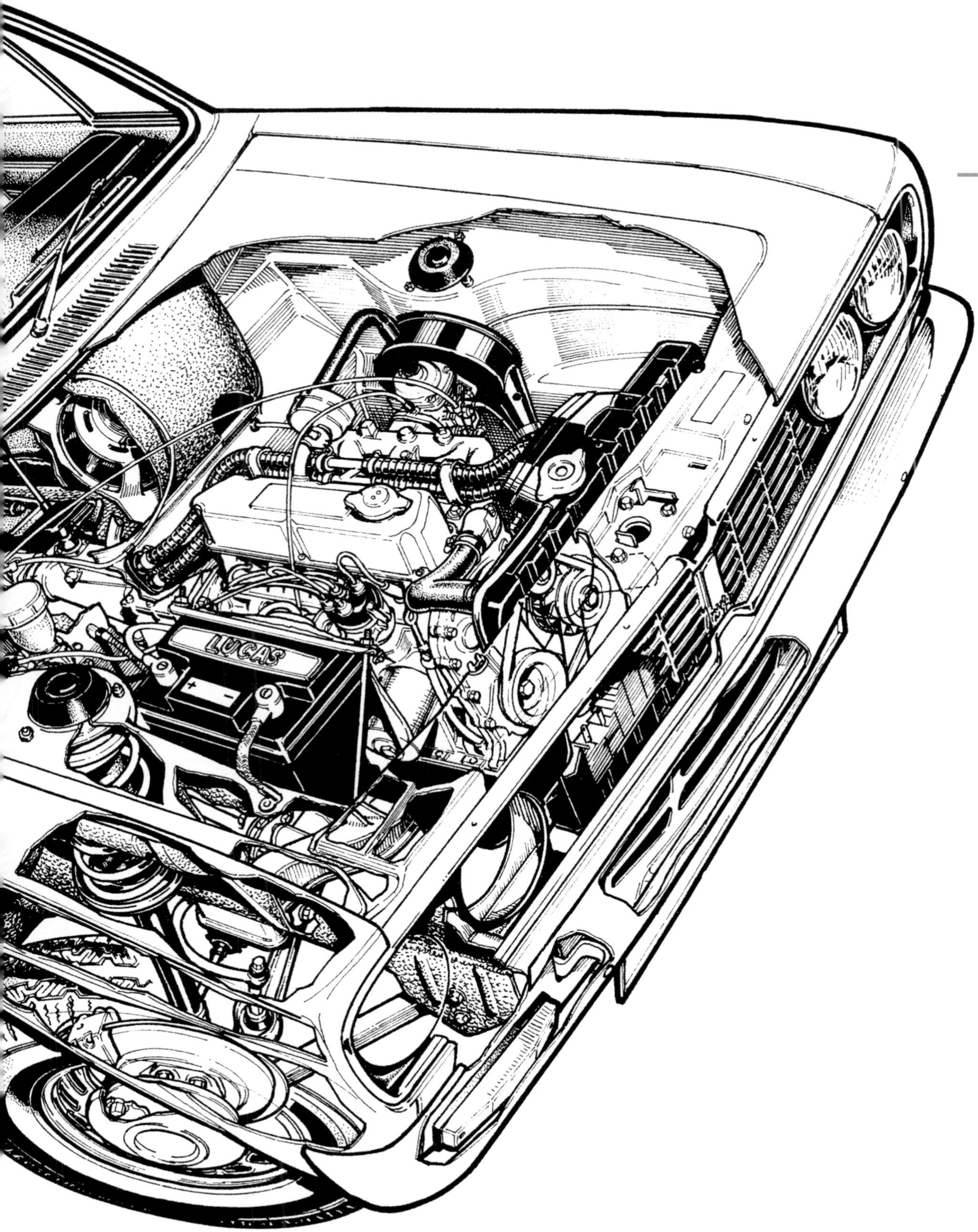

AVENGER
Haynes
Hillman □ Chrysler □ Talbot
1970 to 1982 □ All models
1248 cc □ 1295 cc □ 1498 cc □ 1598 cc
Owners Workshop Manual

HILLMAN HUNTER GLS

YEARS MADE
1972–6

NUMBER MADE
Unknown

ORIGINAL PRICE
£1,320 (in 1972)

MECHANICAL LAYOUT
Front engine, rear-wheel drive

RANGE OF ENGINES
1,725cc, four-cylinder

MOST POWERFUL ENGINE
93bhp (1,725cc)

FASTEST VERSION
105mph (1,725cc)

BEST FUEL ECONOMY
20mpg (1,725cc)

WHEELBASE
2,502mm

LENGTH
4,267mm

NUMBER OF SEATS
5

Here's a truly forgotten performance saloon, made all the more remarkable by the fact that it was a derivative of the Hunter – generally felt to be one of the least charismatic of 1960s/70s family saloons.

In fact, a showy Hunter GT had been available for three years by the time the subtle GLS came along in 1972, which was identifiable from lesser Hunters chiefly by its Rostyle wheels and four round headlamps. But the GLS added a quite highly tuned engine, designed and partly made by racecar engine specialist Holbay. Features like gas-flowed ports and combustion chambers, a high-lift camshaft, superior pistons and a four-branch exhaust manifold – all topped off with twin Weber DCOE 40 carburettors – were usually the talk of the pit lane, yet here it all was in an incongruous saloon.

And the largely unmodified Hunter, despite a tendency to oversteer on wet roads and a crude ride quality, could take the extra power well, offering sparkling acceleration – 0–60mph in 9.7sec, albeit with the live rear axle flailing away merrily under the effort.

Of course, other Hunters were available. Introduced in 1966, the Hunter (and the virtually identical, but lower-spec, Minx) was a credible Cortina alternative that spent 13 years on British sale, latterly as a Chrysler, and then famously put Iran on wheels as the Teheran-built Peykan. But the GLS offered the most sparkle, by a long chalk.

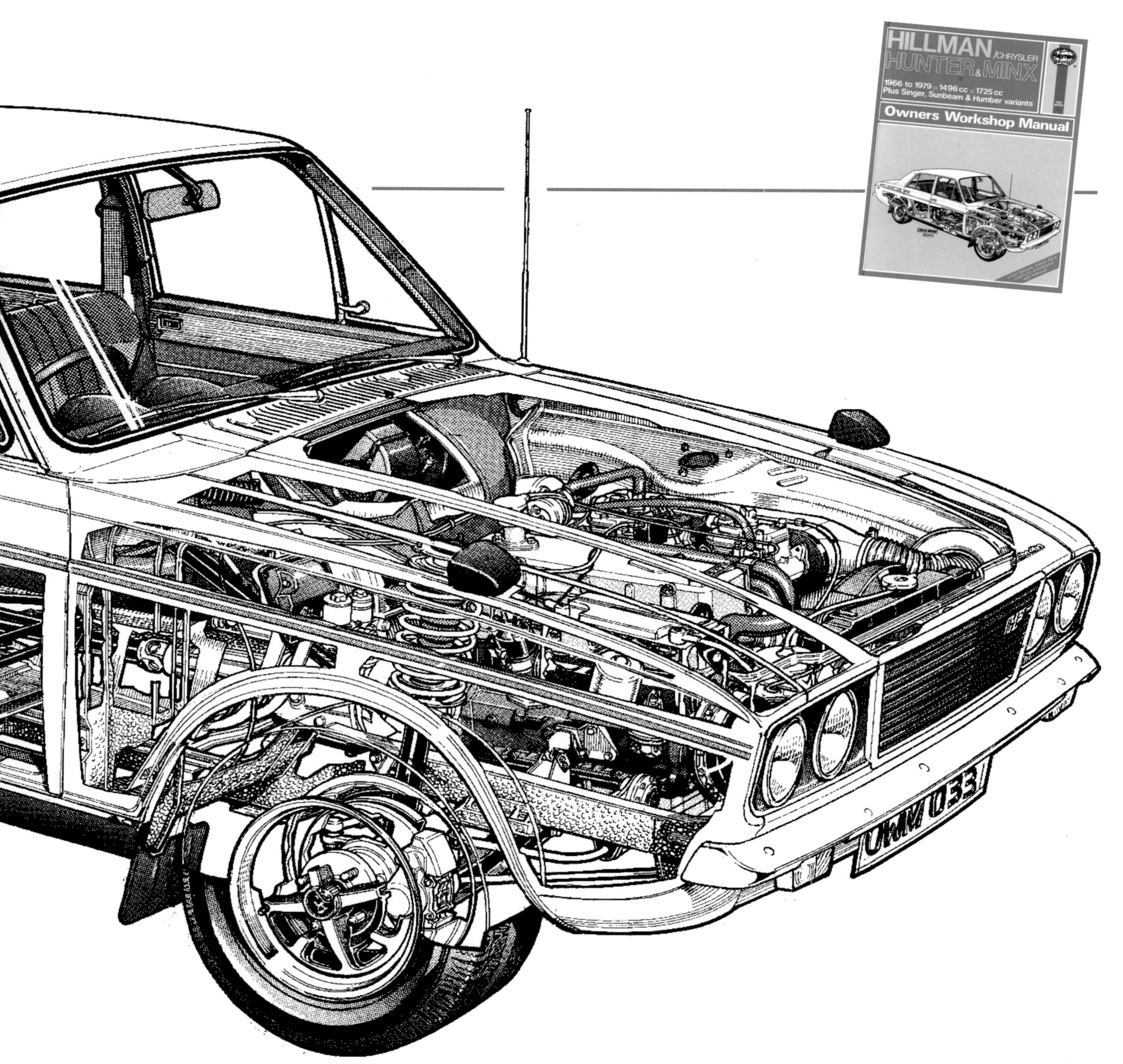
HILLMAN /CHRYSLER
HUNTER & MINX
1966 to 1979 □ 1496 cc □ 1725 cc
Plus Singer, Sunbeam & Humber variants
Owners Workshop Manual

HONDA N600

YEARS MADE
1967–73

NUMBER MADE
1,165,441 (all N-cars)

ORIGINAL PRICE
£589 (in 1968)

MECHANICAL LAYOUT
Front engine, front-wheel drive

RANGE OF ENGINES
599cc, four-cylinder

MOST POWERFUL ENGINE
45bhp (599cc)

FASTEST VERSION
72mph (599cc)

BEST FUEL ECONOMY
36mpg (599cc)

WHEELBASE
2,000mm

LENGTH
3,100mm

NUMBER OF SEATS
4

It's surprising to recall that the first Honda car to go on sale in the UK was the S800 sports car in 1967. However, far more successful, in volume terms, were the tiny N360 and N600, two cramped and raucous city cars that made their UK debut in 1968.

Bearing an uncanny resemblance to the evergreen Issigonis Mini shape, they also shared the British car's front-wheel drive and transverse engine position. From there, however, the similarity stopped, because these Japanese babies featured air-cooled, four-stroke, twin-cylinder powerpacks, mated to either a four-speed manual or three-speed automatic transmission.

Of course, it was never going to be easy to sell the cars to a nation of Mini lovers but, nonetheless, 1,145 of the little N360s were snapped up from 1968 to 1970, and 7,860 N600s between '69 and '74. N400 and N500 versions – all names referring to engine size in cc – were for other markets.

The 599cc air-cooled twin, a single-overhead camshaft unit, was also used in an intriguing coupé, the Z600 – based entirely on 'N' mechanical parts – which was also a hit with British buyers, despite being sold only in bright orange with a broad black stripe and an all-black interior. A total of 2,502 went to fun-loving UK buyers in three years of sales, including DJ Dave Lee Travis. These small cars helped to set the stage for the phenomenal success Honda was to enjoy from the mid-1970s onwards.

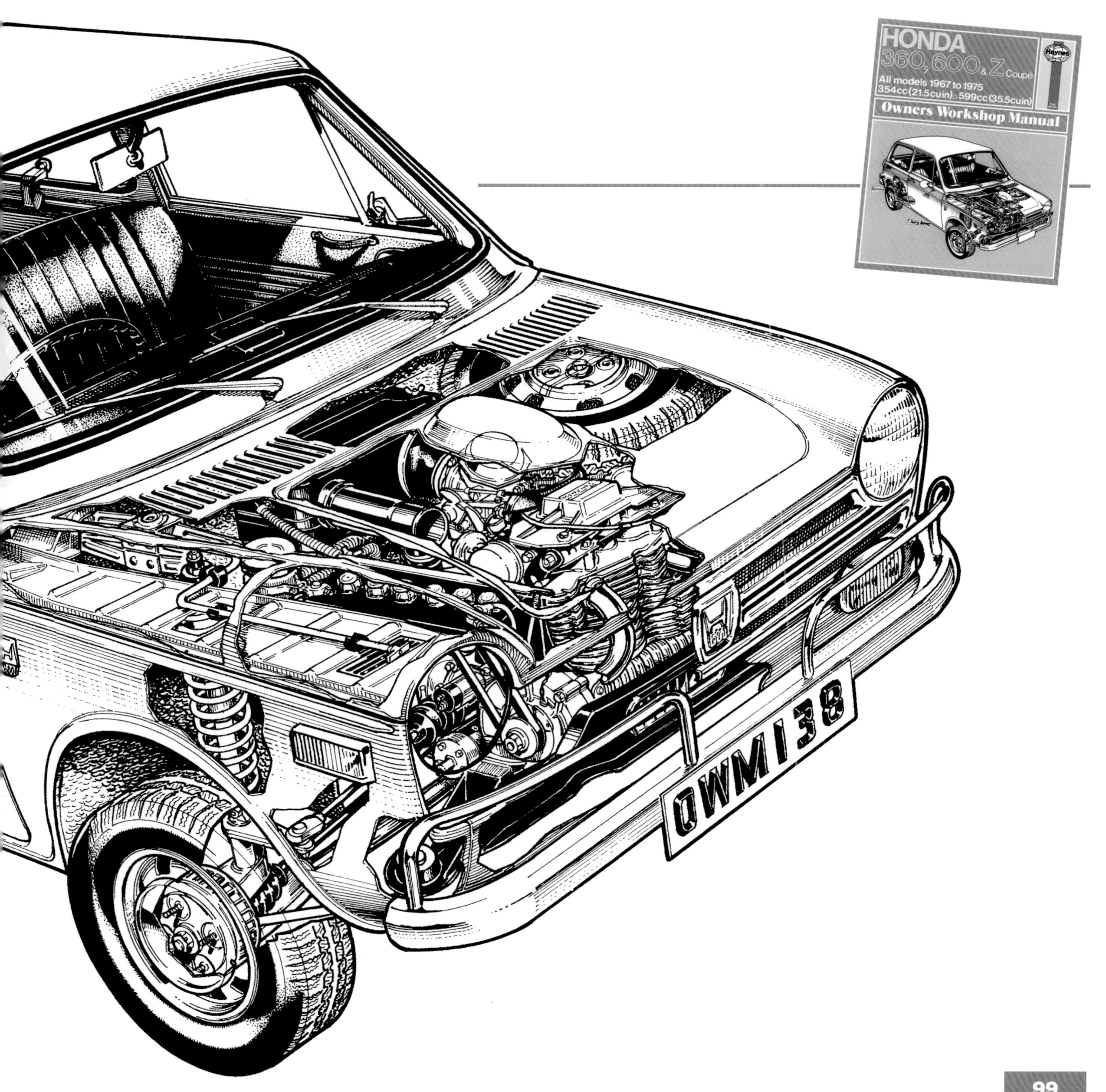
HONDA
360, 600 & Z Coupé
All models 1967 to 1975
354cc (21.5cuin) & 599cc (35.5cuin)
Owners Workshop Manual
Haynes
OWM 138

HONDA CIVIC MK1

YEARS MADE
1972–9

NUMBER MADE
2,000,000 approx

ORIGINAL PRICE
£999 (1200 two-door in 1973)

MECHANICAL LAYOUT
Front engine, front-wheel drive

RANGE OF ENGINES
1,170–1,488cc, four-cylinder

MOST POWERFUL ENGINE
70bhp (1,488cc)

FASTEST VERSION
90mph (1,488cc)

BEST FUEL ECONOMY
30mpg (1,170cc)

WHEELBASE
2,190–2,281mm

LENGTH
3,405–4,060mm

NUMBER OF SEATS
4

The first Civic of 1972 was a really good little car. It offered a well-resolved front-wheel-drive package, lightness of controls and great refinement, front and rear independent suspension, and excellent build quality. But there was more than just a sea-change on the showroom floor: the decision to develop the Civic saw company founder Soichiro Honda sidelined because he favoured technically interesting, but unpopular, air-cooled engines – and the water-cooled Civic was meant to satisfy the widest possible customer base.

The Civic was the right car for the time, as the world plunged headlong into a severe fuel crisis. Honda developed an alternative engine for it, the CVCC (for Compound Vortex Controlled Combustion), with a head design enabling such clean combustion that the car needed neither a catalytic converter nor unleaded petrol to meet stringent emissions rules in Japan and, especially, in the US. It was also thrifty, with 40mpg easily available, and the automatic version did away with a costly, fuel-sapping torque converter. Not surprisingly, the Civic saw a veritable sales explosion, helped by Detroit-built rivals that were mostly rubbish.

We didn't get that CVCC motor in the UK, but in 1973 we did get a Civic with a hatchback, making it a supermini rival to Europeans from Renault and Fiat. A five-speed gearbox, 1.5-litre engine and a five-door option followed as the Civic's legendary reputation was formed.

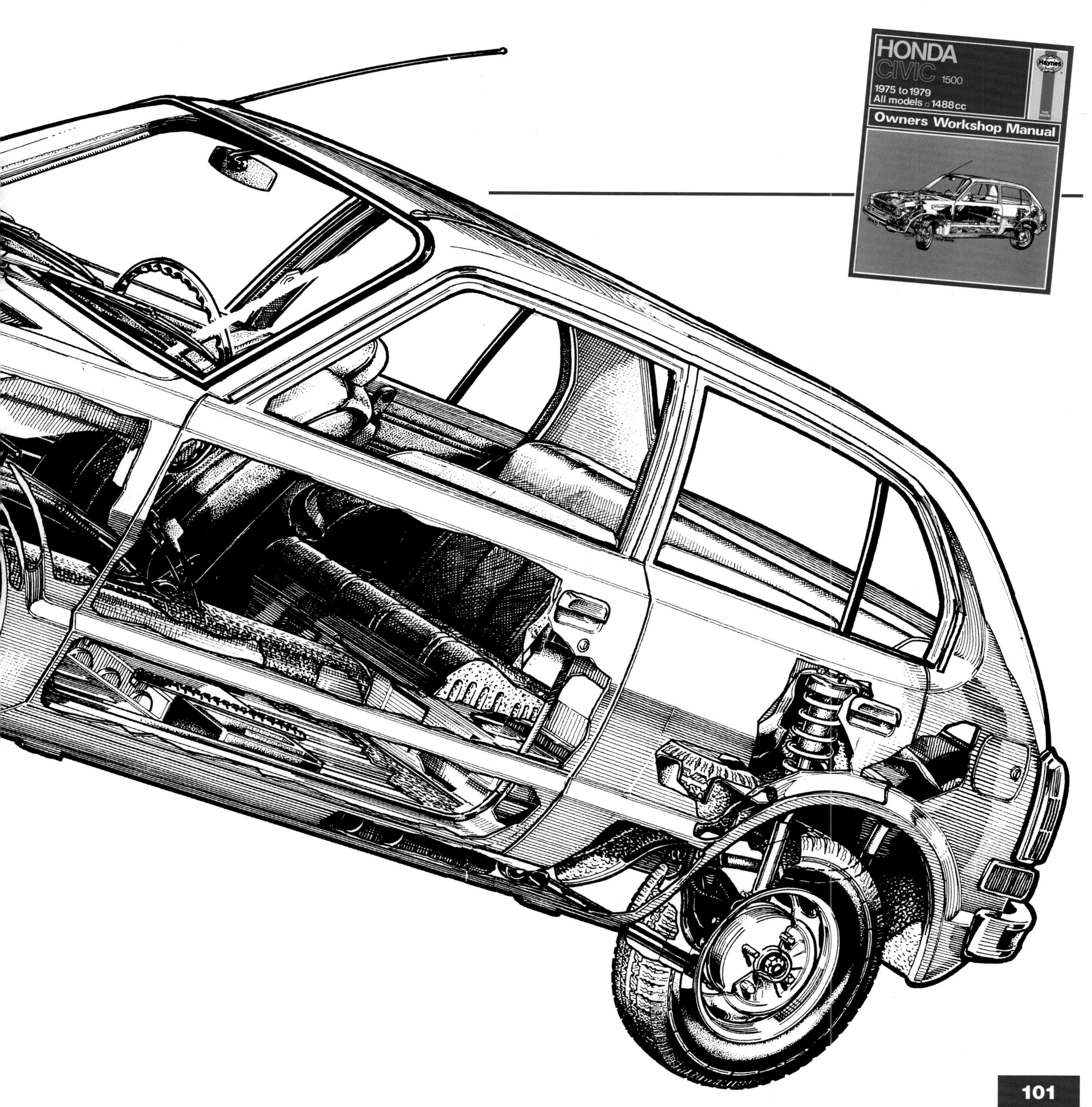

HONDA
CIVIC 1500
1975 to 1979
All models □ 1488cc
Owners Workshop Manual

JAGUAR MK1/2

YEARS MADE
1955–69

NUMBER MADE
128,619

ORIGINAL PRICE
£1,529 (2.4-litre in 1956)

MECHANICAL LAYOUT
Front engine, rear-wheel drive

RANGE OF ENGINES
2,483–3,781cc, six-cylinder

MOST POWERFUL ENGINE
220bhp (3,781cc)

FASTEST VERSION
125mph (3,781cc)

BEST FUEL ECONOMY
23mpg (240, 2,483cc)

WHEELBASE
2,718–2,730mm

LENGTH
4,559–4,597mm

NUMBER OF SEATS
5

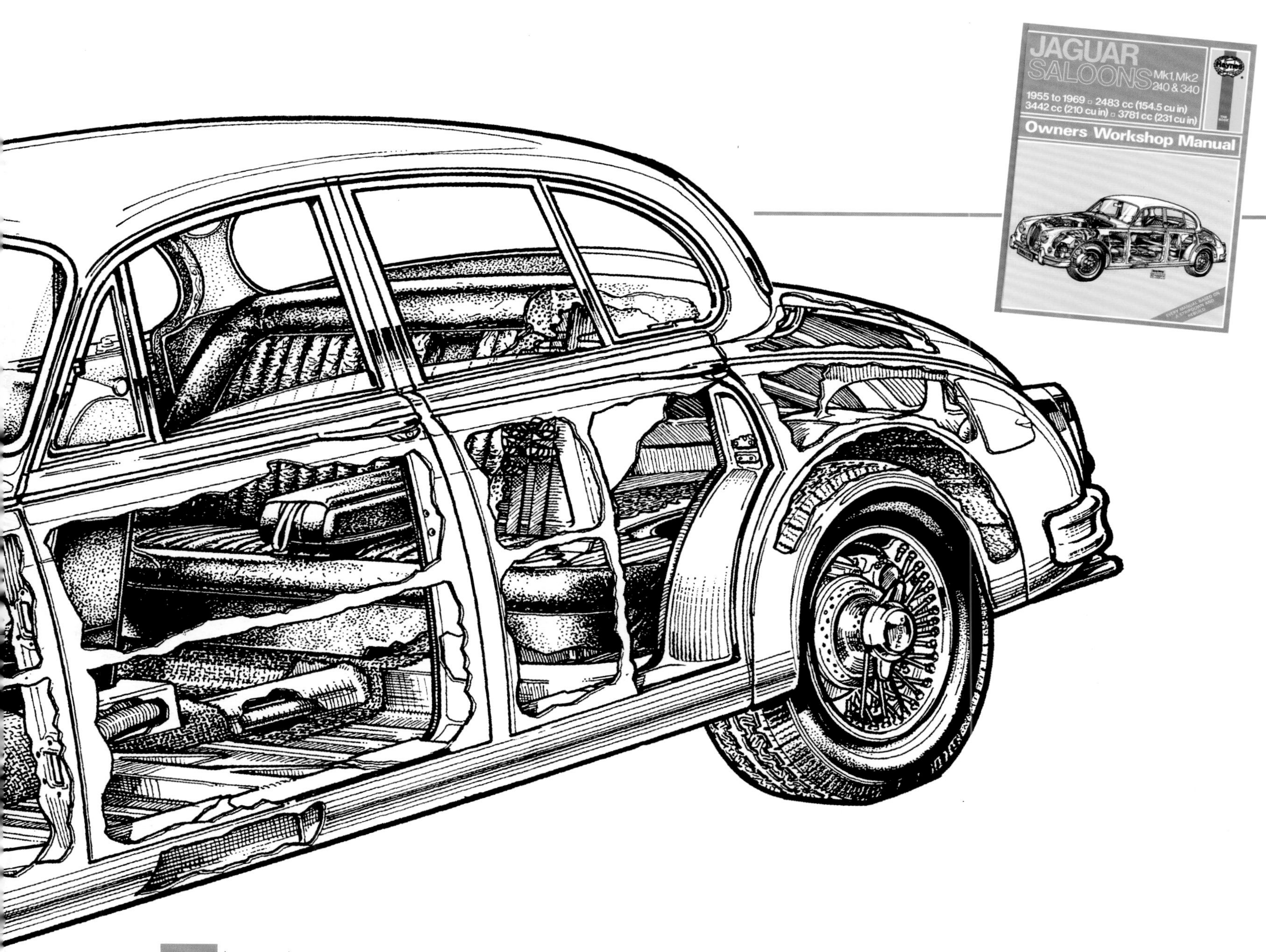

The question anyone might reasonably ask while drooling over the lithe, chrome-encrusted and leather-lined Jaguar Mk2 in our illustration, is: 'What about the Mk1?'

There is no Mk1, of course. That's a retrospective title applied to the Jaguar 2.4-litre, introduced in 1955 – the first Jaguar with unitary-construction instead of a separate chassis.

It looked rather slug-like with its tapering tail and 'spats' sealing the rear wheels (4in closer together than the fronts) into the bodywork. It had sporty handling but was fairly heavy and, because of that, its engine felt gutless. Stung into reaction, Jaguar created a 3.4-litre rendition, effectively installing the power unit from its D-type racer. It could manage 120mph, sensational in 1957, but 210bhp through a narrow back axle together with drum brakes made for a frightening machine if driven hard.

None of which should have boded well for Jaguar. Yet the Mk2 revealed in 1959 sorted the drawbacks and emerged as an unlikely all-time great.

The fundamental handling problems were fixed with a widened rear track, new back axle, revised suspension and standard disc brakes all round. Meanwhile, a masterful facelift produced slimmer roof pillars and larger, more graceful windows.

The company felt confident enough to offer a 3.8-litre engine too, conjuring up the ultimate 1960s sports saloon, a blistering 125mph performer. Renamed 240 and 340 (the 3.8 was axed) in 1967, the cars survived two more years.

JAGUAR E-TYPE

YEARS MADE
1961–75

NUMBER MADE
72,507

ORIGINAL PRICE
£2,096 (in 1961)

MECHANICAL LAYOUT
Front engine, rear-wheel drive

RANGE OF ENGINES
3,781–4,235cc, six-cylinder; 5,343cc, V12-cylinder

MOST POWERFUL ENGINE
272bhp (V12)

FASTEST VERSION
150mph (V12)

BEST FUEL ECONOMY
18mpg (3.8-litre Series 1 coupé)

WHEELBASE
2,438–2,667mm

LENGTH
4,453–4,783mm

NUMBER OF SEATS
2 or 2+2

There's something almost emotional about the shape of any E-type. Sexy, certainly. No wonder when Frank Sinatra saw one, he said: 'I want that car and I want it now!'

In 1961 the E-type was an instant classic, an exercise in cool aerodynamic theory completed with unashamed showmanship. It was the era's most beautiful roadster and, at over 140mph, by far Britain's fastest production car. Moreover, it undercut the price of its nearest rival, Aston Martin's DB4, by a third.

That curvy shape, inspired by the Le Mans-winning Jaguar D-type racer, covered an immensely strong frame, and wishbone and coil spring independent suspension gave limo ride comfort with leech-like roadholding. The 3.8-litre XK engine was well worthy of the new chassis, the clunky four-speed gearbox a little less so.

In 1964, a bigger 4.2 engine offered extra torque. Gearbox, brakes and cockpit were all improved, making the 4.2 Series 1 E the best of the bunch. A roomier two-plus-two version followed in 1966 and optional automatic transmission. But by the time the Series 2 was launched in 1968, emission controls demanded by North American legislation had smothered its power so that, by 1970, the car was a shadow of its snarling former self.

The final Series 3 introduced Jaguar's awesome V12 engine. It was deliciously smooth and very fast once again, even if its softer, fatter body shape lacked the original E's fierce beauty.

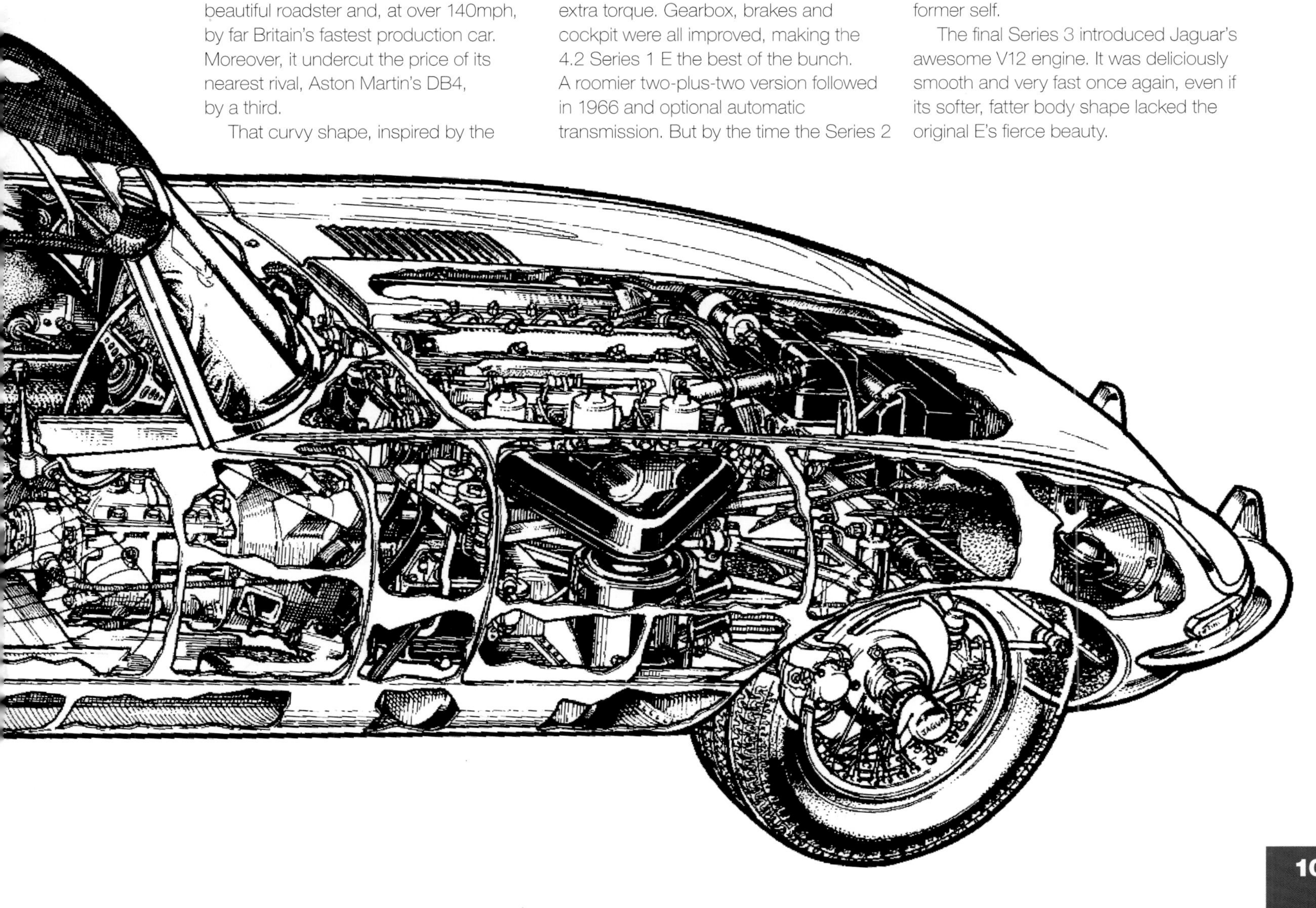

JAGUAR XJ6 SERIES 1-3

YEARS MADE
1968–87

NUMBER MADE
281,176

ORIGINAL PRICE
£1,797 (2.8 in 1968)

MECHANICAL LAYOUT
Front engine, rear-wheel drive

RANGE OF ENGINES
2,792–4,235cc, six-cylinder

MOST POWERFUL ENGINE
205bhp (Series 3, 4,235cc)

FASTEST VERSION
131mph (Series 3, 4,235cc)

BEST FUEL ECONOMY
18mpg (Series 1, 2,792cc)

WHEELBASE
2,765–2,865mm

LENGTH
4,816–4,951mm

NUMBER OF SEATS
5

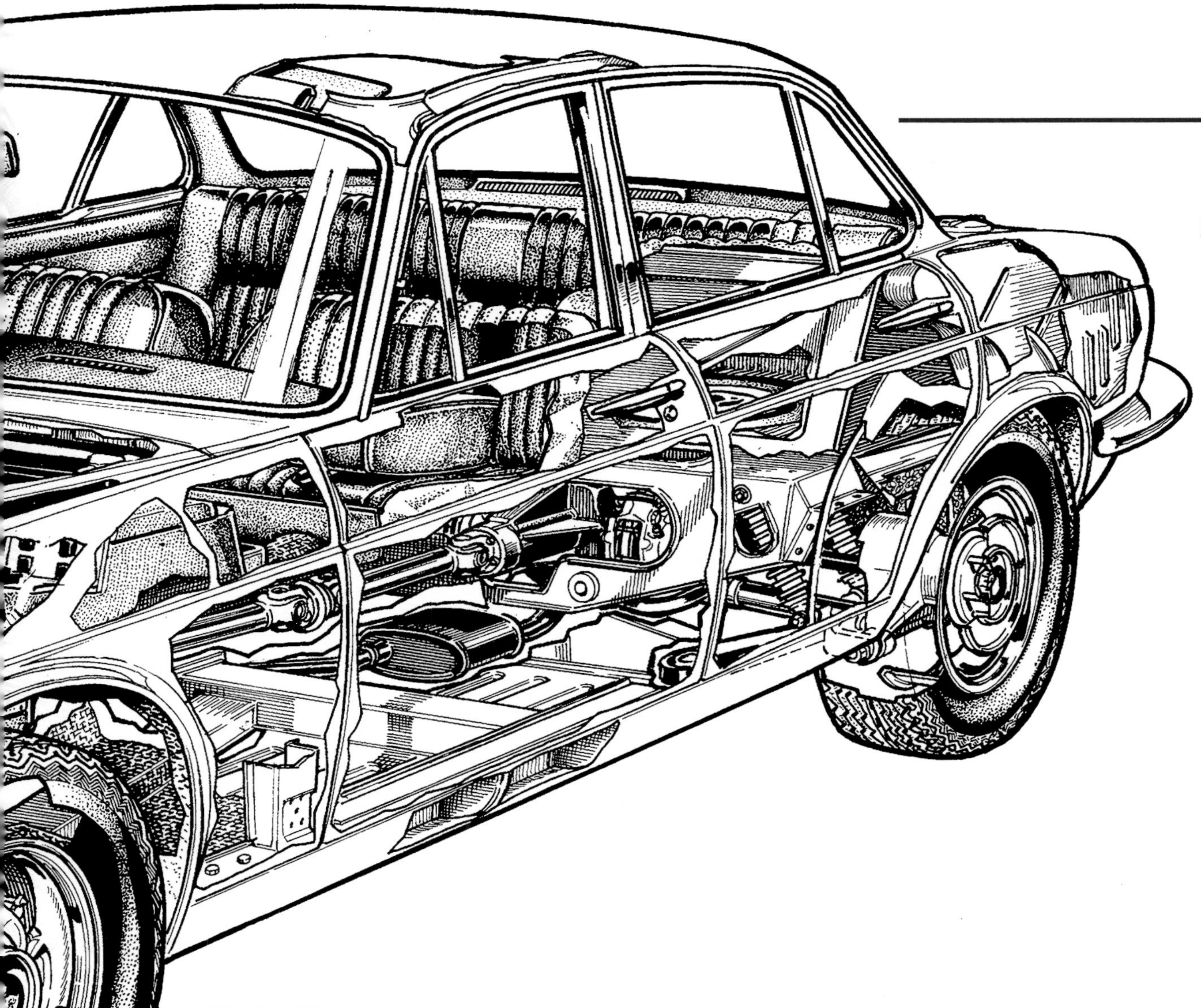

When Jaguar launched the XJ6, it rewrote the luxury car rulebook. Not with anything radical, mind: the XJ6 was a conventional saloon, front-engined, rear-driven, coil-sprung; instead, it did it by masterful fine-tuning.

Jaguar combined standards of ride comfort, silence, handling and roadholding – qualities previously thought irreconcilable in a luxury car – that eclipsed Europe's best and set the pace for two decades. On its plump tyres, specially designed for it by Dunlop, this new British world-beater would out-manoeuvre Jaguar's own E-type and beat Rolls-Royce for ride quality. It had beauty too, a feline aggression that proved amazingly enduring.

Initially using the proven six-cylinder XK engine (a V12-powered XJ12 arrived in 1972) most XJ6s were automatic, all had power steering, and Jaguar built some with a short-stroke 2.8-litre engine to beat European tax laws. Like all previous Jags, the XJ6 was a bargain, often undercutting comparable Mercedes models by 50 per cent.

The XJ6 wasn't perfect, of course. Standards of build looked pretty flaky by the time the facelifted Series 3 came along in 1979. But in March 1980 John Egan was appointed to 'fix' Jaguar. As his quality drive took hold, flagging sales were arrested, and Jaguar enjoyed a spectacular privatisation and stock market flotation in 1984. The very last of these XJs, an XJ12, was built in 1992; wistful aficionados regarded it as the last of the old-style Jags.

LADA 1500

YEARS MADE
1977–84

NUMBER MADE
Unknown

ORIGINAL PRICE
£1,676 (in 1973)

MECHANICAL LAYOUT
Front engine, rear-wheel drive

RANGE OF ENGINES
1,452cc, four-cylinder

MOST POWERFUL ENGINE
75bhp (1,452cc)

FASTEST VERSION
94mph (1,452cc)

BEST FUEL ECONOMY
28mpg (1,452cc)

WHEELBASE
2,426mm

LENGTH
4,039mm

NUMBER OF SEATS
5

Take yourself back to 1974. You'll find you're in the thick of a worldwide oil crisis, strikes and power cuts abound, and – in car showrooms – once-popular British marques are rapidly losing out to reliable Japanese opposition.

Into this maelstrom entered Russia's Lada. After months of evaluation the 1,200cc saloon and estate went on sale for the first time, and by the end of 1974 2,364 had found buyers. The cars were hard to tell apart from the Fiat 124, just made obsolete in Italy. Britain's motor trade might have scoffed, but by 1979 nearly 70,000 cars had been sold and Lada regularly swiped 1 per cent of the total car market.

The reason for this popularity was dead simple: the Ladas were so competitively priced they made even some used cars look expensive. Any lack of refinement was compensated for by sheer toughness.

Fiat helped the Russian state establish the Volzhsky Motor Works, 600 miles south-east of Moscow, in 1966. Its first car was made in 1970, essentially a Fiat 124 but with Russian, Moskvich-derived engines and a reinforced body. This 1.5-litre model followed in 1977.

By the time Ladas were withdrawn from UK sale – as they no longer met emissions laws – some 330,000 cars had been sold. But the Lada 1500, lightly redesigned in 1982 to become the Riva, is still on sale in Russia to this day.

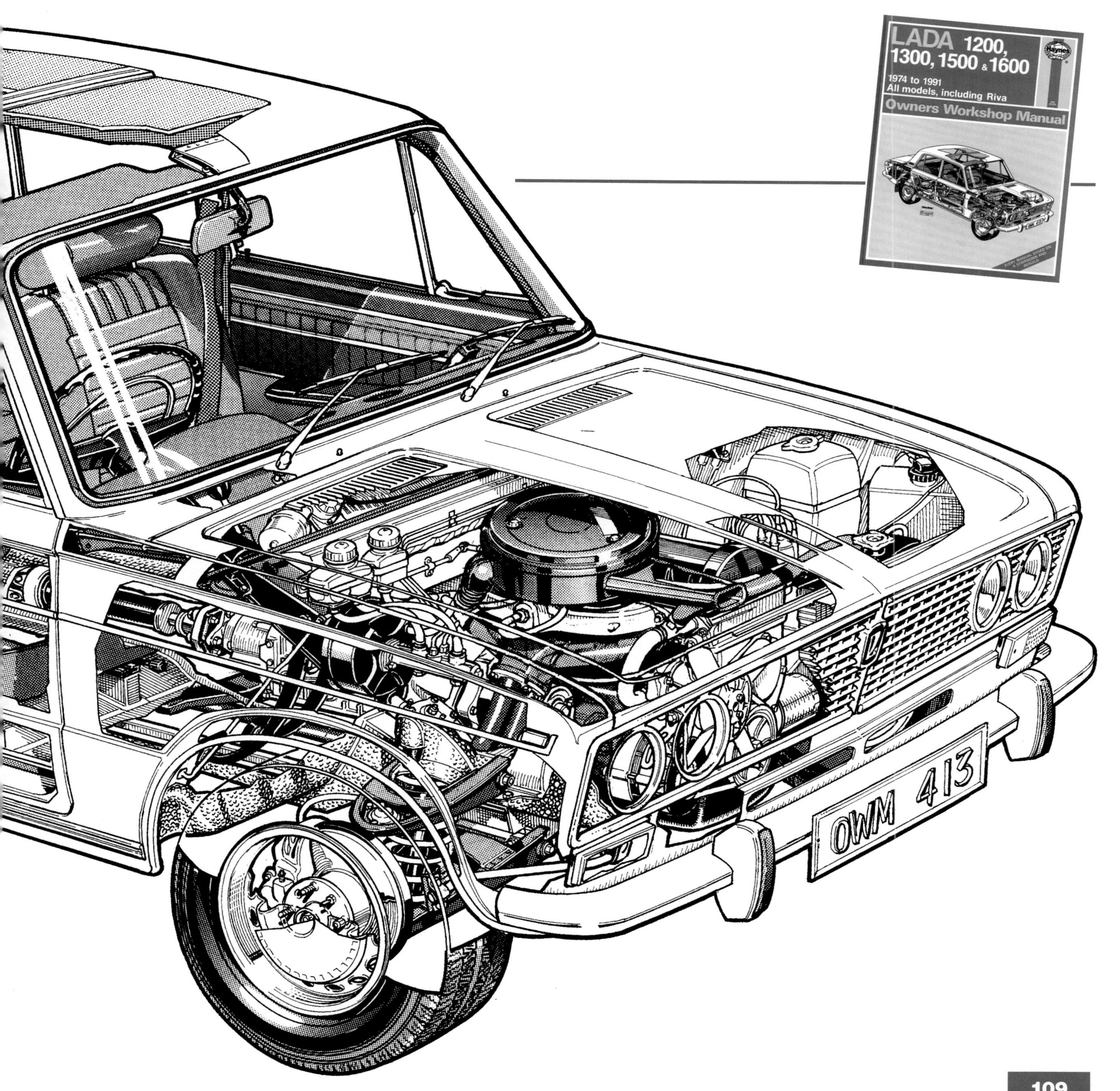
LADA 1200,
1300, 1500 & 1600
1974 to 1991
All models, including Riva
Owners Workshop Manual
Haynes
OWM 413

LAND ROVER SERIES I-III

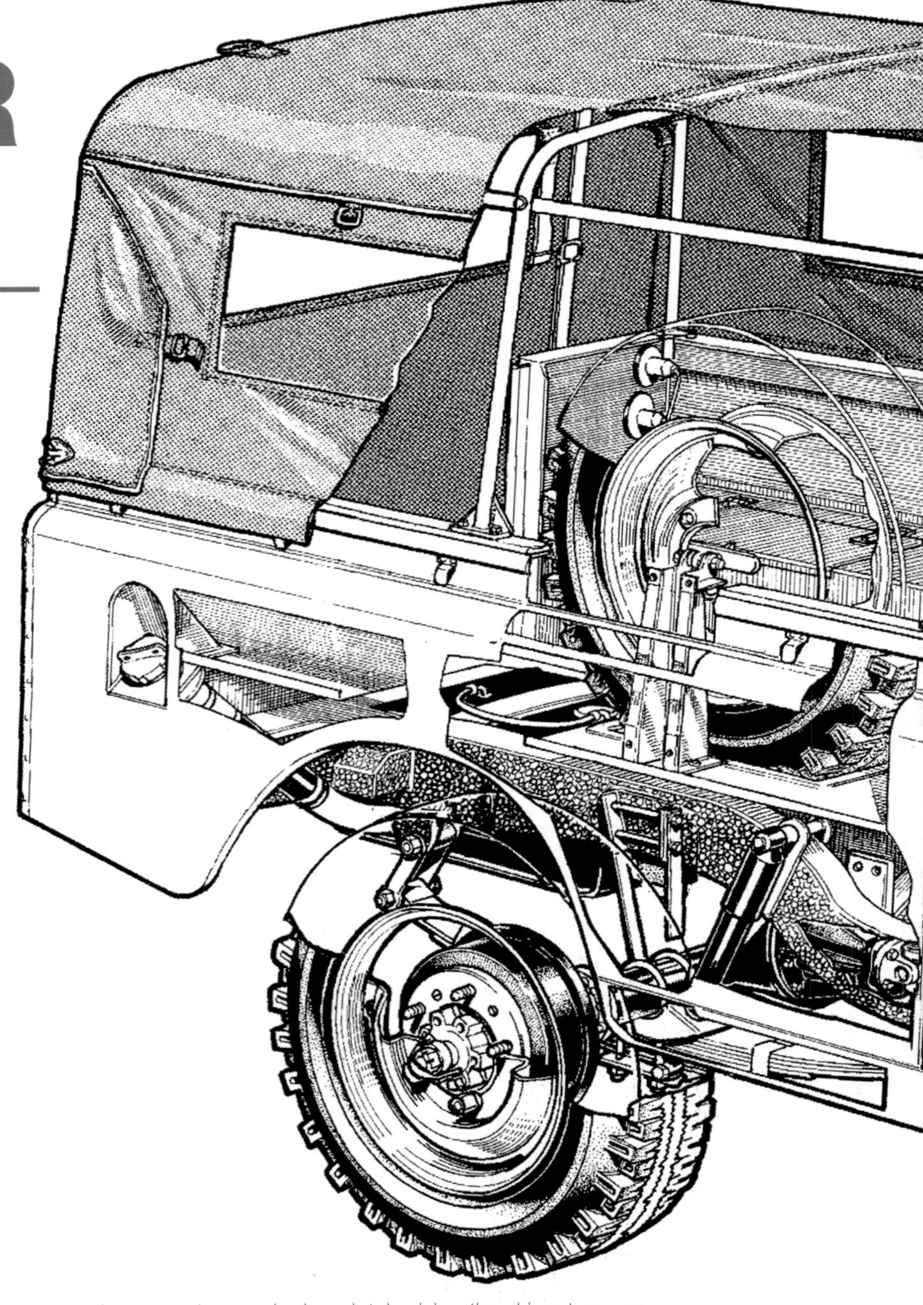

YEARS MADE
1948–84

NUMBER MADE
1,295,000 approx

ORIGINAL PRICE
£450 (in 1948)

MECHANICAL LAYOUT
Front engine, four-wheel drive

RANGE OF ENGINES
1,595–2,625cc, four- and six-cylinder petrol, 3,528cc V8 petrol, 2,052–2,625cc four-cylinder diesel

MOST POWERFUL ENGINE
114bhp (3,528cc)

FASTEST VERSION
84mph (Series III LWB, 3,528cc)

BEST FUEL ECONOMY
21mpg (Series 1 2-litre petrol)

WHEELBASE
2,032–2,768mm

LENGTH
3,353–4,445mm

NUMBER OF SEATS
3 to 8

After World War 2, Rover director Maurice Wilks bought an army-surplus Jeep as a runabout for his Anglesey farm. It needed constant repairs but Wilks couldn't choose a 4x4 alternative because there weren't any. Hence his Eureka moment: Rover would build its own. 'It must be along the lines of the Willys Jeep,' Wilks decreed, 'but much more versatile, more useful as a power source, be able to do everything.'

The resulting 'Land Rover' used mostly Rover car componentry, except for a specially-designed power transfer case, in a structure made from lightweight, rustproof aluminium. Wheelbase was 80in…oddly the same as the wartime Jeep's!

At first, Land Rovers had a curious permanent four-wheel-drive system with no central differential and a freewheel in the front drive to reduce tyre scrub. This was fine for going up hills but not so good for coming down, where the wheels turned at different speeds. In 1950 a dogleg clutch giving the driver two- or four-wheel drive fixed the problem.

Within months, Rover was making more Land Rovers than cars. By the time our artist produced this superb cutaway in the early 1970s, the basic Land Rover was in Series IIA/III guise, having reached 750,000 civilian and military sales. Changes in engine, wheelbase and equipment had been many and frequent, but the vehicle's off-road supremacy was unrivalled and – in Defender form today – remains so.

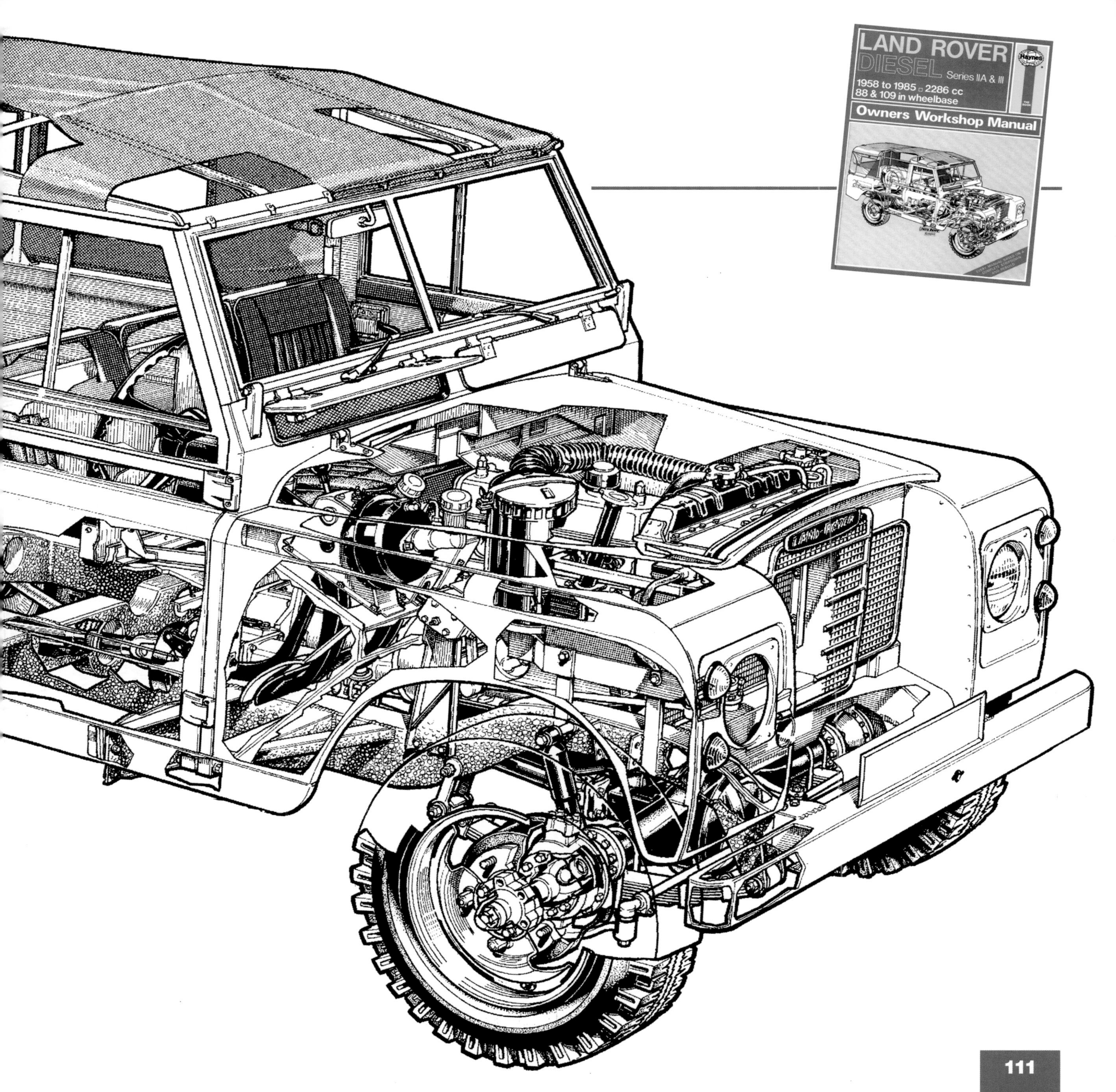
LAND ROVER
DIESEL Series IIA & III
1958 to 1985 □ 2286 cc
88 & 109 in wheelbase
Owners Workshop Manual
Haynes
LAND-ROVER

MAZDA RX3

YEARS MADE
1971–8

NUMBER MADE
285,887

ORIGINAL PRICE
£1,612 (RX3 Coupé in 1972)

MECHANICAL LAYOUT
Front engine, rear-wheel drive

RANGE OF ENGINES
1,964–2,292cc equivalent, rotary twin-rotor

MOST POWERFUL ENGINE
120bhp (2,292cc equivalent)

FASTEST VERSION
110mph (2,292cc equivalent)

BEST FUEL ECONOMY
18.5mpg (1,964cc equivalent)

WHEELBASE
2,286mm

LENGTH
4,064mm

NUMBER OF SEATS
4/5

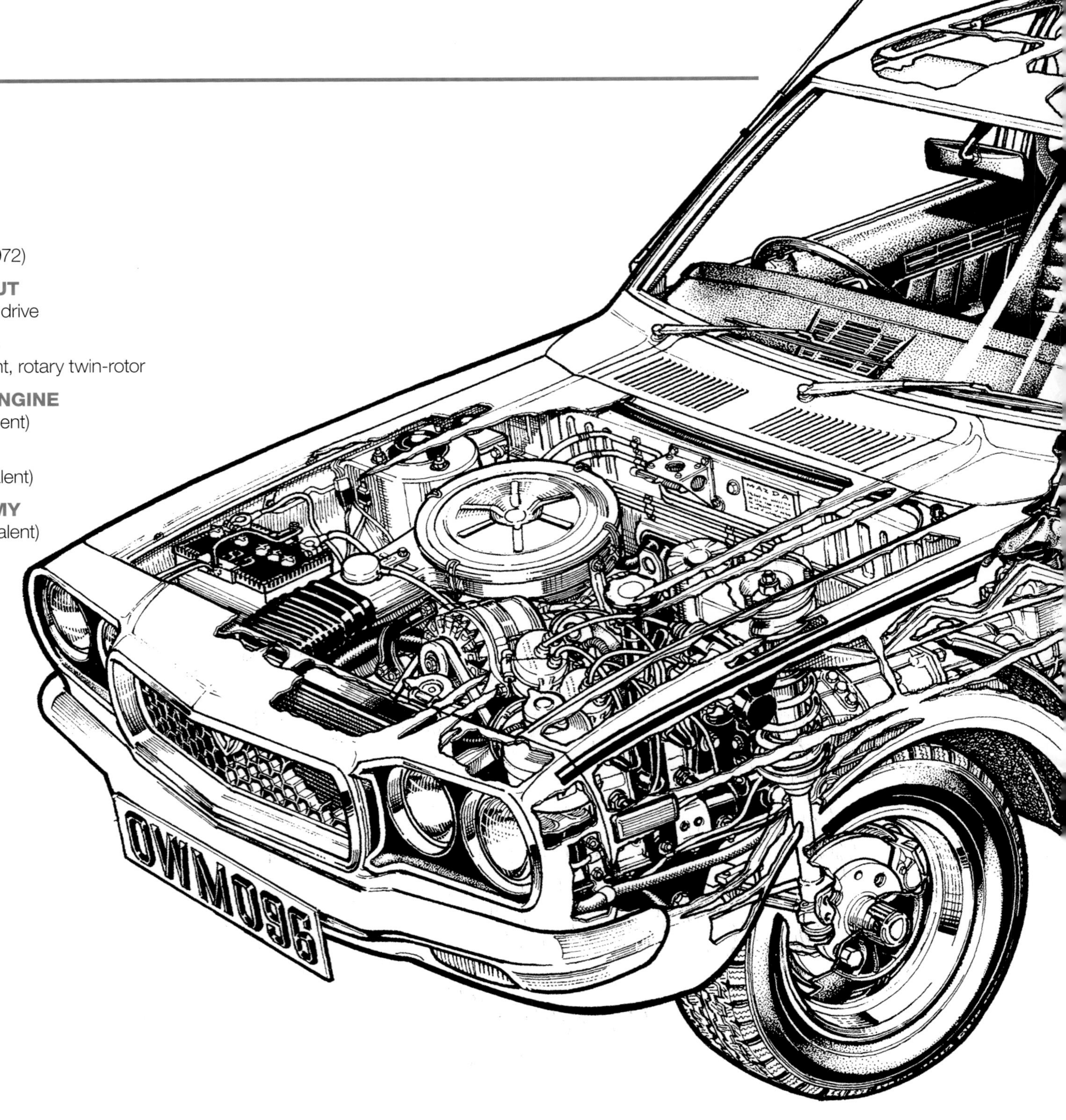

The rotary engine, invented by German engineer Dr Felix Wankel, caused a sensation in the NSU Wankel Spider in 1963. The replacement of reciprocating pistons in the combustion chamber by a rotor, and no need for a crankshaft, made for an exceptionally smooth, refined and quiet engine offering superb power delivery. But Japan's Mazda really embraced rotary engines. It licensed the technology from NSU, and by 1973 offered a rotary-engined version in every range apart from its Carol city car.

The RX3 laid bare here was based on the Mazda 818, about the same size as the Ford Escort, and like all Wankel-powered Mazdas of the time it had a twin-rotor engine giving a capacity equivalent to a 2-litre conventional piston engine; an even bigger power unit was available in North America.

Critics praised its turbine-like power delivery, slick gearchange and good driving position, generally also liking its road manners. Four-door saloon, five-door estate and this two-door coupé were offered.

But there was no escaping the major penalty owners paid for such mechanical sophistication – the RX3, like all rotary cars, had a heavy thirst for petrol. As it was launched on the cusp of a worldwide fuel crisis, its prospects were not good in the market, no matter that the RX3 enjoyed great success in saloon car racing. The last ones arrived in the UK in 1975.

MERCEDES-BENZ 250/280SL

YEARS MADE
1966–71

NUMBER MADE
29,081

ORIGINAL PRICE
£3,850 (250SL in 1966)

MECHANICAL LAYOUT
Front engine, rear-wheel drive

RANGE OF ENGINES
2,496–2,778cc, six-cylinder

MOST POWERFUL ENGINE
170bhp (2,778cc)

FASTEST VERSION
121mph (280SL, 2,778cc)

BEST FUEL ECONOMY
18.5mpg (250SL, 2,496cc)

WHEELBASE
2,850mm

LENGTH
4,285mm

NUMBER OF SEATS
2

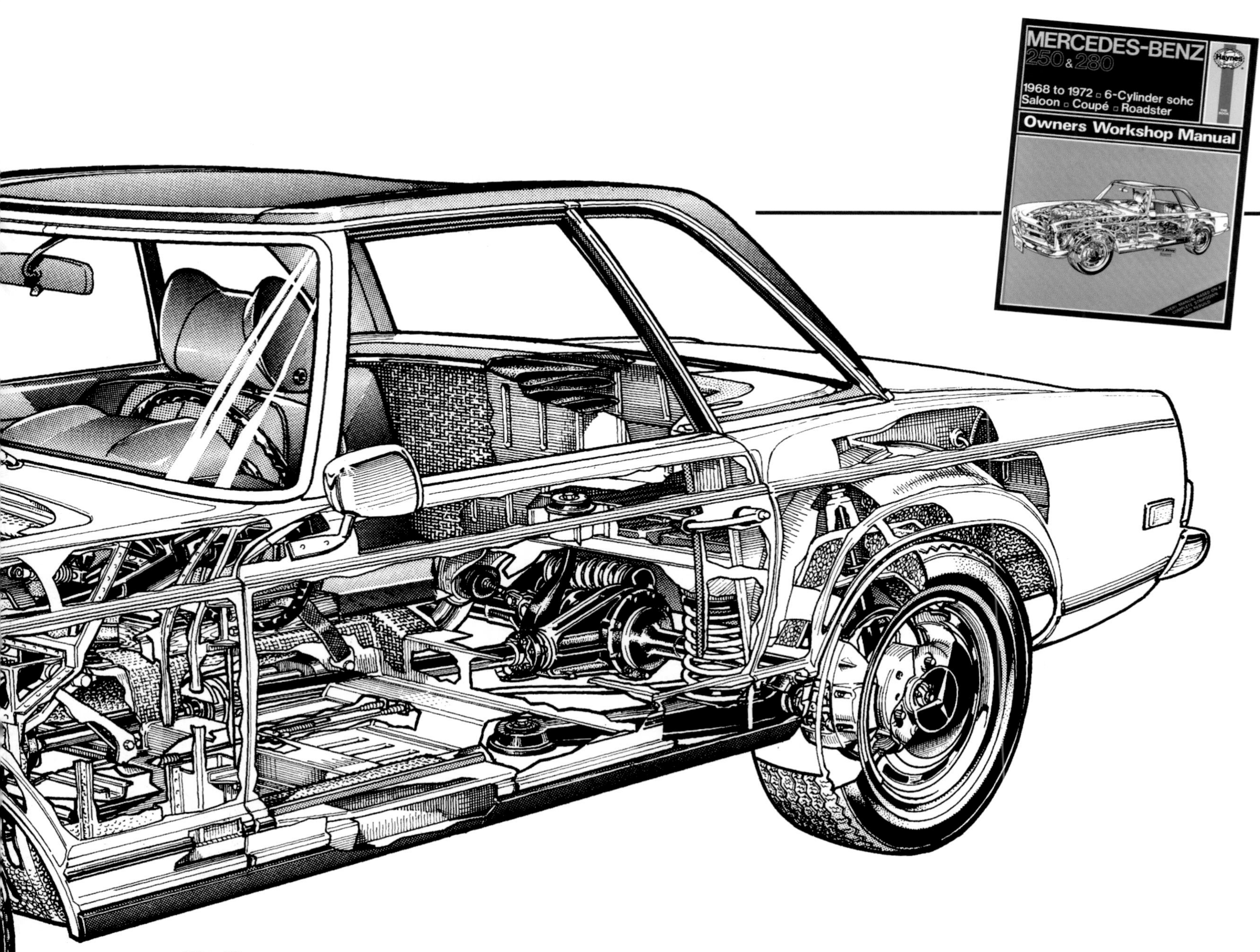

Never mind engine oil; most cars need gallons of metaphorical moisturiser to stop them feeling dated after even ten years, much less 40. Looked at like this, the so-called 'Pagoda-roof' Mercedes-Benz SL is startlingly wrinkle-free. There's barely a crow's foot on its urbane and handsome visage. Its road manners are nostalgia-tinged contemporary, and it has marvellous, Jaguar-shaming build quality.

The 1963 230SL replaced the race-bred 300SL and the pretty, if gutless, 190SL in one fell swoop. The 2.3-litre, six-cylinder, fuel-injected engine offered a fiery 150bhp. Thanks to an abnormally wide track, well sorted suspension, fat tyres and a ground-hugging stance, its handling and roadholding were fantastic. It could also do 120mph…and yet cost double the price of a 150mph Jaguar E-type.

A wide grille, stacked headlights and flared wheelarches were massaged into an elegant shape, while the layered bumpers, chrome bedecked dashboard, ivory steering wheel and hubcaps matched to the bodywork colour oozed cachet. Every SL came with its own detachable metal hardtop. Unusually, Merc offered its excellent automatic gearbox on the SL and, with this available, few people opted for the notchy manual.

Progressively larger engines, first in the rare 1966 250SL and then in the 1968 280SL, gave the car enhanced cruising prowess. Softer suspension and better refinement made it feel more luxurious, and four-wheel disc brakes were now on hand should panic stations strike.

MERCEDES-BENZ 250/280 (W123-TYPE)

YEARS MADE
1975–84

NUMBER MADE
2,996,316 (all W123-type cars)

ORIGINAL PRICE
£5,789 (250 in 1976)

MECHANICAL LAYOUT
Front engine, rear-wheel drive

RANGE OF ENGINES
2,525–2,746cc, six-cylinder

MOST POWERFUL ENGINE
185bhp (2,746cc)

FASTEST VERSION
124mph (280E, 2,746cc)

BEST FUEL ECONOMY
20mpg (250, 2,525cc)

WHEELBASE
2,790mm

LENGTH
4,720mm

NUMBER OF SEATS
5

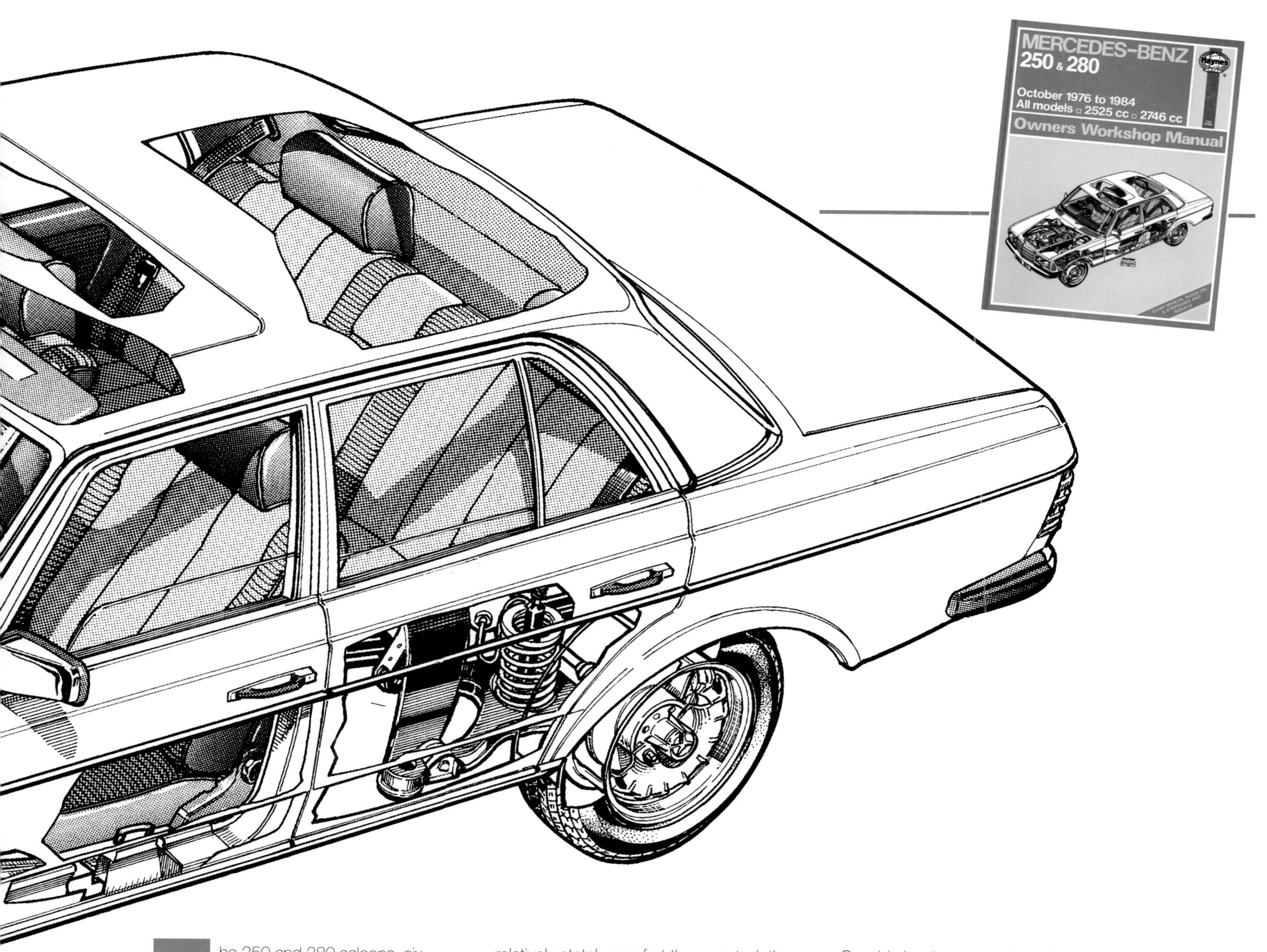

The 250 and 280 saloons, six-cylinder cars offering a single-camshaft 2.5-litre and a twin-cam 2.8 engine respectively, were but one section of the Mercedes line-up in its W123 range.

First seen in 1975, the W123 was destined to be Mercedes-Benz's most successful car to date, with literally millions finding appreciative owners. These buyers could be anyone from private family motorists to business executives to taxi drivers and chauffeurs: if it was the ultimate in high quality, reliability, and relatively stately comfort they wanted, then here it was in spades.

The range began with the 2-litre 200 although, with a top speed of barely 100mph, it was a sluggish ox beside the fleet, 125mph 280E. The car's excellent suspension and damping were well up to the extra urge. However, the unbelievably rugged diesel options also available were even more tortoise-like. As well as the saloons, there were coupés, estates and even the rarity of factory-built long-wheelbase limos.

Considering the steep prices demanded for all this German metal, standard W123s came sparsely equipped. You paid extra for gadgets, in-car entertainment and luxury trim. In 1970s Britain, though, this was no deterrent, and these six-cylinder cars usually left showrooms groaning with optional equipment.

'Over-engineered' is a term that might have been invented for these Mercs. They're built like tanks, and still eminently usable – if thirsty – for daily running nowadays.

MGA

YEARS MADE
1955–62

NUMBER MADE
101,081

ORIGINAL PRICE
£844 (A roadster in 1955)

MECHANICAL LAYOUT
Front engine, rear-wheel drive

RANGE OF ENGINES
1,489–1,622cc, four-cylinder

MOST POWERFUL ENGINE
108bhp (A Twin-Cam, 1,588cc)

FASTEST VERSION
110mph (A Twin-Cam)

BEST FUEL ECONOMY
27mpg (1,489cc)

WHEELBASE
2,388mm

LENGTH
3,962mm

NUMBER OF SEATS
2

A close ancestor of the MGA actually raced at Le Mans in 1951 yet the car wasn't on sale until 1955. It was cheap, stylish and fun, revitalising MG's image and selling at five times the rate of its predecessor, the MG TF.

The A's new, more rigid chassis hosted a 72bhp version of the British Motor Corporation's 1,492cc 'B'-series engine. Its twin carburettors meant a 95mph top speed and spirited acceleration – 0–60mph in 15.6sec. A Triumph TR2 was quicker, but the MGA was cheaper and more civilised.

The 1600 came with a 1,588cc engine, 80bhp and front disc brakes in 1961, and could brush 100mph, but, while mid-range torque was better, acceleration was unchanged. High performance came in the MGA Twin Cam, fitted with a new 1,588cc, 108bhp double overhead-camshaft engine – over 110mph and 0–60mph in, for 1958, a blistering 9.1sec. It had disc brakes all round and its Dunlop centre-lock wheels were just like the Jaguar D-type's.

This special engine was a double-edged sword. It needed high-octane petrol or else the pistons could burn out, and such fuel wasn't common. Worse, it gulped oil like nobody's business. Sales dwindled after word spread, and the Twin Cam was quietly canned.

All MGAs were available as hardtop coupés, as depicted in our artwork, but only one in ten cars were actually ordered like this.

MGA
1955 to 1962
All models ▫ ohv ▫ dohc
Owners Workshop Manual
Haynes
OWM 475

MGB

YEARS MADE
1962–80

NUMBER MADE
526,943

ORIGINAL PRICE
£950 (B roadster in 1962)

MECHANICAL LAYOUT
Front engine, rear-wheel drive

RANGE OF ENGINES
1,798cc, four-cylinder; 3,528cc V8-cylinder

MOST POWERFUL ENGINE
137bhp (3,528cc)

FASTEST VERSION
125mph (3,528cc)

BEST FUEL ECONOMY
21mpg (1,798cc)

WHEELBASE
2,311–2,375mm

LENGTH
3,884–4,019mm

NUMBER OF SEATS
2+2

The MGB was, at 18 years, the longest-running MG ever, and the most popular by a country mile. It did more to establish Britain as the sports car maker than any other.

It had unitary, chassis-less construction but relied on familiar hardware by retaining the MGA suspension and live rear axle. There was extra passenger and luggage space, and the MGA's familiar overhead-valve B-series engine was enlarged to 1,798cc, giving 94bhp.

Performance easily licked the MGA. Top speed was 110mph and 0–60mph took 11.4sec. Road behaviour, meanwhile, was exhilarating: solid roadholding shifting to entertaining handling when you pushed it.

The MGB was sales dynamite, and strong American demand spurred production. Paddy Hopkirk and Alan Hutcheson drove one to 12th place at Le Mans in 1963; in 1964 Hopkirk and Andrew Hedges only managed 19th but, after averaging 99.9mph, grabbed the trophy for fastest British car. In 1965 the MGB came 11th.

The pretty fastback MGB GT arrived in 1965, while the 1973 MGB GT V8 proved the car could handle more power. The 137bhp Rover 3.5-litre V8 was installed, providing 125mph and 0–60mph in 8.6sec.

The MGB grew old gracelessly. US regulations foisted upon it a 1.5in height rise (headlight rules), an engine detune (emissions) and gross polyurethane bumpers (safety). Performance and dynamics suffered and the B went out on a whimper.

MGB
Haynes
1962 to 1980
Roadster □ GT Coupe □ 1798 cc
Owners Workshop Manual

MG
MIDGET MK3

YEARS MADE
1966–74

NUMBER MADE
100,345

ORIGINAL PRICE
£684 (in 1966)

MECHANICAL LAYOUT
Front engine, rear-wheel drive

RANGE OF ENGINES
1,275cc, four-cylinder

MOST POWERFUL ENGINE
65bhp (1,275cc)

FASTEST VERSION
95mph (1,275cc)

BEST FUEL ECONOMY
30mpg (1,275cc)

WHEELBASE
2,032mm

LENGTH
3,495mm

NUMBER OF SEATS
2

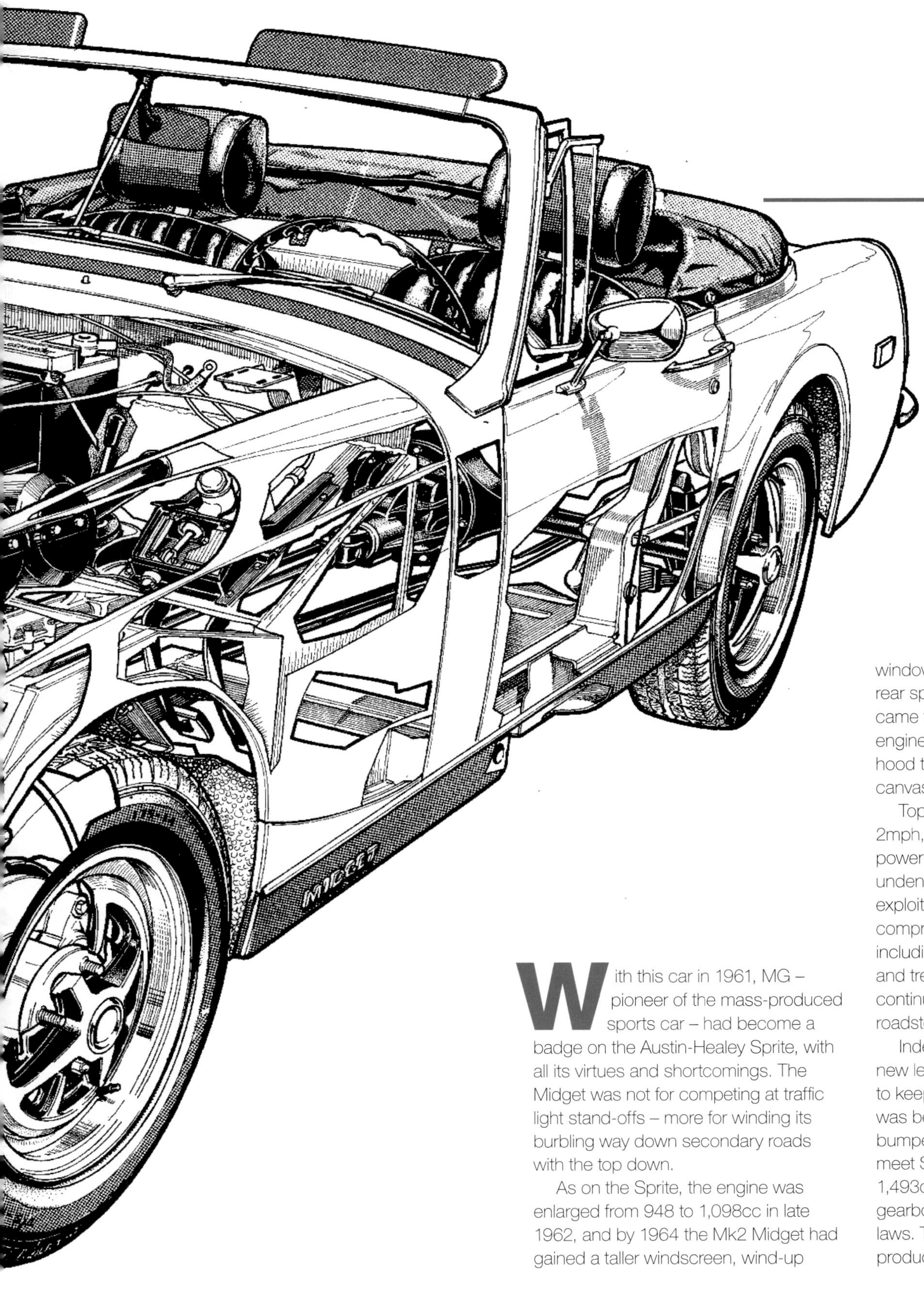

With this car in 1961, MG – pioneer of the mass-produced sports car – had become a badge on the Austin-Healey Sprite, with all its virtues and shortcomings. The Midget was not for competing at traffic light stand-offs – more for winding its burbling way down secondary roads with the top down.

As on the Sprite, the engine was enlarged from 948 to 1,098cc in late 1962, and by 1964 the Mk2 Midget had gained a taller windscreen, wind-up windows and door locks, semi-elliptical rear springs and an extra 3bhp. In 1966 came the Mk3, with a 1,275cc 65bhp engine and a permanently attached hood to replaced the rather flimsy canvas and tube affair of the early cars.

Top speed improved by only 2mph, but it gave more mid-range power that really meant the Midget's undeniable driving fun could be fully exploited. In 1969 came a comprehensive cosmetic makeover, including rounded rear wheelarches and trendy Rostyle wheels, and sales continued apace despite the little roadster's creaking design.

Indeed, the Midget got yet another new lease of life four years later when, to keep the car saleable in the USA, it was bestowed with prominent plastic bumpers, an increased ride height to meet Stateside safety laws, and the 1,493cc Triumph Spitfire engine and gearbox which could meet emissions laws. The Midget continued in production until 1979.

MORRIS MINOR 1000

YEARS MADE
1956–71

NUMBER MADE
847,491

ORIGINAL PRICE
£669 (Deluxe four-door in 1956)

MECHANICAL LAYOUT
Front engine, rear-wheel drive

RANGE OF ENGINES
948–1,098cc, four-cylinder

MOST POWERFUL ENGINE
48bhp (1,098cc)

FASTEST VERSION
76mph (1,098cc)

BEST FUEL ECONOMY
36mpg (1,098cc)

WHEELBASE
2,184mm

LENGTH
3,759mm

NUMBER OF SEATS
4

You can keep a Minor running indefinitely. Every component you'll ever need is cheap and plentiful. That's why Minors are still ubiquitous and possibly, to many enthusiasts who thrive on the battle to keep their cars alive, a little bit unchallenging. They're not fast and they're definitely not sexy.

In 1948, the box-fresh, £358 Morris Minor was an economy car designed by Alec Issigonis that drove, steered and handled outstandingly yet was still roomy and affordable. The engine was set well forward for a better centre of gravity, there was rack-and-pinion steering, and torsion bar independent front suspension, giving the Minor a less jarring ride than rivals.

Its ancient 918cc sidevalve engine, however, meant the Minor huffed and puffed to its maximum speed of just 60mph. Matters slightly improved in 1953 after the car gained the 803cc overhead valve engine from its corporate stablemate, the Austin A30. Then, in 1956, its engine size boosted to 948cc, it become the Morris Minor 1000, with capacity increasing again to 1,098cc in 1962. Never a punchy car, at least now it wasn't too painfully slow.

When designing the commodious Minor Traveller, Alec Issigonis showed remarkable carpentry skills. He devised the rear of the bodywork as a timber frame clad with aluminium panels. Along with van-like doors and flat glass, the 80 structural parts fitted together with Lego-like simplicity.

MORRIS
MINOR 1000
All models 1956 to 1971
948 cc (57.8 cu in) □ 1098 cc (67 cu in)
Owners Workshop Manual
Haynes
MORRIS
DWM 024

MORRIS MARINA

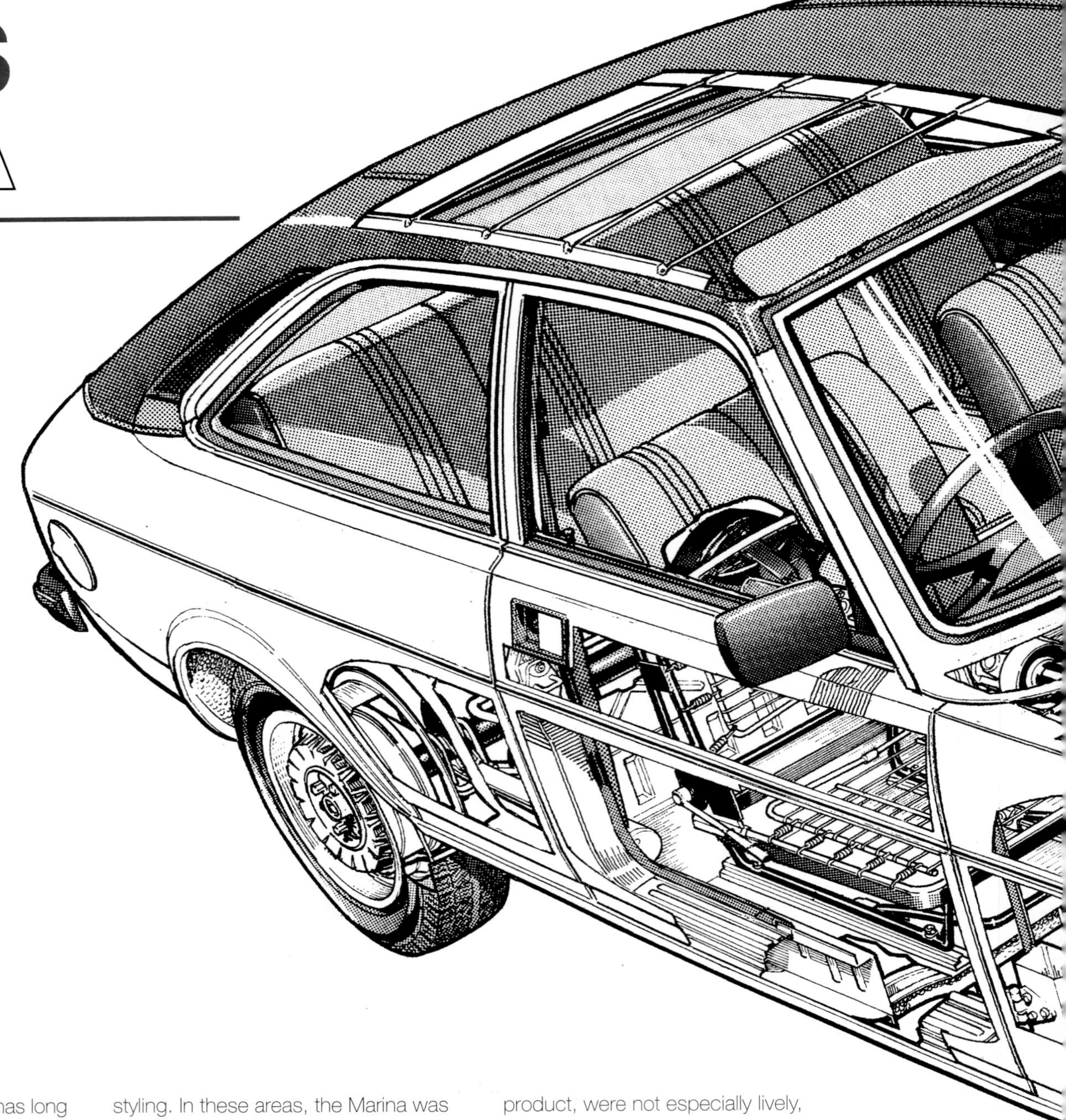

YEARS MADE
1971–80

NUMBER MADE
1,163,116

ORIGINAL PRICE
£994 (1.3 Super four-door in 1971)

MECHANICAL LAYOUT
Front engine, rear-wheel drive

RANGE OF ENGINES
1,275–1,798cc, four-cylinder petrol; 1,489cc, four-cylinder diesel

MOST POWERFUL ENGINE
95bhp (1,798cc)

FASTEST VERSION
100mph (1.8 TC Coupé, 1,798cc)

BEST FUEL ECONOMY
27mpg (1.3 Super four-door)

WHEELBASE
2,439mm

LENGTH
4,143–4,256mm

NUMBER OF SEATS
5

The humble Morris Marina has long been the object of derision among car enthusiasts and, indeed, it was planned to be boringly conventional from the start. This was the first all-new car created by the bosses of the newly formed British Leyland, and it had one critical function: to lure customers away from Ford.

That meant, in essence, copying the sort of cars Ford made, and those tended to be rear-drive, reliable, boxy, roomy, and vaguely American in their styling. In these areas, the Marina was spot-on, but where the Morris fell down was in the technological corner-cutting British Leyland imposed. The Marina's front suspension, for example, was a lever-arm set-up derived from the long-serving Morris Minor, and its limitations endowed early examples with bad understeer and disconcerting road behaviour in sudden manoeuvres. Smaller-engined models, using the faithful 1,275cc A Series engine found in many a British Leyland product, were not especially lively, and there were only ever four-speed gearboxes.

But…the Marina actually sold quite well, passing the magic million sales post in 1978 soon after BL's new 1.7-litre O Series engines made their debut in the car. The estates, introduced in 1972, probably offered the best value. Despite the basic car's obvious mediocrity as it aged, a major stylistic revamp in 1980 that turned it into the Ital meant four more years on sale.

MORRIS
MARINA 1.3 & 1300
Haynes
1971 to 1980 □ 1098 cc □ 1275 cc
Saloon □ Coupe □ Van □ Pick-up □ Estate
Owners Workshop Manual
MORRIS
UWM U73

NISSAN BLUEBIRD

YEARS MADE
1986–90

NUMBER MADE
167,671

ORIGINAL PRICE
£6,699 (1.6 four-door in 1986)

MECHANICAL LAYOUT
Front engine, front-wheel drive

RANGE OF ENGINES
1,598–1,973cc, four-cylinder petrol;
1,952cc, four-cylinder diesel

MOST POWERFUL ENGINE
114bhp (1,973cc)

FASTEST VERSION
112mph (1,973cc)

BEST FUEL ECONOMY
34mpg (1,952cc)

WHEELBASE
2,550mm

LENGTH
4,365–4,460mm

NUMBER OF SEATS
5

This Nissan Bluebird is a truly historic car, although one unlikely to generate much enthusiasm from the collectors of the future.

One of these (in fact, a white Bluebird 2-litre GSX saloon) was the very first Nissan manufactured at the company's British plant in Sunderland. The date was 8 July 1986, and that year it was among some 24,000 Bluebirds to roll off the production line – the first Japanese cars made by a Japanese company in the UK.

It was a pet project of Prime Minister Margaret Thatcher, to stimulate employment and kick inefficient domestic manufacturers up the backside. No wonder she opened the plant…and no doubt was delighted when the place rapidly became first Britain's, and then Europe's, most productive car factory.

That's the politics: what about the Bluebird itself? Well, 'unremarkable' would be an accurate description, although certainly a well-built motor car.

The British Bluebird was a lightly updated version of the straight-laced Japanese model introduced in 1984, most notable for being Nissan's first transverse-engined, front-wheel-drive effort in this Sierra-rivalling class. The British range (called the Auster in non-European markets) alone included a five-door hatchback, plus 1.6-litre petrol and 2-litre diesel engines, and five-speed gearboxes throughout.

The cars became legendary for durability and rust-resistance, so naturally appealed hugely to Britain's minicab drivers – and there can be no more difficult-to-impress stratum of motorists.

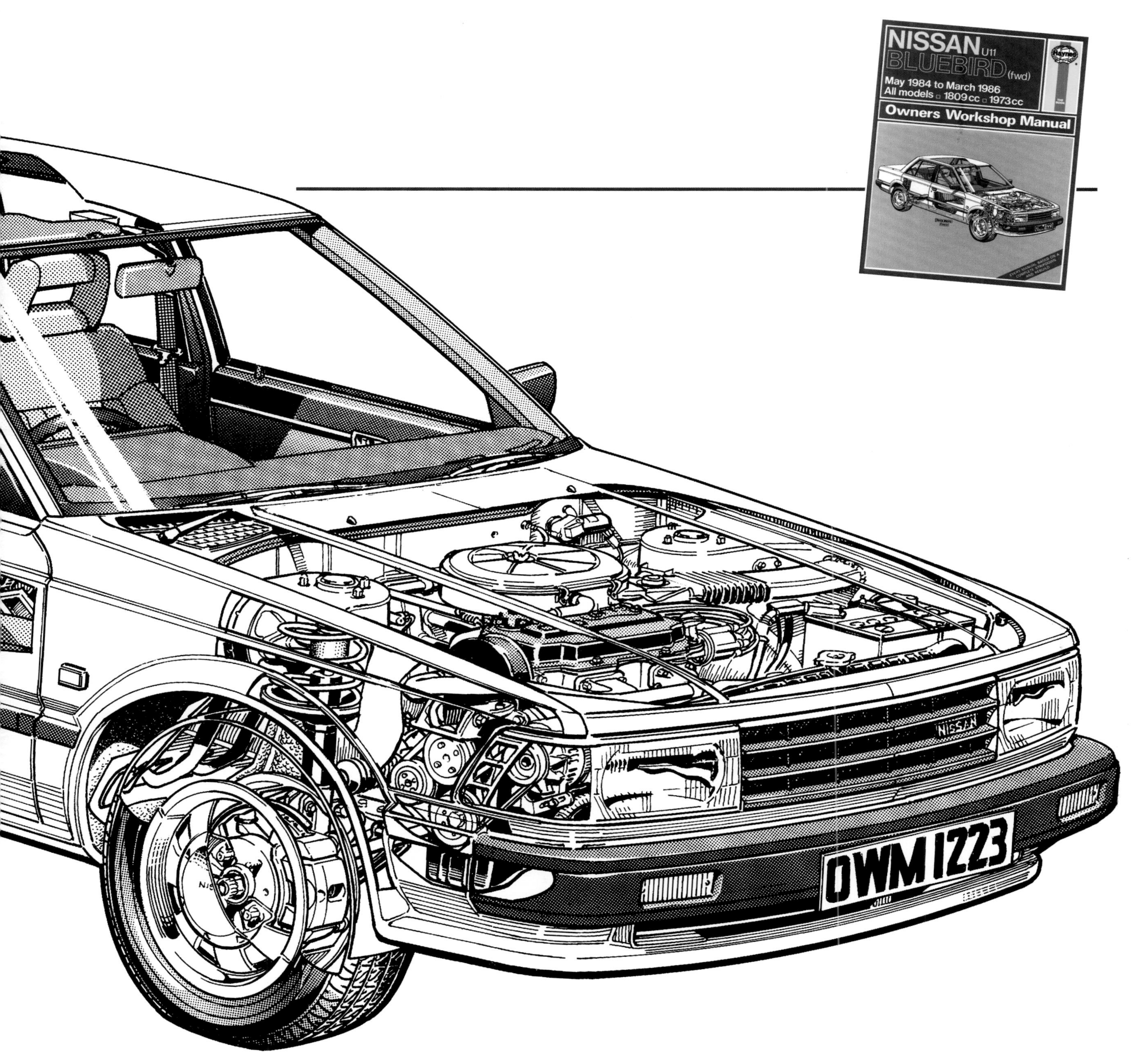
NISSAN U11
BLUEBIRD (fwd)
May 1984 to March 1986
All models □ 1809cc □ 1973cc
Owners Workshop Manual
NISSAN
OWM 1223

OPEL
MANTA MK1

YEARS MADE
1970–6

NUMBER MADE
498,553

ORIGINAL PRICE
£1,600 (1600 in 1970)

MECHANICAL LAYOUT
Front engine, rear-wheel drive

RANGE OF ENGINES
1,196–1,897cc, four-cylinder

MOST POWERFUL ENGINE
105bhp (1,897cc)

FASTEST VERSION
116mph (1,897cc)

BEST FUEL ECONOMY
26mpg (1,597cc)

WHEELBASE
2,430mm

LENGTH
4,292mm

NUMBER OF SEATS
4

Opel's Manta was one of the closest rivals to the Ford Capri in the first half of the 1970s, and some reckoned its well-proportioned fastback lines were, if anything, even more stylish.

Underpinning the Manta was the floorpan and drivetrain of the Opel Ascona, a Cortina-size car popular on the Continent but fairly rare in the UK. The Manta and Ascona, therefore, shared an identical wheelbase, all coil-spring suspension, and choice of camshaft-in-head engines, although in both cases the smallest 1.2-litre unit wasn't offered for the picky British market.

For the final two years of the car's life, there was also a fuel-injected 1.9-litre engine in the GT/E model that gave this civilised tourer real sporting glint. Even more specialised was the option of turbocharging, a British conversion offered through Opel dealers here.

In a way, though, these higher-performance Mantas strayed from the spirit of the original, which was not to be an out-and-out sports car but more a sleek and responsive GT to make everyday ownership of a 'family' car that little less dreary for cool dads with young children!

A new Mk2 Manta, arriving in 1975 alongside an all-new Ascona, updated the concept, and was offered in both two-door coupé and three-door hatchback forms, plus a 2-litre engine option. These found even more British favour, especially since Vauxhall-liveried models were available too.

PEUGEOT 504

YEARS MADE
1968–83 (in Europe)

NUMBER MADE
3,276,288

ORIGINAL PRICE
£1,499 (1.8 four-door in 1969)

MECHANICAL LAYOUT
Front engine, rear-wheel drive

RANGE OF ENGINES
1,796–1,971cc, four-cylinder petrol;
1,948–2,304cc, four-cylinder diesel

MOST POWERFUL ENGINE
104bhp (1,971cc, fuel-injected)

FASTEST VERSION
100mph (1,971cc, fuel-injected)

BEST FUEL ECONOMY
30mpg (2,112cc diesel)

WHEELBASE
2,740mm

LENGTH
4,490–4,803mm

NUMBER OF SEATS
5–7

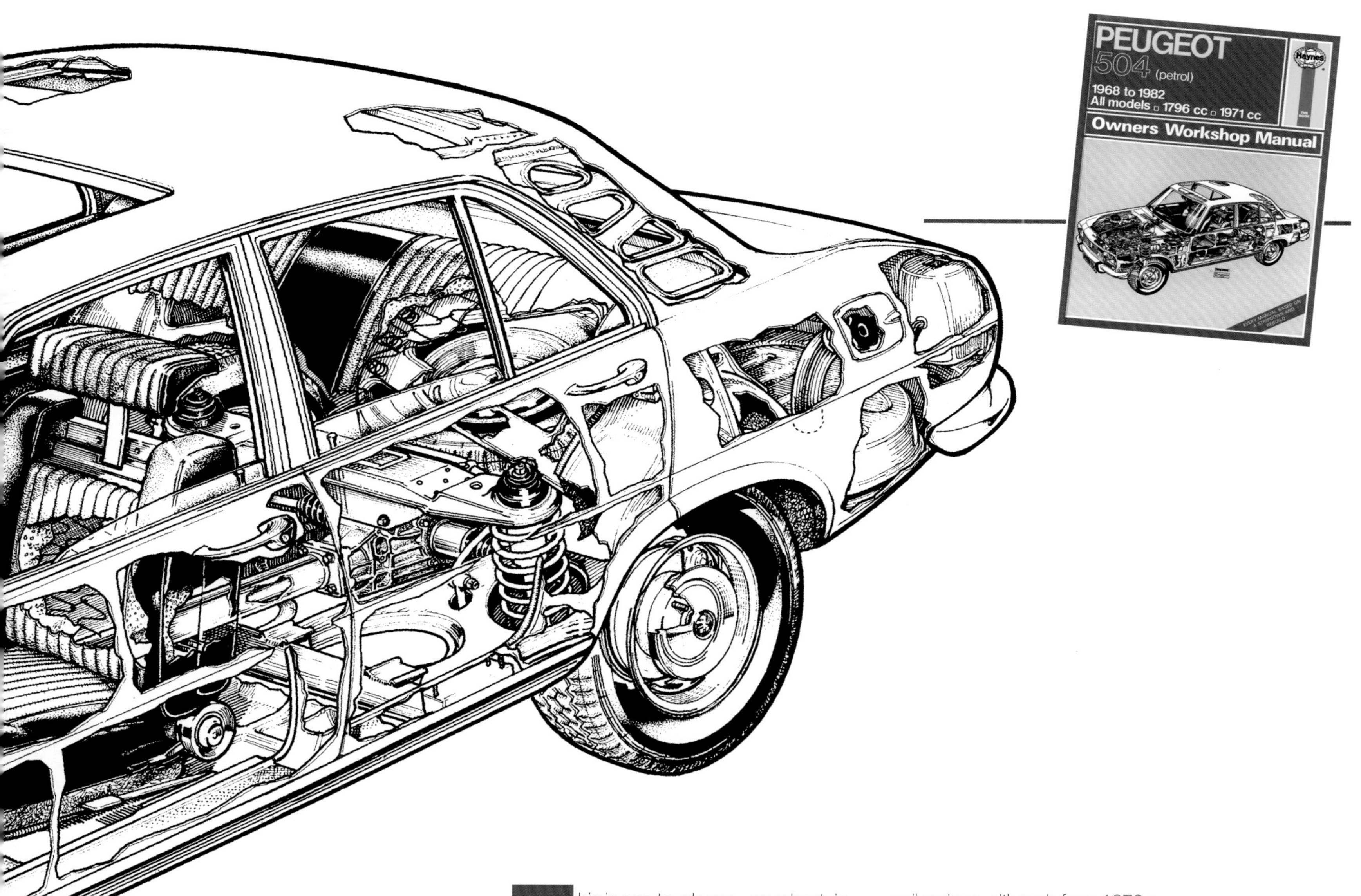

This is one tough car – so robust, in fact, that it continued to be made in Kenya and, latterly, Nigeria until 2006, which was a full 23 years since it last rolled off a production line in its native France…and 26 since it was supposed to be replaced by the 505.

It's hard to put a finger on the one element of the 504 that made it so eminently suitable for the roads of Africa. After all, it was very much a 'First World' design when it made its debut in 1968, so good that it nabbed the 1969 European Car Of The Year award. The 504 was rear-driven with in-line engines, boasted rack and pinion steering, and came with all-round independent suspension by MacPherson struts and coil springs, although from 1973 a cut-price edition was offered with a live axle at the rear and disc brakes only at the front, and minus the usual standard sunroof.

It seems Peugeot simply offered an exceptional all-round level of engineering excellence and mechanical simplicity in the 504. Its estates, added in 1971, were the most cavernous family load-carriers around, and yet the range-topping fuel-injected saloon – not to mention the rare, Pininfarina-built coupé and cabriolet – was a rather chic machine. Then again, the diesel-engined versions offered levels of frugality and longevity that virtually no British competitors could match.

PEUGEOT 205

YEARS MADE
1983–98

NUMBER MADE
5,278,050

ORIGINAL PRICE
£3,895 (1.0 three-door in 1984)

MECHANICAL LAYOUT
Front engine, front-wheel drive

RANGE OF ENGINES
954–1,905cc, four-cylinder petrol; 1,769–1,905cc, four-cylinder diesel

MOST POWERFUL ENGINE
130bhp (1,905cc, without catalytic converter)

FASTEST VERSION
122mph (GTi 1.6 in 118bhp tune, 1,580cc)

BEST FUEL ECONOMY
54mpg (1,769cc diesel)

WHEELBASE
2,420mm

LENGTH
3,705mm

NUMBER OF SEATS
4

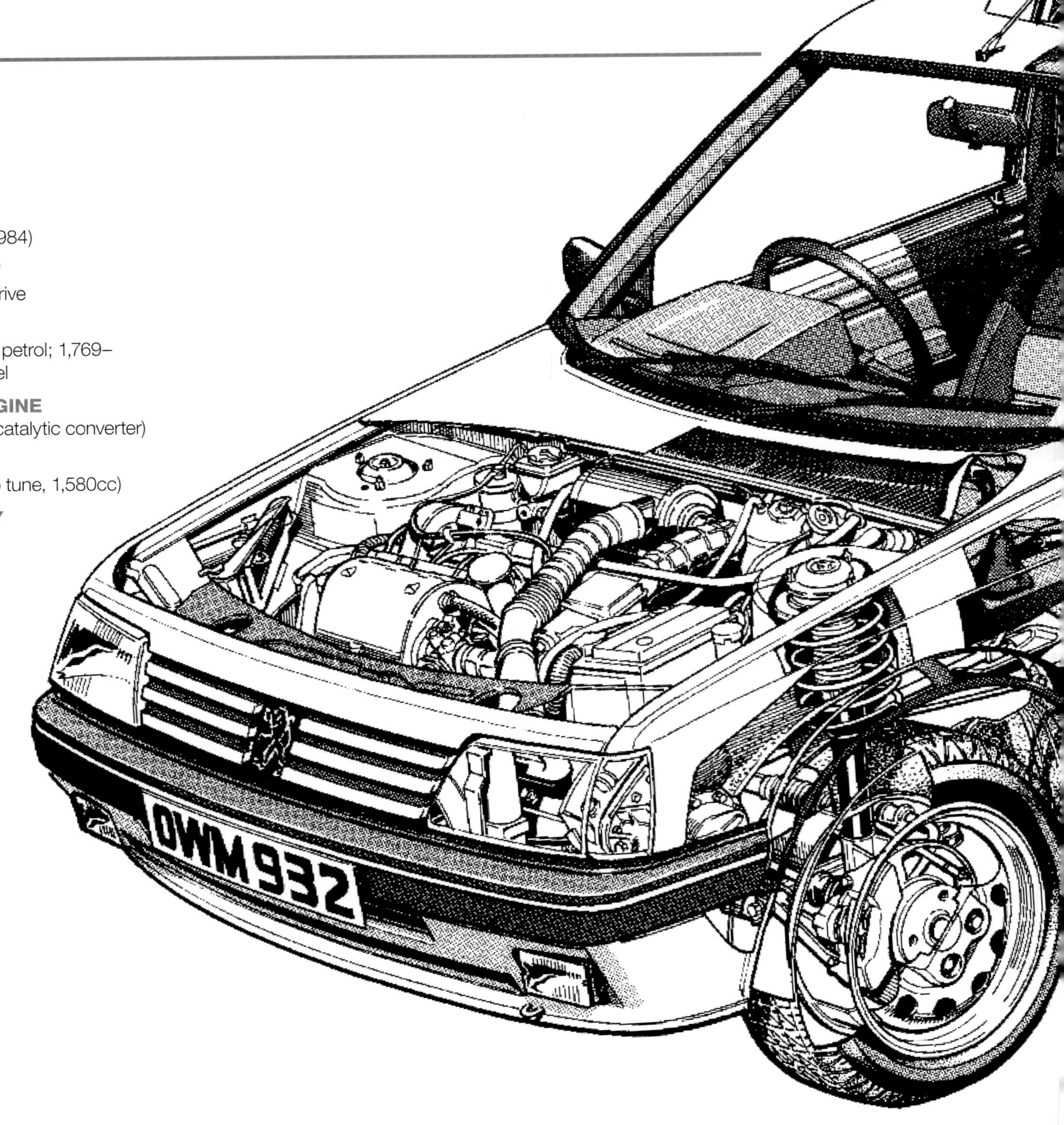

The little 205's position as the 11th best-selling single car design of all time is impressive; the acclaim it won during its whole lifetime is extraordinary.

Car magazine, for example, anointed it as the single best car the 1980s produced, while seasoned hacks at rival *Autocar* stated in 1991 it was 'still the best small car' – and that for a lowly 1.1 model tested against Ford's all-new Fiesta. That year, too, the eight-year old car accounted for 3 per cent of the whole UK market. And, throughout its 15 years on sale, it was never once facelifted.

The neat and timeless Pininfarina styling was certainly a factor in its appeal, but the overall rightness of the 205 won people over – the superbly roomy cabin thanks to compact torsion bar suspension, the supple ride, the lightness that meant even the smallest engines felt punchy. Perhaps most of all, it was the high-torque XUD7 diesel engine available in the car, a motor so quiet and powerful it single-handedly turned sentiment in favour of small diesels.

Meanwhile, the 205 GTi (depicted in our artwork), with its lowered suspension and widened wheelarches, grabbed the hot hatchback baton from Volkswagen and sprinted with it. Once again, its legacy lingers: the most powerful 1.6-litre edition remains a yardstick of driver satisfaction, acceleration and handling by which modern fun cars are still measured.

PORSCHE 911

YEARS MADE
1963–97

NUMBER MADE
439,235

ORIGINAL PRICE
£3,538 (in 1963)

MECHANICAL LAYOUT
Rear engine, rear- or four-wheel drive

RANGE OF ENGINES
1,991–3,600cc, flat-six-cylinder

MOST POWERFUL ENGINE
430bhp (911 Carrera GT2, 3,600cc)

FASTEST VERSION
184mph (911 Carrera GT2, 3,600cc)

BEST FUEL ECONOMY
26mpg (911T, 2,341cc)

WHEELBASE
2,210–2,277mm

LENGTH
4,160–4,250mm

NUMBER OF SEATS
2+2

Hmm: say 'Porsche 911' and you could be talking about any of dozens of different rear-engined sports cars from Stuttgart, but we've drawn the line for our data panel at 1997, when the venerable road racer-cum-status symbol underwent the most radical change ever to its winning formula – the switch from air-cooled to water-cooled engines.

Even then, the original 911 came in myriad varieties. When Terry Davey produced this beautiful illustration of the car for us in the 1970s, he was using the stunning 911 Carrera 2.7 as his subject – not quite the seminal example of the period (because of those energy-absorbing bumpers fitted to the car from 1974), but almost.

Spoilers and fat wheelarches cluttered the 911's elegant profile as the 1970s wore on but performance also developed apace, as there seemed to be almost limitless development potential for the superb flat-six that hung out the other side of the rear wheels; there's a massive 200bhp difference, for instance, between the original 911 Turbo and the last air-cooled car.

Rewarding, tail-happy handling has always been part of the 911's mystique, although those with worries could go for the late-model Carrera 4 with grippy power to the front wheels too. Build quality and reliability are more than legends, though: since the mid-'70s all 911s have been built from non-rusting galvanised steel. Porsche 911s were always costly, but generally worth it.

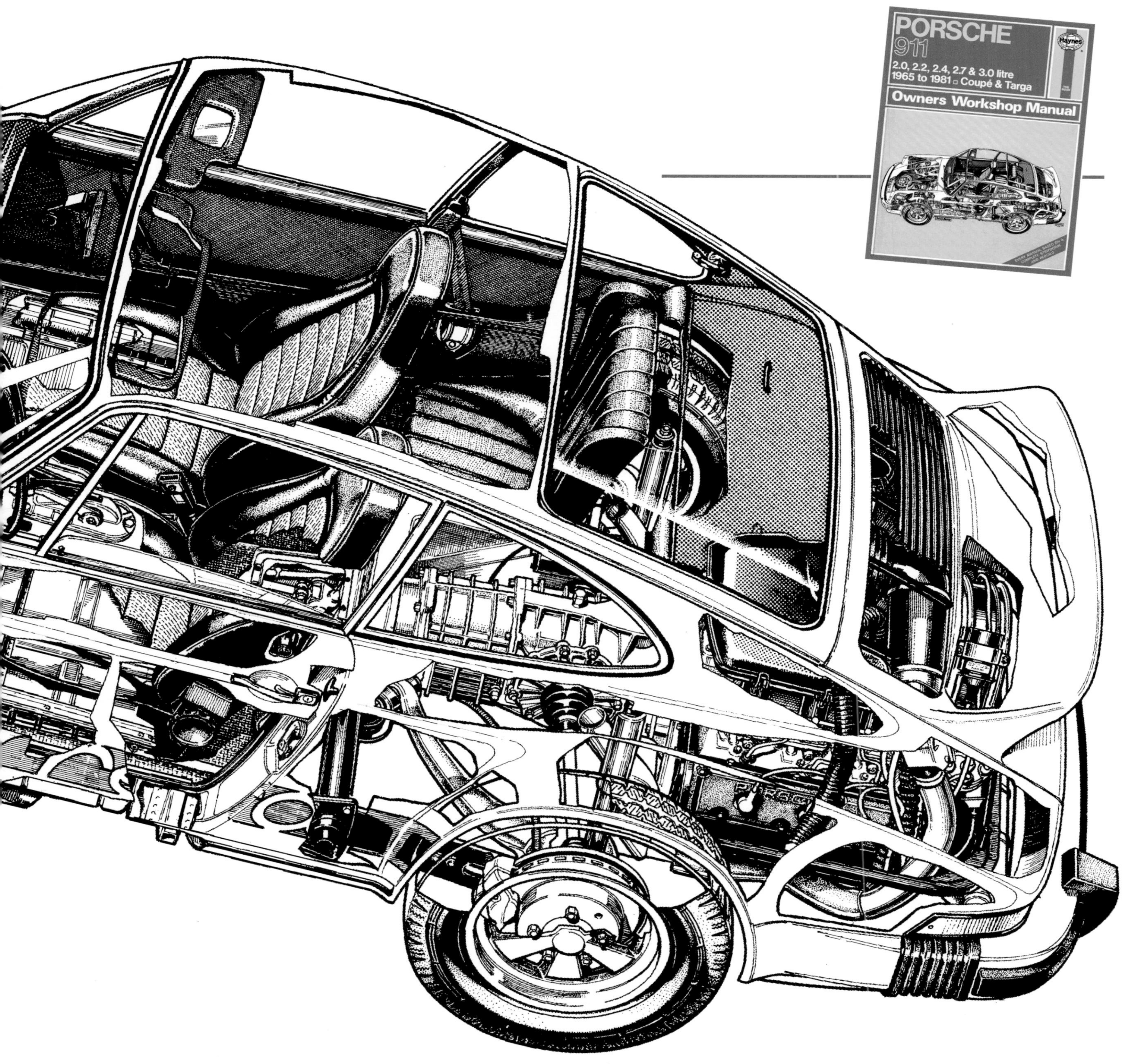
PORSCHE
911
2.0, 2.2, 2.4, 2.7 & 3.0 litre
1965 to 1981 □ Coupé & Targa
Haynes
Owners Workshop Manual

RELIANT ROBIN

YEARS MADE
1973–81

NUMBER MADE
61,000 approx

ORIGINAL PRICE
£801 (in 1973)

MECHANICAL LAYOUT
Front engine, rear-wheel drive

RANGE OF ENGINES
748–848cc, four-cylinder

MOST POWERFUL ENGINE
40bhp (848cc)

FASTEST VERSION
80mph (848cc)

BEST FUEL ECONOMY
50mpg (748cc)

WHEELBASE
2,159mm

LENGTH
3,327mm

NUMBER OF SEATS
4

A fiscal loophole in British law allowed Reliant three-wheeler cars to flourish for almost 50 years.

A little-visited page of the lawbook states that a 'tricycle' is classed as a motorbike as long as it keeps its unladen weight down to 500kg. That means the owner can drive it on a motorbike licence, pay tiny amounts of road tax, and, with such lightness, enjoy (if that's the right word) tiny fuel consumption. Running a Reliant was an object lesson in cheap motoring.

Tom Williams, the company's founder, first introduced a four-seater Reliant Regal car alongside his popular Reliant Regent vans in 1952. It featured Reliant's own 747cc engine copied from the Austin Seven's; four years later it gained glass fibre bodywork and, in 1962, the new Reliant Regal 3/25 boasted Reliant's all-new light alloy 600cc engine.

As other three-wheelers faded away, Reliant went from strength to strength. In 1973 industrial designer consultancy Ogle was hired to reinvent its staple three-wheeled car, and the resulting Robin proved even more successful than its predecessors, especially during 1970s fuel crises when an attentive Robin driver could squeeze 70 miles of motoring from one precious gallon of fuel. Its engine was increased in capacity to 750cc, and later 850cc. Princess Anne, a fan of Reliant's Scimitar sports car, had one as a Gatcombe Park runabout, although more usual owners were former bikers working in factories and mines.

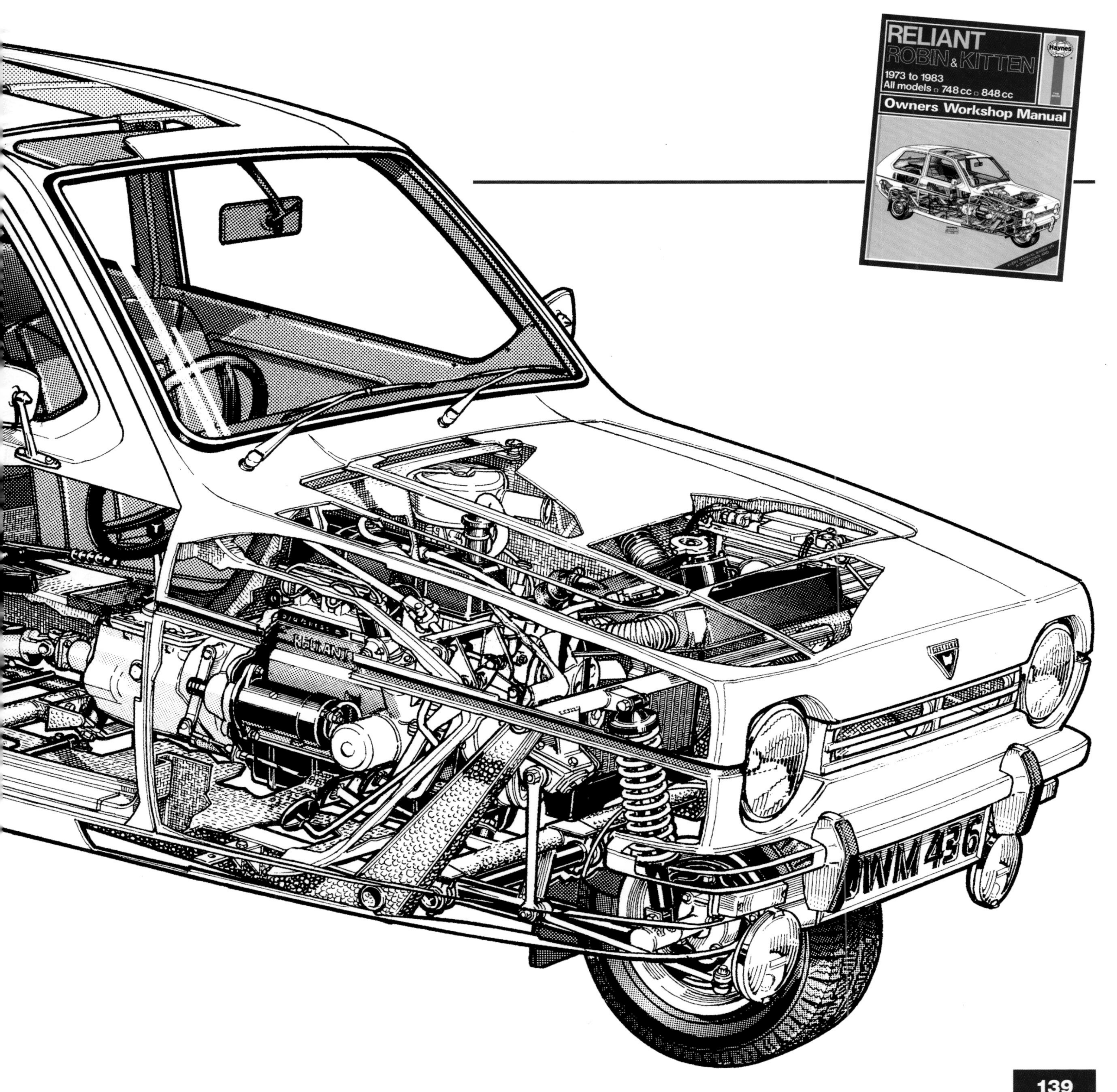
RELIANT
ROBIN & KITTEN
1973 to 1983
All models 748 cc 848 cc
Haynes
Owners Workshop Manual
RELIANT
WM 436

RENAULT

YEARS MADE
1961–93

NUMBER MADE
8,135,422 approx

ORIGINAL PRICE
£549 (750 in 1962)

MECHANICAL LAYOUT
Front engine, front-wheel drive

RANGE OF ENGINES
747–1,108cc, four-cylinder

MOST POWERFUL ENGINE
27bhp (1,108cc)

FASTEST VERSION
82mph (1,108cc)

BEST FUEL ECONOMY
43mpg (747cc)

WHEELBASE
2,401 (left) & 2,449mm (right)

LENGTH
3,668mm

NUMBER OF SEATS
4

As Renault's response to the utilitarian Citroën 2CV, the 4 was a long time coming, making its debut 13 years after the minimalist Citroën delivered motoring to millions of French drivers for the first time. Then again, for Renault, the car entered new territory on several fronts.

For a start it was the company's first front-wheel-drive car. Also, it pioneered the concept of a five-door hatchback with folding rear seats. It had several smaller innovations, like a different wheelbase on each side – with no adverse effect on handling – to facilitate a simple, cheap torsion bar rear suspension as part of the all-independent set-up. This was a key reason the car had such tight roadholding despite its propensity to lean alarmingly in any corner taken rapidly. A gearlever sprouting from the dashboard gave a flat, uncluttered floor for driver and passenger.

The frugal and friendly 4 was so much appreciated that it eventually became the biggest-selling French car ever. But it was basic to the end in 1993 (in Britain the last imports arrived in '85), which meant it stuck with features like sliding windows. The 1.1-litre-engined GTL arrived in 1978, much more tolerable on long trips with higher gearing, bigger drum brakes and cloth seats. Its grey plastic trimmings – plus, oh joy, longer wiper blades – set it apart from its millions of older doppelgangers around Europe.

RENAULT 16

YEARS MADE
1965–80

NUMBER MADE
1,846,000 approx

ORIGINAL PRICE
£949 (GL in 1962)

MECHANICAL LAYOUT
Front engine, front-wheel drive

RANGE OF ENGINES
1,470–1,647cc, four-cylinder

MOST POWERFUL ENGINE
83bhp (TX, 1,647cc)

FASTEST VERSION
105mph (TX, 1,647cc)

BEST FUEL ECONOMY
27mpg (1,470cc)

WHEELBASE
2,717 (left) & 2,650mm (right)

LENGTH
4,240mm

NUMBER OF SEATS
5

Seats folding down into beds were but one aspect of this Renault's marvellous, if sometimes quirky, package. The car is a motoring milestone: the first thoroughly conceived large family hatchback. So much of what we take for granted on today's Renault Laguna was right there in the 16. No wonder it was voted 1965 European Car Of The Year.

Renault engineers provided a brand new, all-aluminium, 1,470cc four-cylinder engine driving through the front wheels, with long-travel independent suspension by torsion bars giving a softly cosseting – some might say, today, sick-making – ride. An anomaly, however, was a manual gearlever mounted on the steering column – the 16 would be the world's last car to retain this feature when production ceased in January 1980.

And then there was the hatchback. By today's standards, the sill was absurdly high, but the luggage accommodation was extraordinary compared to a typical British family car of the time, like a Vauxhall Victor 101.

Renault constantly improved the 16. In March 1968 a sporty TS came with a gutsier 1,565cc engine, giving 83bhp instead of the 1,470cc's 55. There was an automatic transmission option a year later and then, in September 1973, the ultimate 16 arrived in the shape of the quad-headlamp TX with a five-speed gearbox, electric front windows, central locking, a roof spoiler, and rear screen wiper.

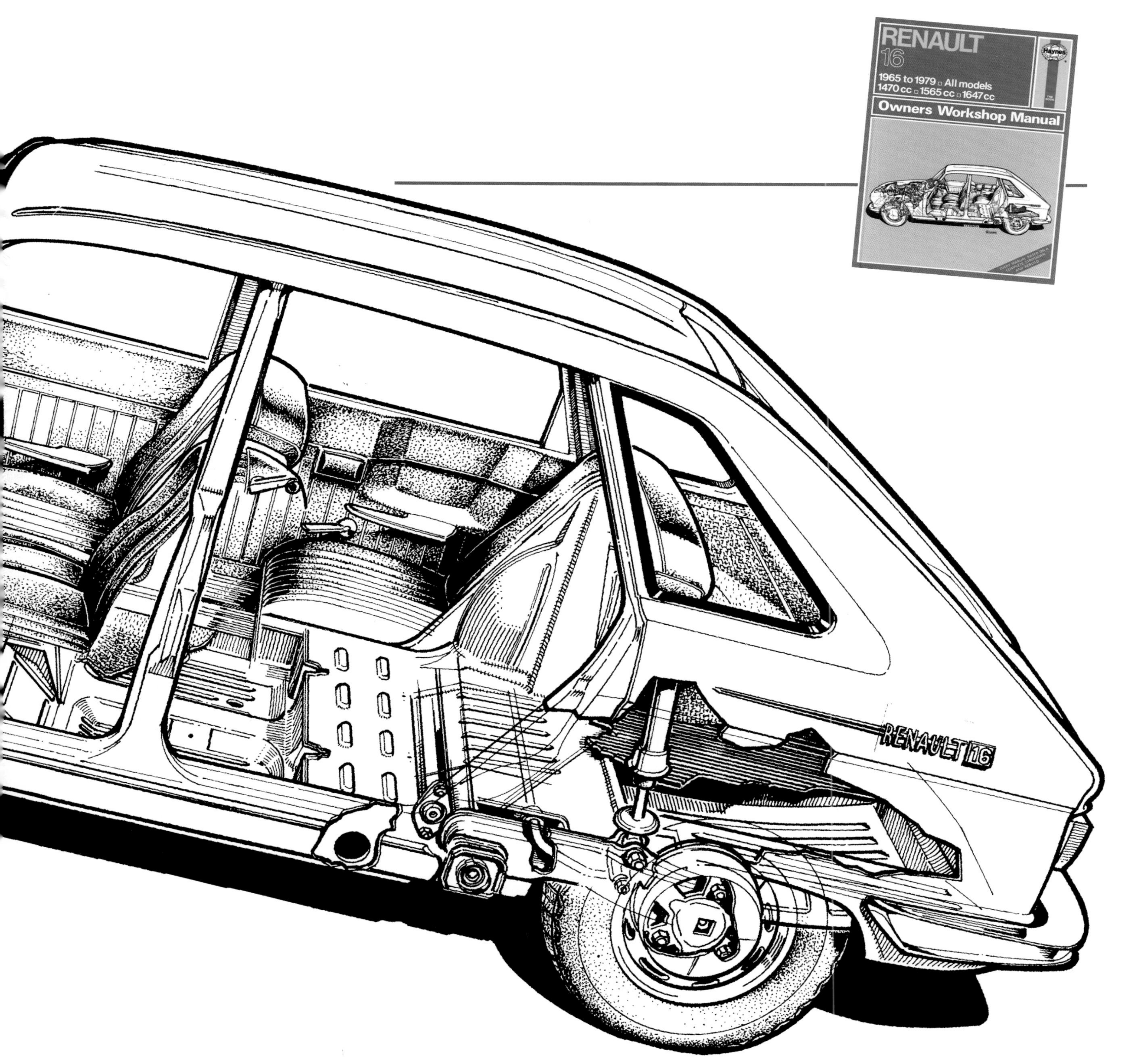
RENAULT
16
1965 to 1979 □ All models
1470 cc □ 1565 cc □ 1647 cc
Owners Workshop Manual
Haynes
RENAULT 16

RENAULT 5 MK1

YEARS MADE
1972–84

NUMBER MADE
5,471,701 approx

ORIGINAL PRICE
£939 (TL in 1972)

MECHANICAL LAYOUT
Front engine, front-wheel drive

RANGE OF ENGINES
782–1,397cc, four-cylinder

MOST POWERFUL ENGINE
110bhp (Gordini Turbo, 1,397cc)

FASTEST VERSION
112mph (Gordini Turbo, 1,397cc)

BEST FUEL ECONOMY
40mpg (782cc)

WHEELBASE
2,420mm

LENGTH
3,520mm

NUMBER OF SEATS
4

A third of new cars sold in the UK today are 'superminis' – the ultra-practical, easy-to-drive front-drive small hatchback is part of Europe's motoring fabric. The supermini has been with us for over 35 years, and here's the vehicle that defined it – the Renault 5.

The little French car, with its crisp profile, easy-access third rear door and safe, enjoyable handling, was actually predated by the 1971 Fiat 127. That one was slightly roomier inside (thanks to its compact transverse engine – the 5's was longitudinally-mounted) but not every model came with a hatchback, and those that did had a stupidly high sill.

The 5 set the benchmark because its hatchback opened down to bumper level and it had brilliant visibility; very '70s novelties were moulded plastic bumpers and dashboard. In 1979 Renault once again set the pace for this type of car by offering a five-door option in the same wheelbase and length – something widely copied during the 1980s.

Nor was performance overlooked, as there was a racy 93bhp 5 Alpine in 1976 (the name changed to 5 Gordini in the UK to avoid a trademark rumpus with Chrysler), made even hotter with the addition of a turbocharger in 1982.

Sadly, though, the brilliant designer behind the classlessly stylish 5's looks, Michel Boué, died in 1971 aged 35, before his clever baby was launched.

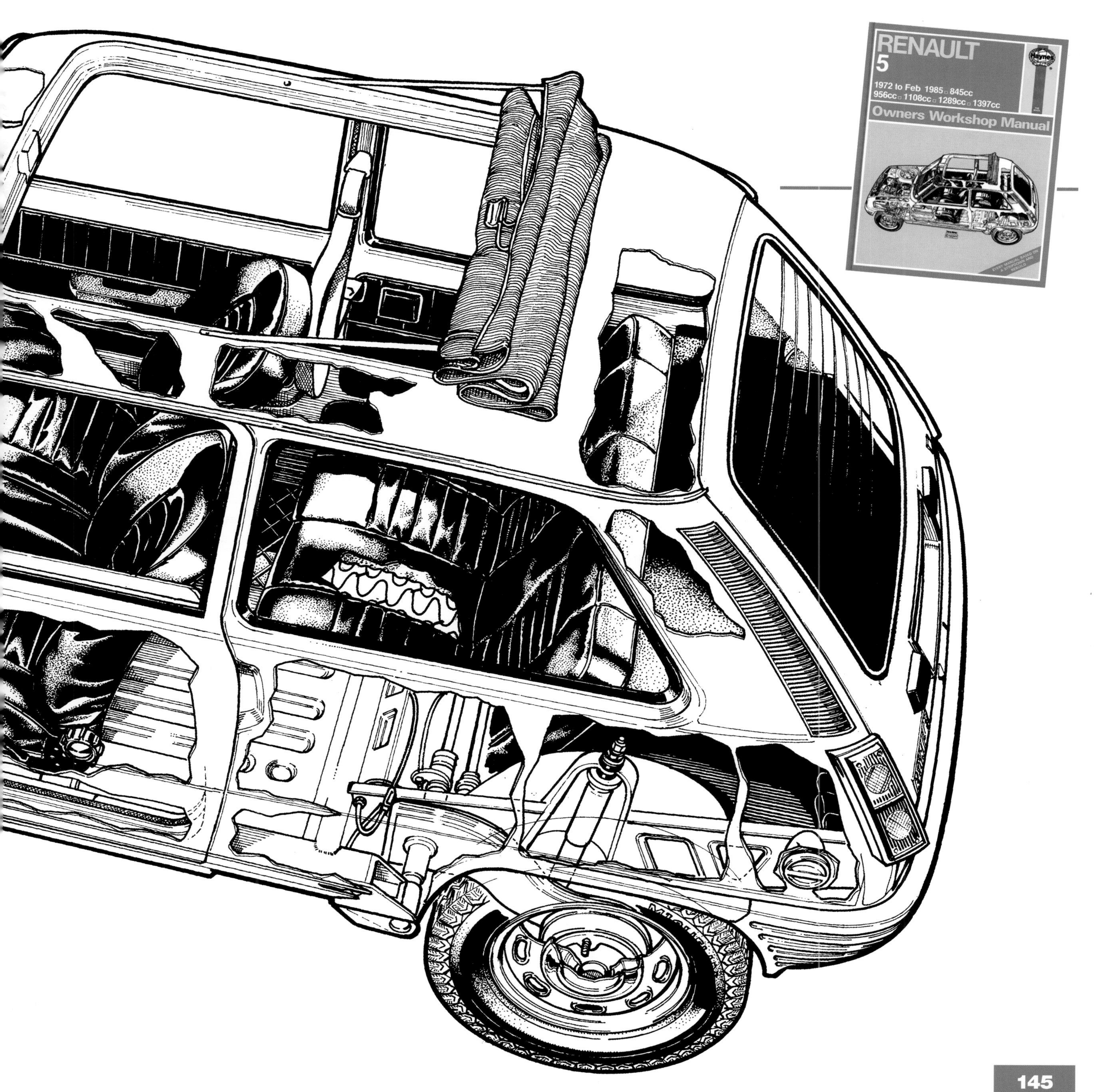
RENAULT
5
1972 to Feb 1985 □ 845cc
956cc □ 1108cc □ 1289cc □ 1397cc
Owners Workshop Manual

RENAULT 20 TS

YEARS MADE
1977–84

NUMBER MADE
201,401

ORIGINAL PRICE
£5,153 (in 1978)

MECHANICAL LAYOUT
Front engine, front-wheel drive

RANGE OF ENGINES
1,995cc, four-cylinder

MOST POWERFUL ENGINE
109bhp (1,995cc)

FASTEST VERSION
107mph (1,995cc)

BEST FUEL ECONOMY
26mpg (1,995cc)

WHEELBASE
2,660mm

LENGTH
4,520mm

NUMBER OF SEATS
5

All but a tiny handful of the Renault 20TSs sold in the UK have departed for that great scrapyard in the sky, so don't worry if this car is unfamiliar to you – it's an irrelevance today. Possibly the most important thing to recall about it in a British context is its place in popular culture.

In a classic TV ad screened on ITV in 1979, a 20TS pulls up at traffic lights and a policeman on a bicycle taps on the window. 'Who do you think you are – Stirling Moss?' he growls, only for the electric window to slide down… revealing the bemused racing hero himself. Well, it was funny at the time.

And at around that time, the 20 was a swift and popular five-door executive car – indeed, the only 2-litre hatchback on sale. It was an early addition to the 20 range, supplanting the slow 1.6 model with a version powered by an all-alloy 2-litre engine, later shared with Peugeot and Citroën. A five-speed gearbox option in 1979 turned it into a proper motorway cruiser.

The 20 and 30 (V6 power) cars also boasted unusually high levels of safety, incorporating front and rear crumple zones and side impact protection bars long before they were widespread.

A shame, then, that rust and then dilapidation has rendered this excellent car, at best, a rather distant memory.

RENAULT
20
1976 to 1984 □ All models
1647 cc □ 1995 cc □ 2165 cc
Owners Workshop Manual
Haynes

RENAULT 14

YEARS MADE
1976–82

NUMBER MADE
999,093

ORIGINAL PRICE
£2,562 (in 1976)

MECHANICAL LAYOUT
Front engine, front-wheel drive

RANGE OF ENGINES
1,218–1,360cc, four-cylinder

MOST POWERFUL ENGINE
71bhp (1,360cc)

FASTEST VERSION
96mph (TS, 1,360cc)

BEST FUEL ECONOMY
33mpg (1,218cc)

WHEELBASE
2,530mm

LENGTH
4,025mm

NUMBER OF SEATS
5

You might find it surprising to recall that Renault was one of the first manufacturers to recognise the Volkswagen Golf's packaging brilliance, and take a serious tilt at that German motoring masterpiece.

With admirable resourcefulness, it bought in the transverse powerpacks it needed from rival Peugeot, and then mounted the engine in the 14 at an inclined angle of 72° with the gearbox nestling in the sump underneath it. So there was room under the bonnet to position the spare wheel, freeing up maximum luggage space.

With a short stubby nose and an interestingly curvaceous main body, the emphasis in the 14 was therefore on excellent cabin space, the better to exploit the car's coil-sprung (conventional, by Renault standards) ride comfort. The rear seat could be just as easily removed as folded.

Renault goofed in its launch ad campaign by comparing the car's organic shape to that of a pear; ironically, the car would soon prove to rot away almost as fast as the fruit itself, and develop an infuriating tendency not to start on damp mornings. They then switched tack to promoting it as modern industrial sculpture, but the fact remained: many people actively disliked the 14's shape.

None of which detracts from the fact that this car, especially in eager TS form with five-speed gearbox, did indeed make a spiritedly Gallic Golf rival.

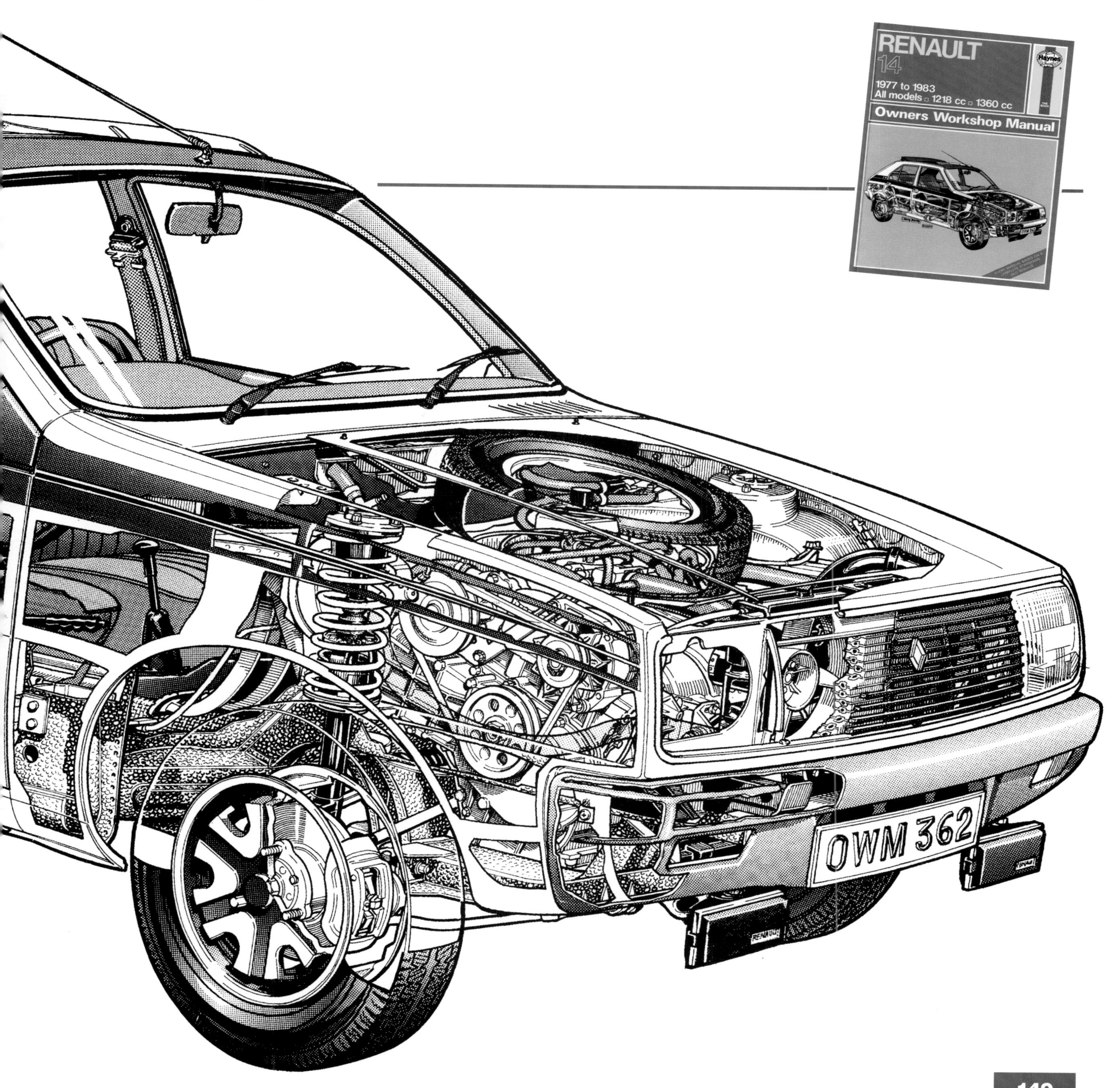
RENAULT
14
1977 to 1983
All models □ 1218 cc □ 1360 cc
Owners Workshop Manual
OWM 362
RENAULT

RENAULT FUEGO

YEARS MADE
1980–93

NUMBER MADE
226,583 (in France – 40,000 more made in Spain and south America)

ORIGINAL PRICE
£4,489 (1.4GTL in 1980)

MECHANICAL LAYOUT
Front engine, front-wheel drive

RANGE OF ENGINES
1,397–1,995cc, four-cylinder petrol; 2,068cc, four-cylinder diesel

MOST POWERFUL ENGINE
132bhp (1.6 Turbo, 1,565cc)

FASTEST VERSION
118mph (1.6 Turbo, 1,565cc)

BEST FUEL ECONOMY
31mpg (1,397cc)

WHEELBASE
2,440mm

LENGTH
4,380mm

NUMBER OF SEATS
4

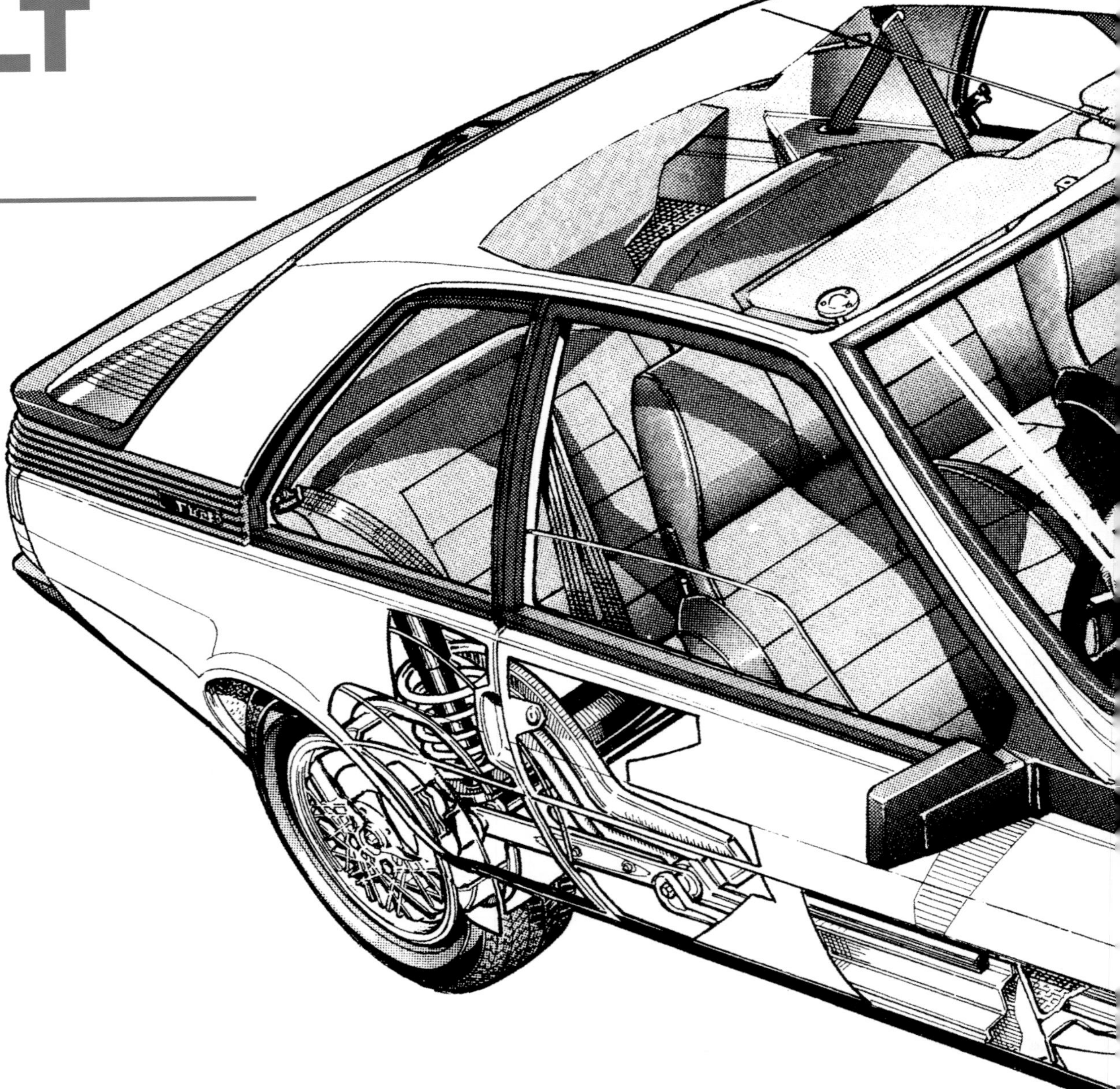

The Fuego (it's Spanish for 'fire') adapted the hardware – and wheelbase – from the mundane Renault 18 saloon into a sleek and aerodynamic sports coupé. That black plastic belt-line encircling the bodywork was distinctive, while the panoramic glass hatchback gave ample headroom in the back for two adults.

Engines ranged from an economical, low-hassle 1.4-litre motor developing 64bhp up to a 110bhp 2-litre. But in 1984 Renault also produced the Fuego Turbo, with a blown 1.6-litre engine putting out 132bhp through the front wheels; the torque-steer was almost as obscene as the huge stickers on the doors reading 'TURBO', for the benefit of anyone who hadn't already twigged.

Nor was the turbo the most interesting engine. A year before, Renault slotted the 18's 2.1-litre turbo-diesel into the Fuego. With 88bhp, it was a modest performer, but is more significant for being the first vaguely sporting car with diesel power.

And the innovations didn't stop there, either. In the electronic spirit of the early 1980s, the Fuego was the first car with a remote central locking system.

In truth, the car was not the committed performance driver's choice. The spongy MacPherson strut suspension, betraying the Renault 18 within, had been devised for comfort rather than agility. However, on smooth, straight roads, the Fuego's stability and ride was excellent, probably thanks also to a low drag factor of just 0.34.

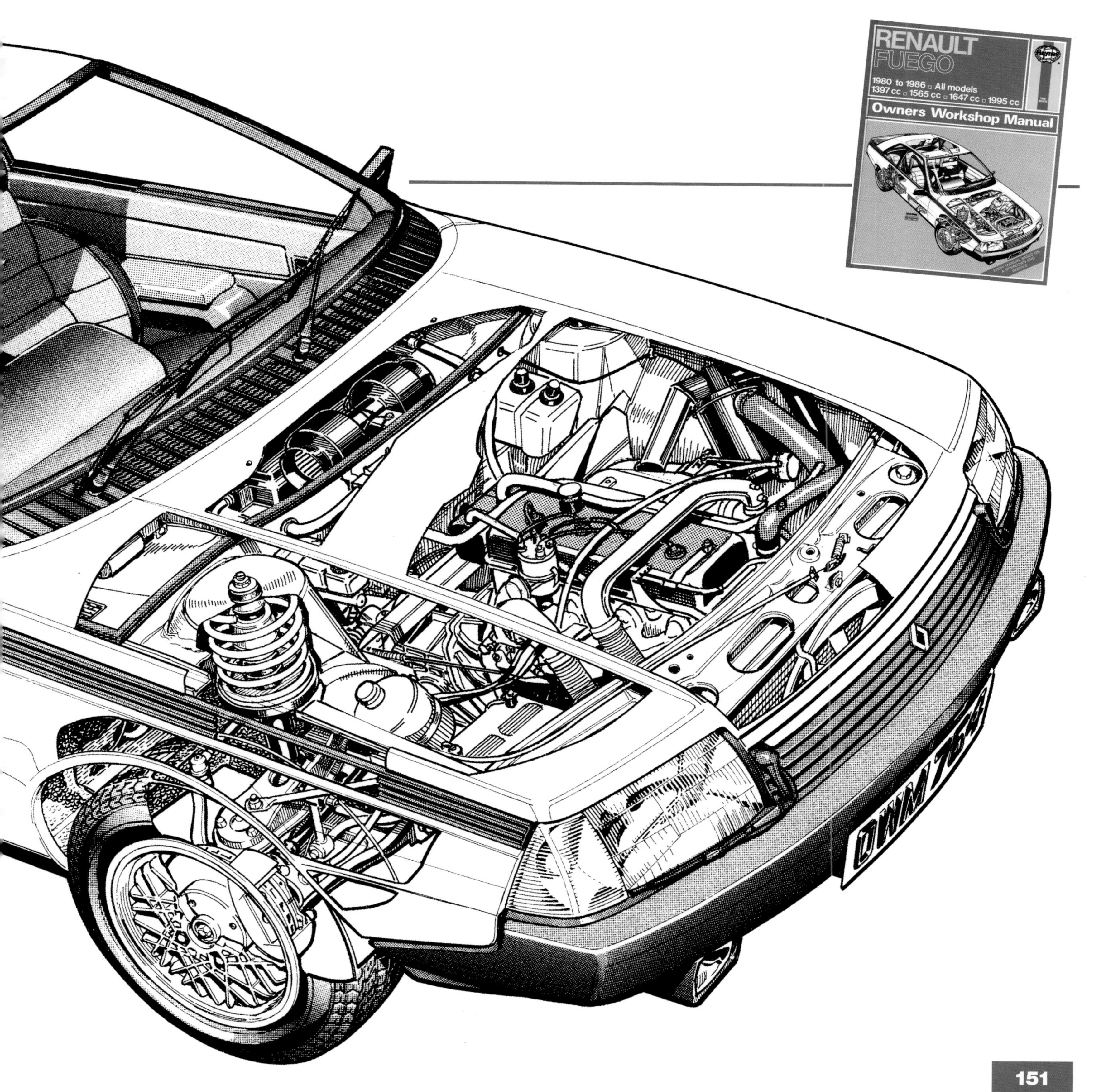
RENAULT
FUEGO
1980 to 1986 □ All models
1397 cc □ 1565 cc □ 1647 cc □ 1995 cc
Owners Workshop Manual

ROVER
3500 P6

YEARS MADE
1968–76

NUMBER MADE
62,942

ORIGINAL PRICE
£1,791 (Three Thousand Five in 1968)

MECHANICAL LAYOUT
Front engine, rear-wheel drive

RANGE OF ENGINES
3,528cc,V8-cylinder

MOST POWERFUL ENGINE
150bhp (3,528cc)

FASTEST VERSION
122mph (3500S, 3,528cc)

BEST FUEL ECONOMY
19mpg (3,528cc)

WHEELBASE
2,625mm

LENGTH
4,554–4,566mm

NUMBER OF SEATS
4

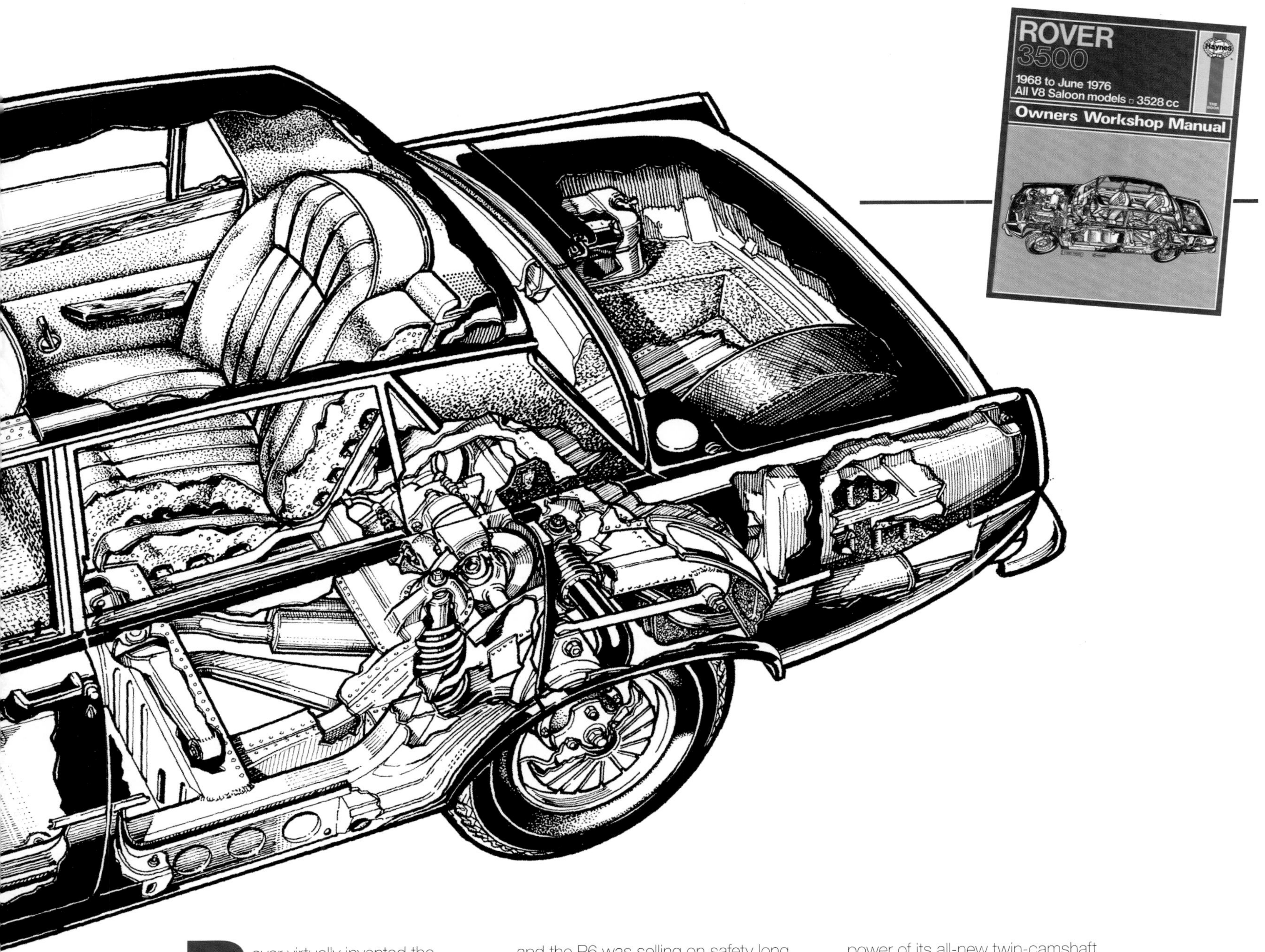

Rover virtually invented the 'executive' car with the 2000, first in its P6 line, a vehicle as mould-breaking in its class as the Mini. It was a 100mph saloon ripe for the dawn of Britain's motorway age that didn't appeal solely – like every previous Rover – to solemn, silver-haired bank managers in bowler hats. And the P6B 3500 that followed was, if anything, an even slicker package.

Here was a compact, young blade's Rover, bristling with new technology, and the P6 was selling on safety long before it was fashionable. It featured a super-strong 'base unit' cage (a steel skeleton to which the unstressed outer panels were attached), four-wheel disc brakes and a well-padded interior.

In fact you stood a good chance of avoiding a crash in the first place because the de Dion rear suspension followed racing car practice, so the smooth-riding 2000 had prodigious grip, and could handle the flexible power of its all-new twin-camshaft engine. American safety campaigner Ralph Nader hailed it as 'how all cars should be built'.

Then Rover truly excelled itself by installing the light-alloy V8 engine it had acquired from General Motors into the 2000, to create what it initially called the Three Thousand Five. This light and powerful motor made it smooth, fast and very desirable, with surprisingly good fuel economy and, in Mk2 3500S form with a manual gearbox, very fast.

ROVER 3500 SD1

YEARS MADE
1976–86

NUMBER MADE
303,345 (all SD1s – around one-third of them 3500s)

ORIGINAL PRICE
£4,750 (3500 in 1976)

MECHANICAL LAYOUT
Front engine, rear-wheel drive

RANGE OF ENGINES
3,528cc,V8-cylinder

MOST POWERFUL ENGINE
190bhp (3,528cc)

FASTEST VERSION
132mph (3500 Vitesse, 3,528cc)

BEST FUEL ECONOMY
20mpg (3,528cc)

WHEELBASE
2,815mm

LENGTH
4,968mm

NUMBER OF SEATS
5

Britain was a proud nation in 1976 when British Leyland finally pulled a decent car out of the hat after a parade of recent duds.

Thanks to a sudden injection of much-needed budget in 1973, Rover's renowned engineering department could finally make their new five-door luxury hatchback a reality, and the 3500 certainly was handsome. Its fastback styling was the height of modernity, with a sexy frontal treatment paying homage to the Ferrari Daytona. Under that sleek bonnet was Rover's familiar V8 engine mated to a brand new five-speed gearbox. Power steering, naturally, was standard, and the crushed velour interior, complete with dials contained in a prominent box atop the dashboard, was a sight to behold. Every schoolboy in British suburbia hoped his dad might be successful enough to get one.

The euphoria was crowned by the big Rover's elevation to European Car Of The Year for 1976. However, in its eight years on sale Rover's SD1 (its project codename, standing for Specialist Division 1, never actually used on any showroom car) endured bumpy fortunes at odds with its own composed road behaviour.

Alternative engines and models proliferated but British Leyland-monitored build quality was dreadful, allowing BMW and even Saab to steal sales. The reputation never quite rebounded, despite a move in 1982 to assembly at Cowley and, that year, the arrival of the storming 190bhp Vitesse.

ROVER
3500 V8
1976 to 1987
All models □ 3528 cc
Owners Workshop Manual

SAAB 96/95 V4

YEARS MADE
1966–79

NUMBER MADE
326,570/77,873

ORIGINAL PRICE
£801 (96 in 1967)

MECHANICAL LAYOUT
Front engine, front-wheel drive

RANGE OF ENGINES
1,498cc, V4-cylinder

MOST POWERFUL ENGINE
65bhp (1,498cc)

FASTEST VERSION
90mph (96, 1,498cc)

BEST FUEL ECONOMY
28.5mpg (1,498cc)

WHEELBASE
2,498mm

LENGTH
4,170–4,230mm

NUMBER OF SEATS
4

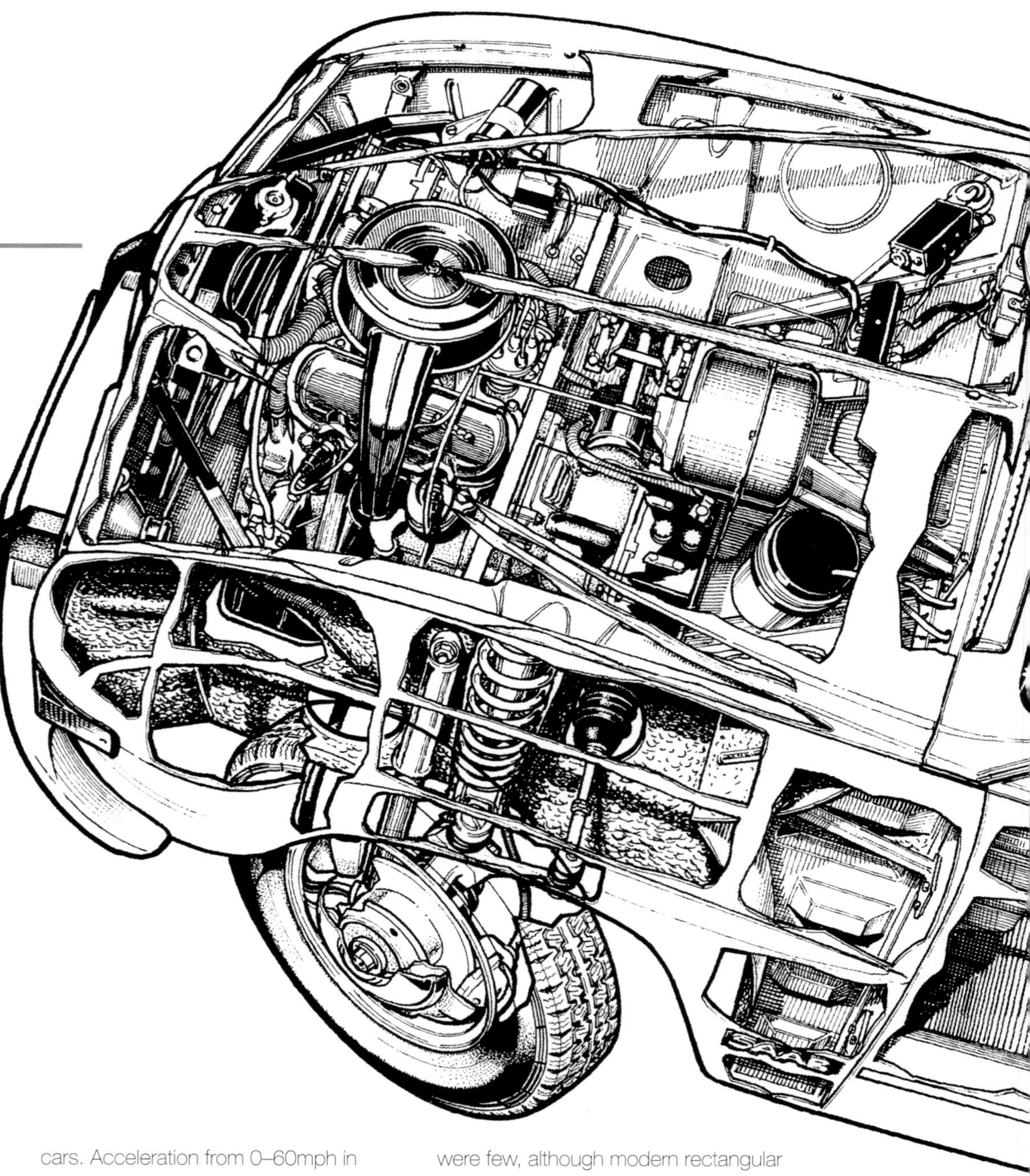

Installing a new engine in the quirky 96, to replace the outmoded two-stroke units that had served Saab cars since their late 1940s inception, was intended as a stopgap measure by the company until the 99 replacement was ready for launch. In the end, the 96 continued on sale alongside the 99 for a dozen years more.

The V4 engine used in the German-made Ford Taunus was chosen, and it turned the 96 saloon and its 95 estate stablemate into sprightly yet economical cars. Acceleration from 0–60mph in 16.6sec and touring fuel consumption of 35mpg weren't bad considering the hefty weight being propelled; the excellent aerodynamics of the little Saabs' shapely bodies must have helped.

More fuel saving was possible when motoring downhill thanks to the freewheel, which cut engine power when the driver's foot came off the accelerator so the car could coast without needing engine-braking.

Changes during the V4 96/95 lifecycle were few, although modern rectangular headlights spruced up the looks in 1969. These also boosted the safety credentials of a car that was already way ahead of most, despite its dated styling. It had a hugely strong body – Saab having pioneered the aerospace-influenced passenger safety cell construction concept – diagonally split, dual-circuit brakes, and a collapsible steering column. It was ideal for winter use, having carburettor pre-heating and, latterly, headlamp wipers and heated front seats.

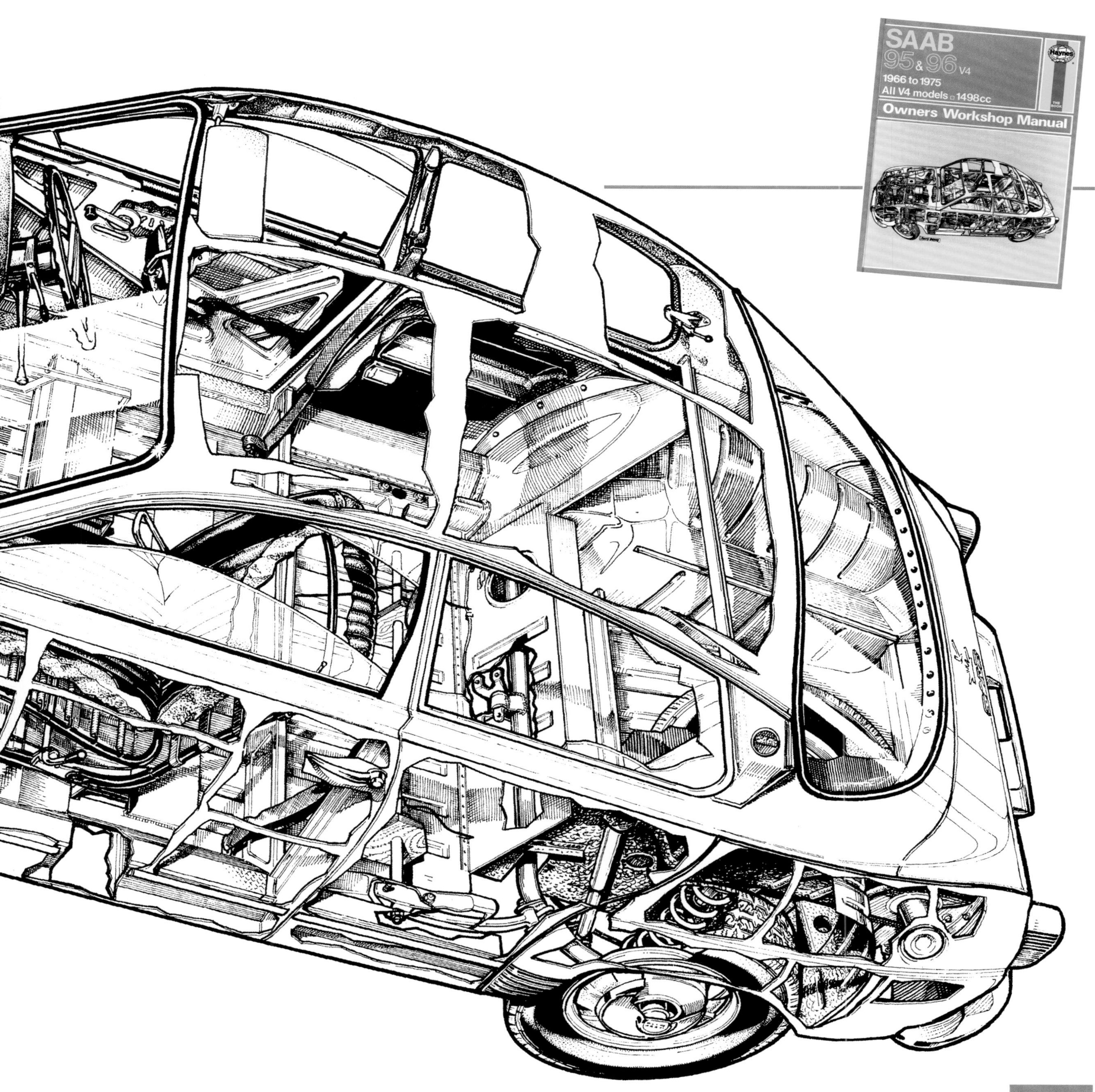
SAAB
95 & 96 V4
1966 to 1975
All V4 models 1498cc
Owners Workshop Manual
Haynes

SAAB 900 TURBO

YEARS MADE
1978–93

NUMBER MADE
202,284

ORIGINAL PRICE
£8,675 (three-door in 1978)

MECHANICAL LAYOUT
Front engine, front-wheel drive

RANGE OF ENGINES
1,985cc, four-cylinder

MOST POWERFUL ENGINE
185bhp (1,985cc)

FASTEST VERSION
133mph (Carlsson three-door, 1,985cc)

BEST FUEL ECONOMY
28mpg (1,985cc)

WHEELBASE
2,515mm

LENGTH
4,680–4,690mm

NUMBER OF SEATS
5

The Saab 900 Turbo turned into a very winning combination of the 900 base car, thoroughly developed from the excellent but shorter 99, and the thrilling performance of the engine from the 99 Turbo.

Saab had broken new ground with the 99 Turbo in 1977, for before that time the technology to use waste exhaust gases to boost engine performance had been restricted to sports cars like Porsche's 911. Here, the turbocharger – manufactured in the UK by Garrett AiResearch – was offered in a highly practical three-door hatchback.

Together with fuel-injection, this lifted the available brake-horsepower of the 2-litre engine from 110 to 145. It was now installed in the 900's three- and five-door bodies (four-door saloons and convertibles would follow), and power leapt to 175bhp when the engine went 16-valve in 1984. The crazy 185bhp motor was found only in the Carlsson limited edition of 1989, named for Saab's rally ace and sometime ambassador Erik Carlsson. Five-speed gearboxes arrived in 1980.

These were strongly built cars offering equally strong urge, and inspiring enormous loyalty because of their safe and surefooted handling, and their extremely comfortable seats and logical controls. Their resistance to decay and owner abuse was also a strong suit. Somehow, with the Vauxhall Cavalier-based range that replaced them in 1993 the unique character and qualities of cars like the original 900 became diluted.

SKODA S110R

YEARS MADE
1970–80

NUMBER MADE
56,902

ORIGINAL PRICE
£1,050 (in 1972)

MECHANICAL LAYOUT
Rear engine, rear-wheel drive

RANGE OF ENGINES
1,107cc, four-cylinder

MOST POWERFUL ENGINE
62bhp (1,107cc)

FASTEST VERSION
85mph (1,107cc)

BEST FUEL ECONOMY
37mpg (1,107cc)

WHEELBASE
2,400mm

LENGTH
4,155mm

NUMBER OF SEATS
4

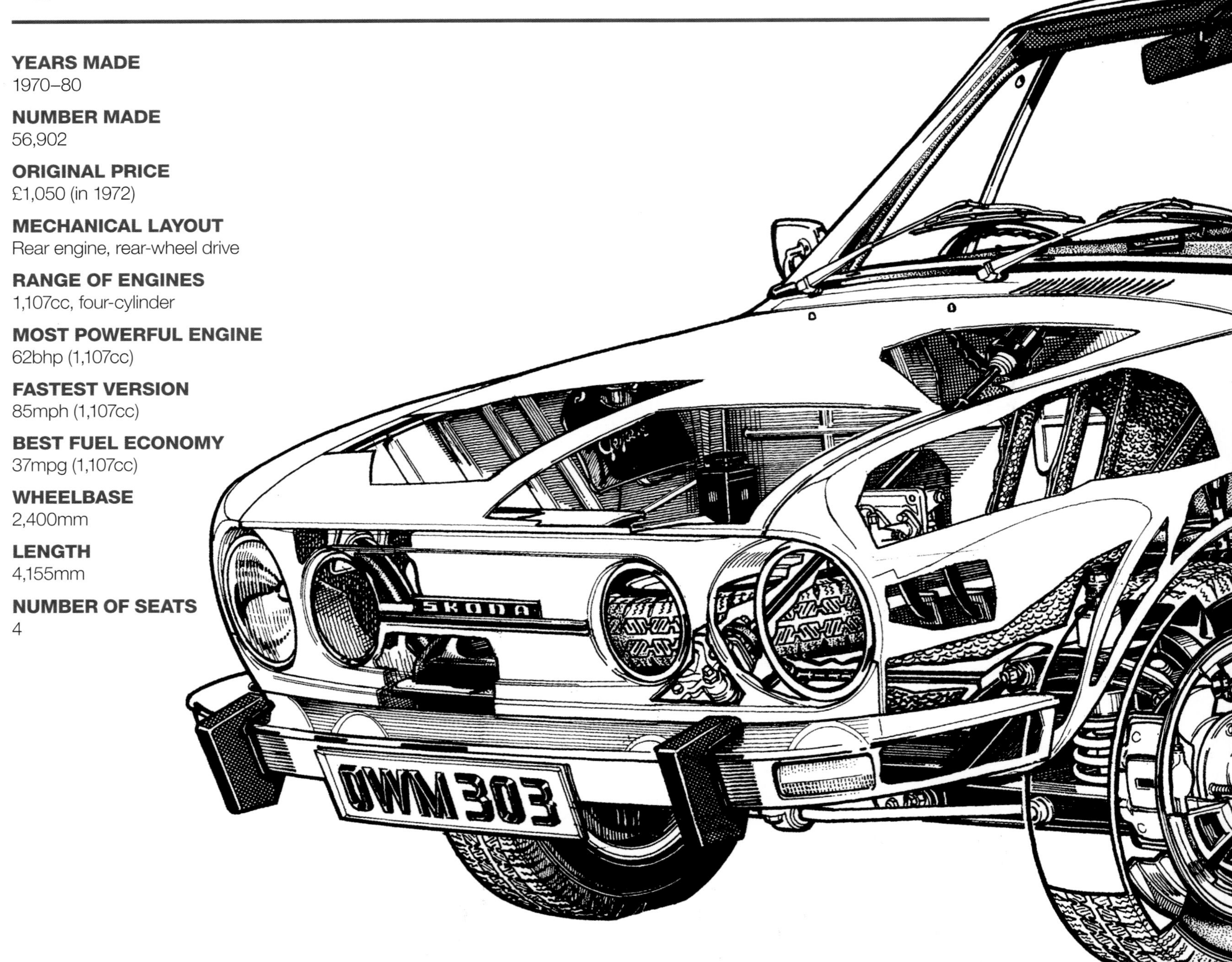

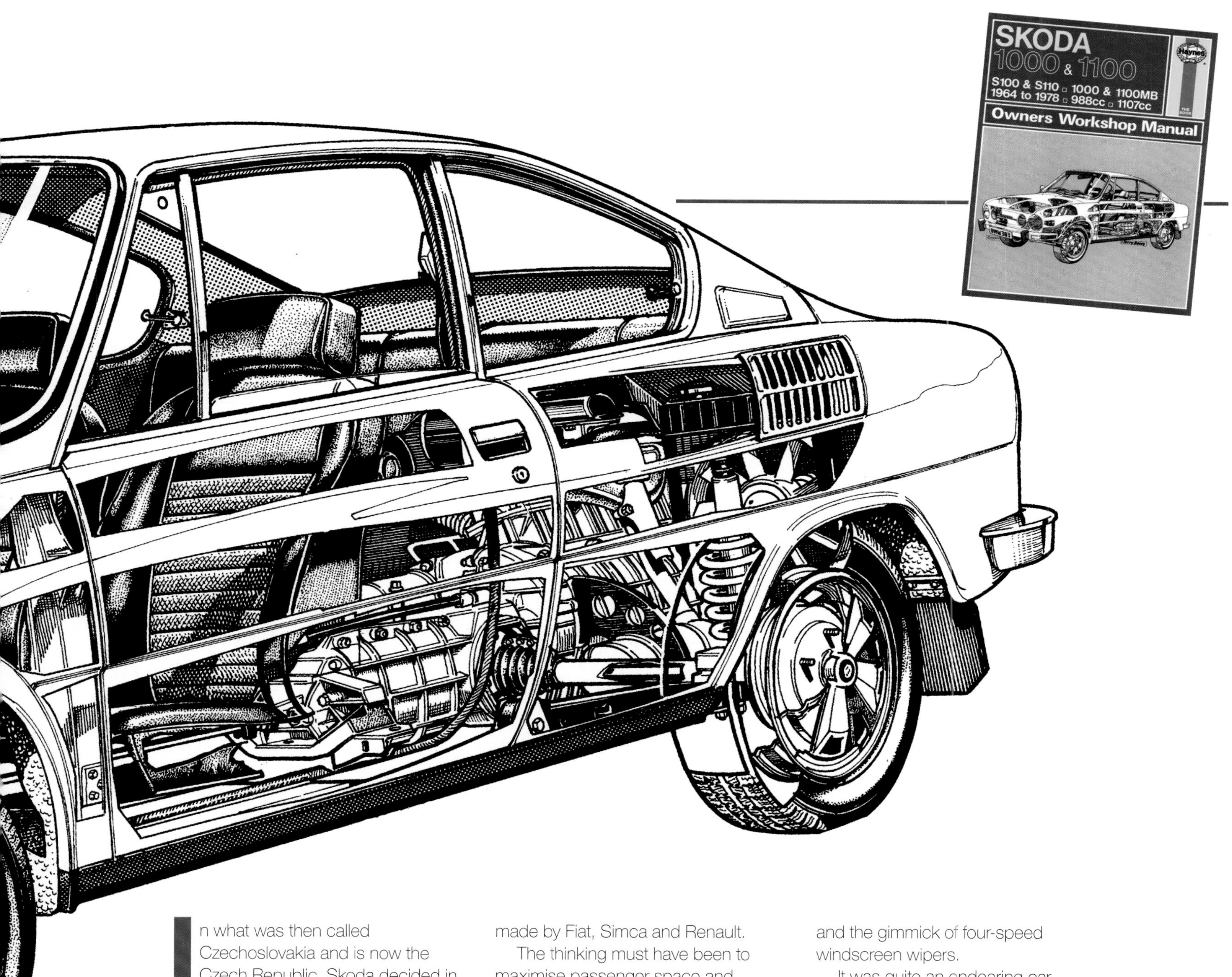

In what was then called Czechoslovakia and is now the Czech Republic, Skoda decided in 1964 to turn convention on its head and transfer the engines in its cars from the front to the back.

From a 21st-century perspective, that might seem bizarre, but at the time it was hard for the company – from behind the restrictive iron curtain of that Cold War period – to ignore the wild success of Volkswagen, and the popularity of small rear-engined cars made by Fiat, Simca and Renault.

The thinking must have been to maximise passenger space and compact the powerpack; it can't have been to achieve excellent handling, because the resulting tail-heavy 1000MB had rear suspension by swing axles, so it could be lethal in the wet or in the hands of the uninitiated.

The basic car was restyled and renamed in 1969, and a year later the cute-looking S110R coupé was added. There were front disc brakes and the gimmick of four-speed windscreen wipers.

It was quite an endearing car, particularly once its road manners had been mastered (modified ones did well in rallying, after all), and offered a slightly scary top speed together with excellent fuel economy when used day-to-day. Still, fittings and controls were coarsely finished, and the seats weren't designed with the wellbeing of the driver's back as a forethought…

SUNBEAM RAPIER

YEARS MADE
1967–76

NUMBER MADE
46,204 (including Alpine version)

ORIGINAL PRICE
£1,200 (in 1968)

MECHANICAL LAYOUT
Front engine, rear-wheel drive

RANGE OF ENGINES
1,725cc, four-cylinder

MOST POWERFUL ENGINE
105bhp (1,725cc)

FASTEST VERSION
106mph (H120, 1,725cc)

BEST FUEL ECONOMY
25mpg (1,725cc)

WHEELBASE
2,502mm

LENGTH
4,432mm

NUMBER OF SEATS
4

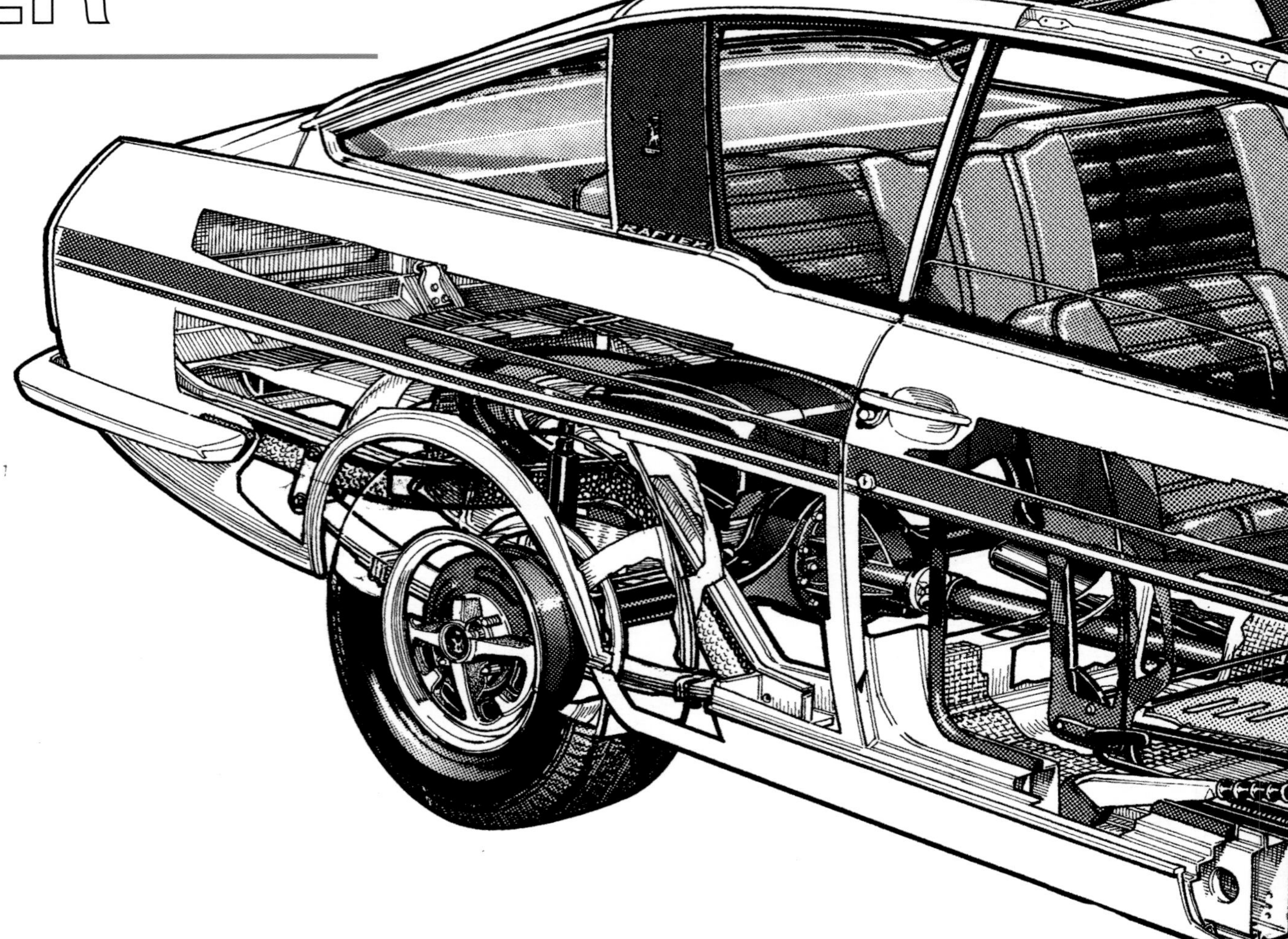

An interesting melding of British hardware and American design trends, the Rapier was entirely based on the Hillman Hunter, but with fastback styling heavily influenced by the new US parent of Britain's Rootes Group, Chrysler. In a dim light, and from a good few yards away, the car was a dead ringer for 1960s style-setter the Plymouth Barracuda!

In 1967 the Rapier set out its stall as a civilised and refined cruiser, capable of 100mph but not at its happiest holding such heady speeds. Overdrive was usually specified on the high-geared four-speed manual gearbox (there were automatics too) while an adjustable steering column meant a relaxed driving position was easy to achieve in the tastefully trimmed cockpit. And if you couldn't quite run to the cost of a Rapier, Rootes offered a poverty version, the Alpine, with 14 less bhp, no overdrive and distinctly unimpressive instrumentation.

And then, just as everyone had become accustomed to the Rapier as pretty uninteresting, there came the H120 spin-off with a hot Holbay-tuned engine and twin carbs. It could now sprint to 60mph in 11sec, snapping away at the heels of the Lotus Cortina, even if the chassis wasn't really well sorted enough to handle the extra oomph. Go-faster stripes, a tail spoiler and Rostyle wheels completed the package and, all things considered, the comfy cruiser crossed the line into boy racer territory convincingly.

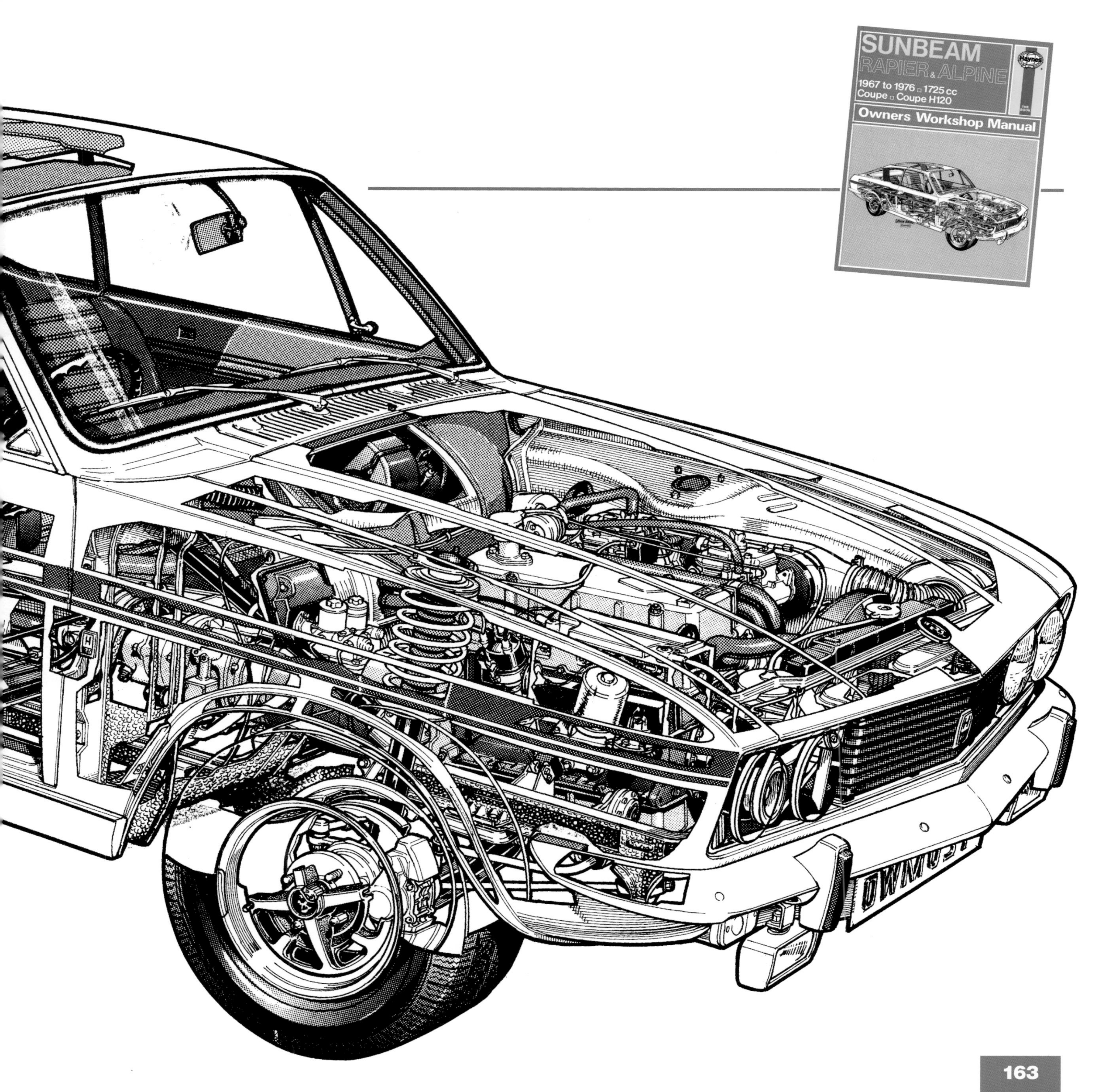
SUNBEAM
RAPIER & ALPINE
1967 to 1976 □ 1725 cc
Coupe □ Coupe H120
Haynes
Owners Workshop Manual

TALBOT HORIZON

YEARS MADE
1977–87

NUMBER MADE
51,230 (UK-built – overall total unknown)

ORIGINAL PRICE
£2,740 (1.1 in 1978)

MECHANICAL LAYOUT
Front engine, front-wheel drive

RANGE OF ENGINES
1,118–1,592cc, four-cylinder petrol;
1,905cc four-cylinder diesel

MOST POWERFUL ENGINE
90bhp (1,592cc – not sold in the UK)

FASTEST VERSION
108mph (1,592cc – not sold in the UK)

BEST FUEL ECONOMY
35mpg (1,905cc)

WHEELBASE
2,520mm

LENGTH
3,960mm

NUMBER OF SEATS
4

This five-door hatchback was envisaged as a 'world' car – hence its presentation simultaneously in Paris and Detroit on 7 December 1977. But this was hollow tokenism. The only thing the Simca and Plymouth Horizons shared was a basic shape and, ironically, that had been created at a design studio in Coventry. Beneath, they were two different cars, one engineered as a replacement for the tinny Simca 1100 and the other as an ultra-compact American runabout.

The five-door Horizon went on British sale in October 1978, badged a Chrysler. It was judged as merely competent because, aside from its neat appearance and all-independent suspension (front torsion bars, rear coil springs), ropey Simca drivetrain and low-geared steering/huge turning circle hampered the car. It was an unworthy winner for European Car Of The Year in 1978; then again, that year's candidates were so lacklustre the Fiat Strada came second! And, soon after healthy sales were under way, Vauxhall's first Astra and Ford's Mk3 Escort upped the game enormously.

Renamed the Talbot Horizon in 1979, the car was an import only until 1981, when it began rolling down Talbot's Coventry production line, although the late-model diesel always came from Spain. Horizons were notable for their crappy electronic gizmos, from a brake pad wear warning light to an 'econometer' to encourage thrifty driving and even, on the upmarket SX, a 'trip computer'.

TALBOT
CHRYSLER
HORIZON
All models 1978 to 1986
1118 cc 1294 cc 1442 cc
Owners Workshop Manual
1·5
OWM 473

TALBOT SAMBA

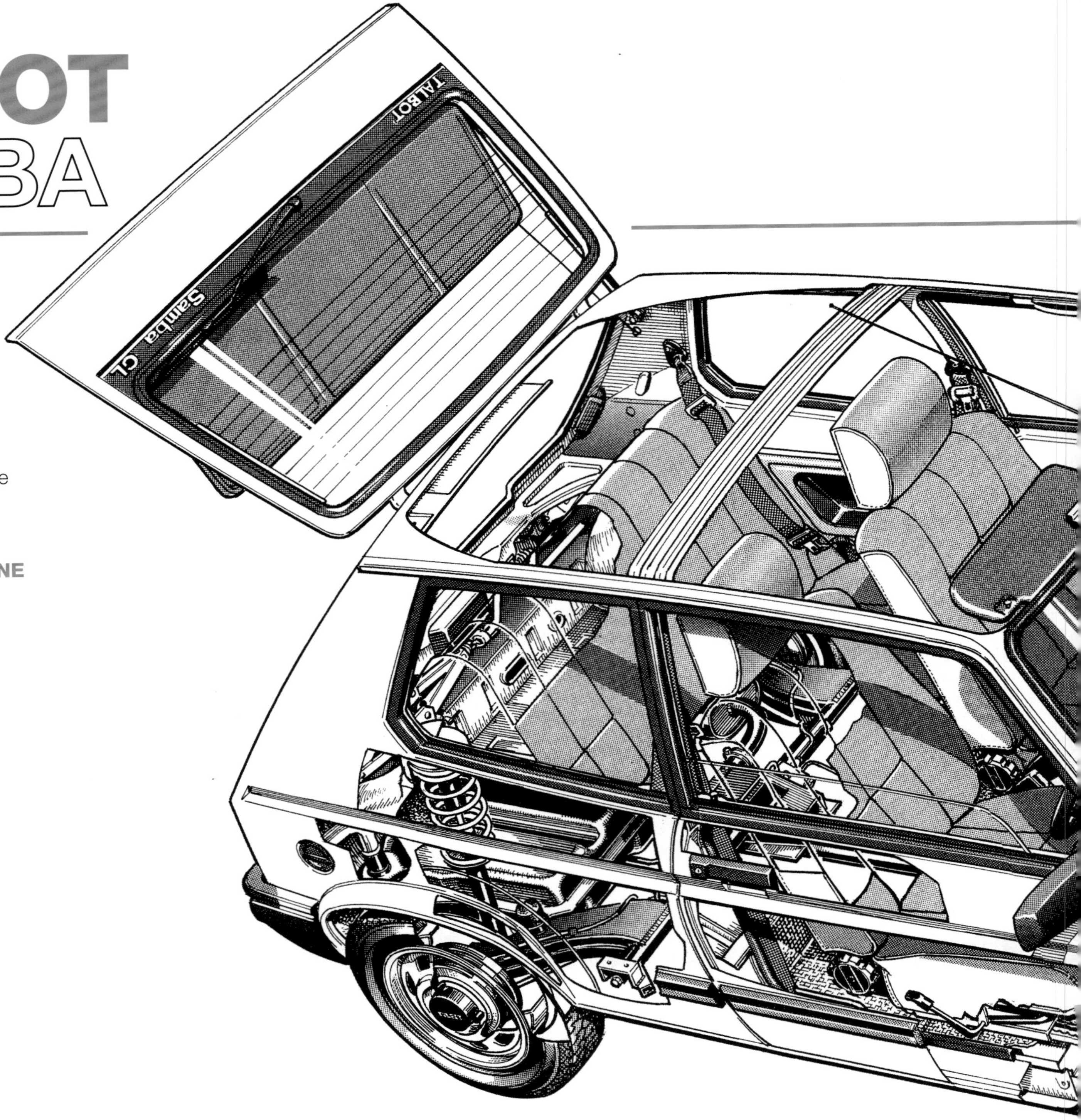

YEARS MADE
1982–6

NUMBER MADE
270,555

ORIGINAL PRICE
£2,995 (1.0 LS in 1982)

MECHANICAL LAYOUT
Front engine, front-wheel drive

RANGE OF ENGINES
954–1,360cc, four-cylinder

MOST POWERFUL ENGINE
79bhp (1,360cc)

FASTEST VERSION
103mph (S, 1,360cc)

BEST FUEL ECONOMY
40mpg approx (1,124cc)

WHEELBASE
2,340mm

LENGTH
3,506mm

NUMBER OF SEATS
4

TRIUMPH
TR5 & 6
1967 to 1975 □ All models □ 2498cc
Owners Workshop Manual
GOODYEAR
RALLY

TRIUMPH 2500

YEARS MADE
1968–77

NUMBER MADE
97,140

ORIGINAL PRICE
£1,450 (2.5PI in 1968)

MECHANICAL LAYOUT
Front engine, rear-wheel drive

RANGE OF ENGINES
2,498cc, six-cylinder

MOST POWERFUL ENGINE
132bhp (2,498cc)

FASTEST VERSION
106mph (2.5PI/2500S, 2,498cc)

BEST FUEL ECONOMY
25mpg (2500TC, 2,498cc)

WHEELBASE
2,693mm

LENGTH
4,420–4,648mm

NUMBER OF SEATS
5

The term 'Triumph 2500' is a useful catch-all for several cars that crowned the British company's saloon car range in the late 1960s and early 1970s. How easy it is to forget this long-defunct marque was then a top choice for wealthy businesspeople – the sort of exalted market position occupied today by Audi and Lexus.

What these Triumphs all share is the same basic 2.5-litre, straight-six engine, a potent and robust power unit that premiered in the TR5 sports car in 1967. It was designed for fuel-injection, a notoriously troublesome piece of kit supplied by Lucas, and, so-equipped, the 2.5PI arrived in 1968, turning the former Triumph 2000 saloon into a veritable hot-rod.

This car, and its estate stablemate, had but a short time in the showrooms because in 1969 the whole big Triumph saloon range received a comprehensive makeover. These Mk2 cars got longer and more graceful nose and (although not for the estates) tail sections, plus a multitude of other refinements including a new dashboard.

When the fuel-injection was working well, the car was a superb long-distance cruiser. But typical Lucas unreliability led to the launch of the 2500TC in 1974, reverting to good old-fashioned carbs. However, it arrived in tandem with the fuel-injected 2500S that – with power steering, overdrive and alloy wheels – made it the ultimate incarnation of these very attractive motor cars.

TRIUMPH Mk I & MK II
2000, 2500 & 2.5
1963 to 1977
All models 1998 cc 2498 cc
Owners Workshop Manual
DWM 336

TRIUMPH SPITFIRE

YEARS MADE
1962–80

NUMBER MADE
314,332

ORIGINAL PRICE
£729 (in 1962)

MECHANICAL LAYOUT
Front engine, rear-wheel drive

RANGE OF ENGINES
1,147/1,296/1,493cc, four-cylinder

MOST POWERFUL ENGINE
75bhp (1,296cc)

FASTEST VERSION
101mph (1500, 1,493cc)

BEST FUEL ECONOMY
31mpg (1,147cc)

WHEELBASE
2,108mm

LENGTH
3,730–3,786mm

NUMBER OF SEATS
2

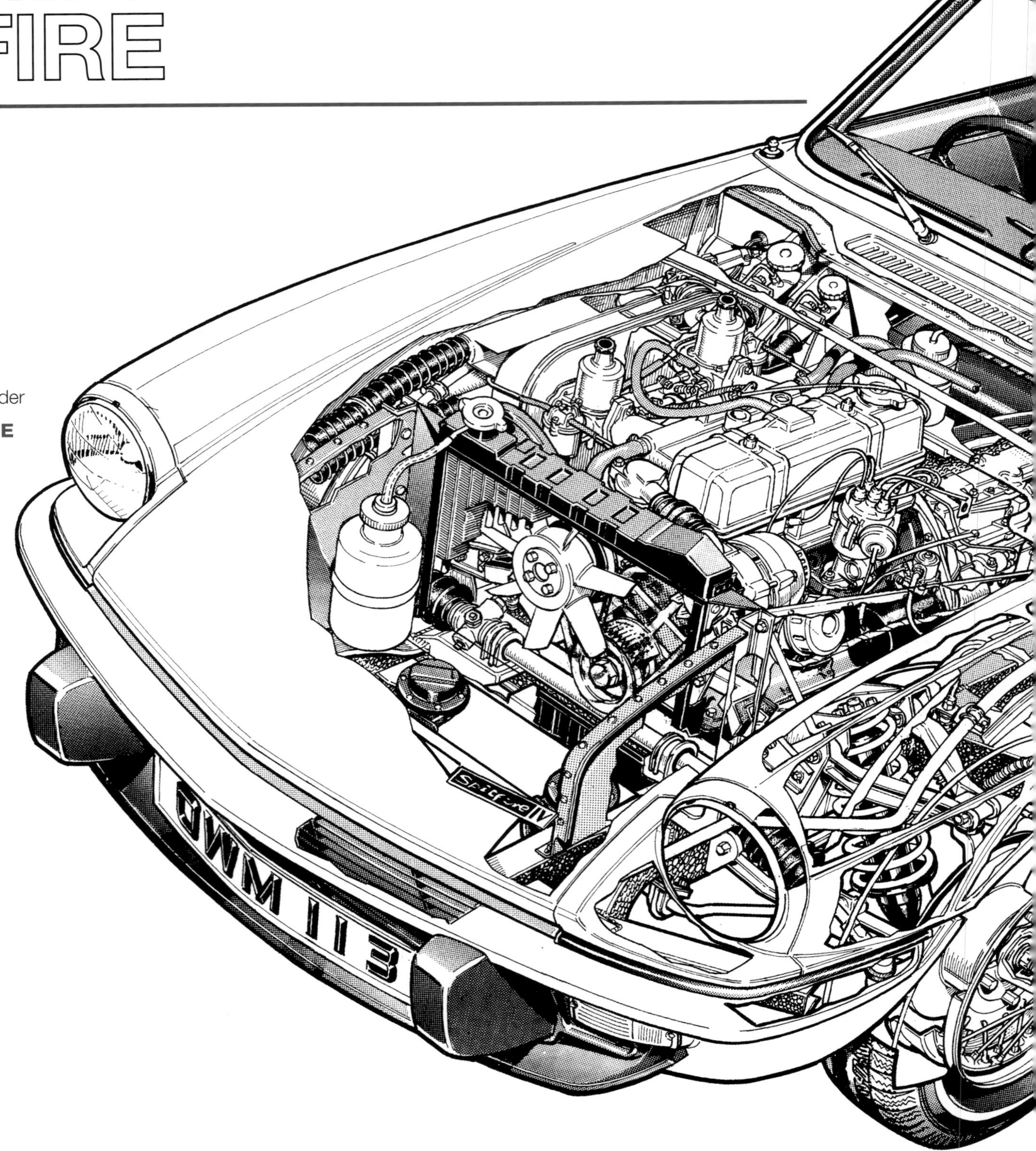

The dinky Spitfire was based wholesale on Triumph's Herald, which featured an old-fashioned and cheap-to-make separate chassis and bolt-on body panels. Yet the Herald also had artfully detailed bodywork, the work of Italian designer Giovanni Michelotti, and he was brought in again to design the 1962 Spitfire, Triumph's MG Midget rival. A lovely job he did too.

The engine was eager enough to out-run the Midget – good for 90mph with 0–60mph in 16.5sec. Front disc brakes, a decent soft-top and roomy boot made it a practical and fun everyday proposition too. In its roadholding, however, the Spitfire inherited the Herald's flawed swing-axle independent rear suspension, making it twitchy in fast, ill-judged corners.

The 1965 Mk2 gained 4bhp from its new 1,296cc engine, and there was 8bhp more for the 1967 Mk3. The Spitfire could now hit the ton, preferably on a dead-straight road…

In 1970 Triumph revamped the car, giving this MkIV – shown in our artwork – new and more elegant bodywork. Best of all, engineers fettled the rear suspension; they now called it 'swing-spring', and it cured the previously wayward tendencies.

The final change to the car came in 1975 when a 1,500cc engine meeting all American anti-smog rules was standardised. In this ultimate guise, the Spitfire 1500 remained on sale until August 1980, ending an amazing 18-year lifespan.

TRIUMPH TOLEDO

YEARS MADE
1970–6

NUMBER MADE
119,182

ORIGINAL PRICE
£889 (1300 in 1970)

MECHANICAL LAYOUT
Front engine, rear-wheel drive

RANGE OF ENGINES
1,296–1,493cc, four-cylinder

MOST POWERFUL ENGINE
65bhp (1,493cc)

FASTEST VERSION
87mph (1500, 1,493cc)

BEST FUEL ECONOMY
32mpg (1,296cc)

WHEELBASE
2,460mm

LENGTH
3,970mm

NUMBER OF SEATS
4

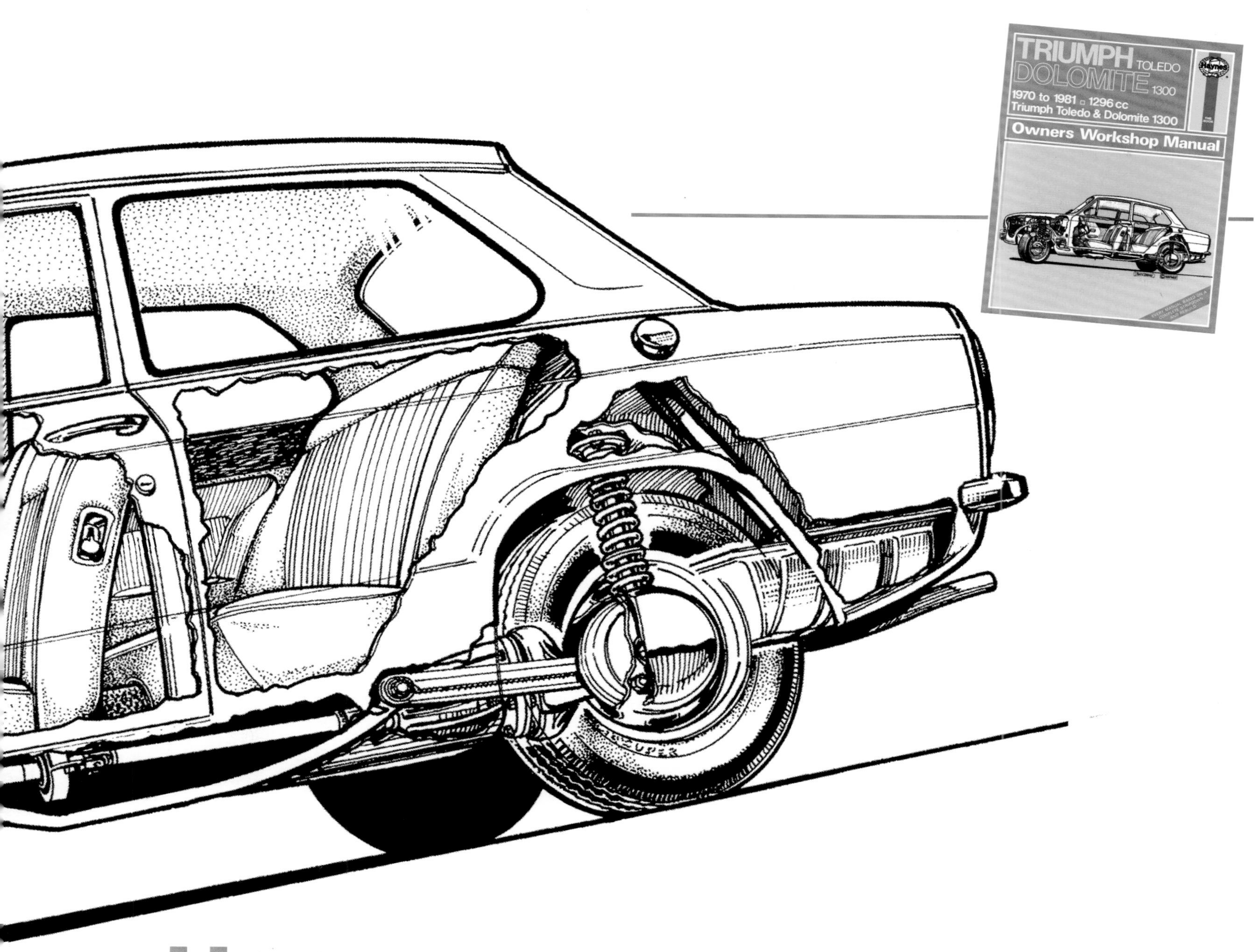

Here's one of the great anomalies of British car history – the car that started out with front-wheel drive and converted to rear-wheel drive.

Launched in 1970, the Toledo was the replacement for Triumph's ageing Herald. Instead of developing an entirely new car – impossible anyway, due to big budgets within British Leyland allocated to the teams creating the Austin Allegro and Morris Marina – the Toledo adapted the body shell of the Triumph 1300. That car, of course, was front-wheel drive, and had also featured independent rear suspension; and the whole drivetrain, despite its modernity, was deemed to be just too expensive to manufacture.

Hence the Toledo had a simple beam rear axle and a propshaft taking the drive to the back wheels. There was more cost-cutting inside, where simpler trim and real woodwork confined solely to the dashboard panel could be found, while the lowly performance aspirations of this little Triumph were reflected in all-drum brakes.

All things are relative, of course, and the Toledo was a decent, superior car despite the economies, and possessed safe and trustworthy handling. Its small rectangular headlamps were distinctive, and there would ultimately be the choice of two or four doors, although the 1,500cc engine was only for export models. The four-door Toledo was finally assimilated into the Dolomite range in 1976, and continued to be popular as Triumph's entry-level saloon.

TRIUMPH STAG

YEARS MADE
1970–7

NUMBER MADE
25,939

ORIGINAL PRICE
£2,093 (in 1970)

MECHANICAL LAYOUT
Front engine, rear-wheel drive

RANGE OF ENGINES
2,997cc, V8-cylinder

MOST POWERFUL ENGINE
145bhp (2,997cc)

FASTEST VERSION
118mph (2,997cc)

BEST FUEL ECONOMY
21mpg (2,997cc)

WHEELBASE
2,540mm

LENGTH
4,420mm

NUMBER OF SEATS
4

There was little to compare the gorgeous Triumph Stag to in 1970; the Mercedes-Benz SL maybe came closest as a stylish open grand tourer, but that was a two-seater.

The padded roll-over bar was unique to the Michelotti design, and the Stag was Triumph's first open car with unitary construction. Front suspension was by MacPherson struts and incorporated an anti-roll bar, while the independent rear was by coil springs and trailing arms. The braking system was dual-circuit and the Stag was the first British car with an inertia-operated fuel cut-off activated during an accident.

The Stag's V8 engine was controversial. A unique engine when Rover's proven 3.5-litre V8 would have done the job, it got the go-ahead in the midst of febrile British Leyland internal politics. Triumph's double overhead-camshaft 3-litre V8 had been under development since 1963 – essentially two Triumph 1.5-litre slant four-cylinder engines joined together on a common crankshaft. Yet overheating became a notorious Stag fault, leading to costly warranty claims.

Ironically, many individuals did convert their Stags to trusty Rover V8 power, in which form the car worked a treat – although a fastidiously maintained 3-litre original can be perfectly reliable.

The Stag was well-behaved around corners, boasted a comfortable ride, and made a refined, civilised cruiser. Most of its problems were cured in the Mk2 of 1973 but, sadly, sales never soared.

TRIUMPH
STAG
1970 to 1978
All models ◻ 2997cc V8
Owners Workshop Manual
TRIUMPH

TRIUMPH DOLOMITE

YEARS MADE
1972–80

NUMBER MADE
204,003

ORIGINAL PRICE
£1,399 (1850 in 1972)

MECHANICAL LAYOUT
Front engine, rear-wheel drive

RANGE OF ENGINES
1,296–1,998cc, four-cylinder

MOST POWERFUL ENGINE
127bhp (1,998cc)

FASTEST VERSION
115mph (Sprint, 1,998cc)

BEST FUEL ECONOMY
32mpg (1,296cc)

WHEELBASE
2,460mm

LENGTH
3,965–4,115mm

NUMBER OF SEATS
5

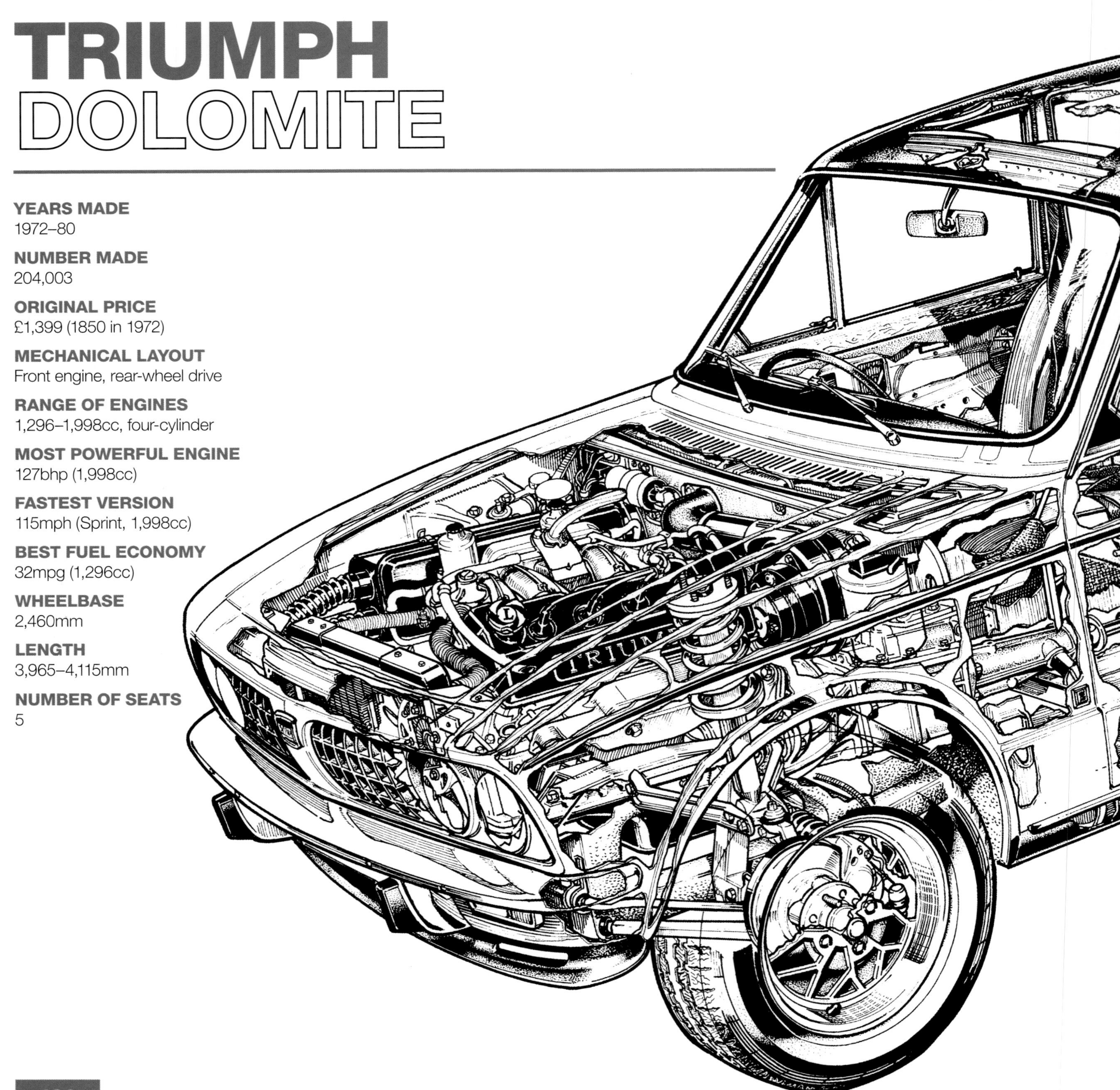

Triumph had BMW firmly in its sights when it devised the original Dolomite, a classic front-engine/rear-drive sports saloon. Just as the Toledo was meant to replace the Herald, so the Dolomite was intended to take over where the well-liked 1960s Vitesse left off.

To produce this rakish, 100mph, four-door saloon, engineers raided the corporate stores for the best bits from their other cars – all centred around a slant-four, overhead camshaft 1.85-litre engine Triumph had previously built exclusively for Saab. The rear-wheel drivetrain came from the Toledo while the body was a smartened-up 1500 with four headlamps.

Just one year after the fine-handling Dolomite made its debut, though, Triumph served up a real cracker in the Dolomite Sprint, featuring an enlarged 2-litre engine with a 16-valve head – run-of-the-mill today but a real innovation back then – delivering its meaty 127bhp through a TR6-style four-speed-plus-overdrive gearbox. It had real alloy wheels, not the usual go-faster fakes of the time, and won genuine acclaim from everyone who tried it.

Triumph tidied up its bewildering range in 1976, when the Toledo became the Dolomite 1300 and the 1500TC the Dolomite 1500. All the cars continued to sell well until 1980, when the Canley, Coventry, plant where they were built was closed. Although the Triumph name continued on the Honda-based Acclaim in 1981, it was a less vivid car entirely.

VAUXHALL VIVA/FIRENZA

YEARS MADE
1970–9 (Viva HC series)

NUMBER MADE
640,863

ORIGINAL PRICE
£851 (two-door Deluxe in 1971)

MECHANICAL LAYOUT
Front engine, rear-wheel drive

RANGE OF ENGINES
1,159–2,279cc, four-cylinder

MOST POWERFUL ENGINE
110bhp (2,279cc)

FASTEST VERSION
100mph (2300SL, 2,279cc)

BEST FUEL ECONOMY
29mpg (1,159cc)

WHEELBASE
2,464mm

LENGTH
4,115mm

NUMBER OF SEATS
4

Vauxhall waved goodbye to its last Viva HC in 1979. By then, despite an excellent reputation for robustness, the new Vauxhall Astra with front-wheel drive and hatchback represented the future.

Vauxhall's first Viva arrived in 1963. Designed for economy, the clean lines were all-British, as was the 1,057cc, four-cylinder engine. It featured a four-speed all-synchromesh gearbox, and precise rack-and-pinion steering. By the time HA Viva production finished in 1966, 307,738 had been built. Its replacement proved even more popular. The all-new Viva HB was longer, lower, wider and roomier, with new coil spring suspension all-round and a bigger (1,159cc), gutsier engine; 556,752 HBs were made until 1970. Then it was all-change again with the HC Viva.

On a slightly longer wheelbase but with otherwise similar HB underpinnings, the HC was even roomier than its forebear, with sleek yet barrel-sided coachwork boosting elbowroom inside. In addition to 1.2- and 1.6-litre engines, Vauxhall engineers managed to shoehorn-in 70bhp 1.8-litre and 110bhp 2.3-litre lumps.

The car was offered in a bewildering number of derivatives: two- and four-door saloons, two-door estate and two-door coupé Vivas; Firenza coupés (as shown in our illustration); and the upmarket Magnum in all three body styles but only with the larger engines. In 1971 the millionth Viva rolled off the Luton production line and, seconds later, the 1,000,001st example was completed at Ellesmere Port.

VAUXHALL
FIRENZA ohv
1971 to September 1973
1159cc □ 1256cc □ De Luxe & SL
Haynes
Owners Workshop Manual
OWM 089

VAUXHALL VICTOR/VX FE

YEARS MADE
1972–8

NUMBER MADE
69,956

ORIGINAL PRICE
£1,317 (1800 Deluxe in 1973)

MECHANICAL LAYOUT
Front engine, rear-wheel drive

RANGE OF ENGINES
1,759–2,279cc, four-cylinder, 3,294cc, six-cylinder

MOST POWERFUL ENGINE
124bhp (3,294cc)

FASTEST VERSION
104mph (3300SL estate, 3,294cc)

BEST FUEL ECONOMY
26mpg (1,759cc)

WHEELBASE
2,667mm

LENGTH
4,554mm

NUMBER OF SEATS
5

These big saloons and estates occupy a rather mournful place in Vauxhall's history: they were the last cars launched that were completely designed, engineered and built in the UK – henceforth, all new Vauxhalls would be versions, either lightly altered or virtually identical, of Opels that were created in Germany.

Of course, that was no bad thing for car buyers because 'British' Vauxhalls had, by the early 1970s, a reputation for mediocrity and, more crucially, rust.

This final Victor, the fifth generation of the famous name, was a handsome car in a transatlantic sort of way, highly conventional in its rear-drive layout and offering well-tried 1.8- and 2-litre engines.

The fastback estate is notable for having near-perfect 50/50 weight distribution with these power units. However, there was also a short-lived estate model propelled by a 3.3-litre straight-six more normally found powering (if that's the right term) Bedford trucks. Considering its large capacity, the top speed and acceleration were terrible and power steering was a very necessary option. A separately-marketed saloon with this engine was called the Vauxhall Ventora, while there was also a 2.3-litre twin-carb FE-type performance model called the VX4/90: despite a near-1,000cc difference between them, performance was roughly similar.

In 1976 the cars were relabelled as simply the VX range, and given a plethora of detail trim changes. In this form they survived for two years.

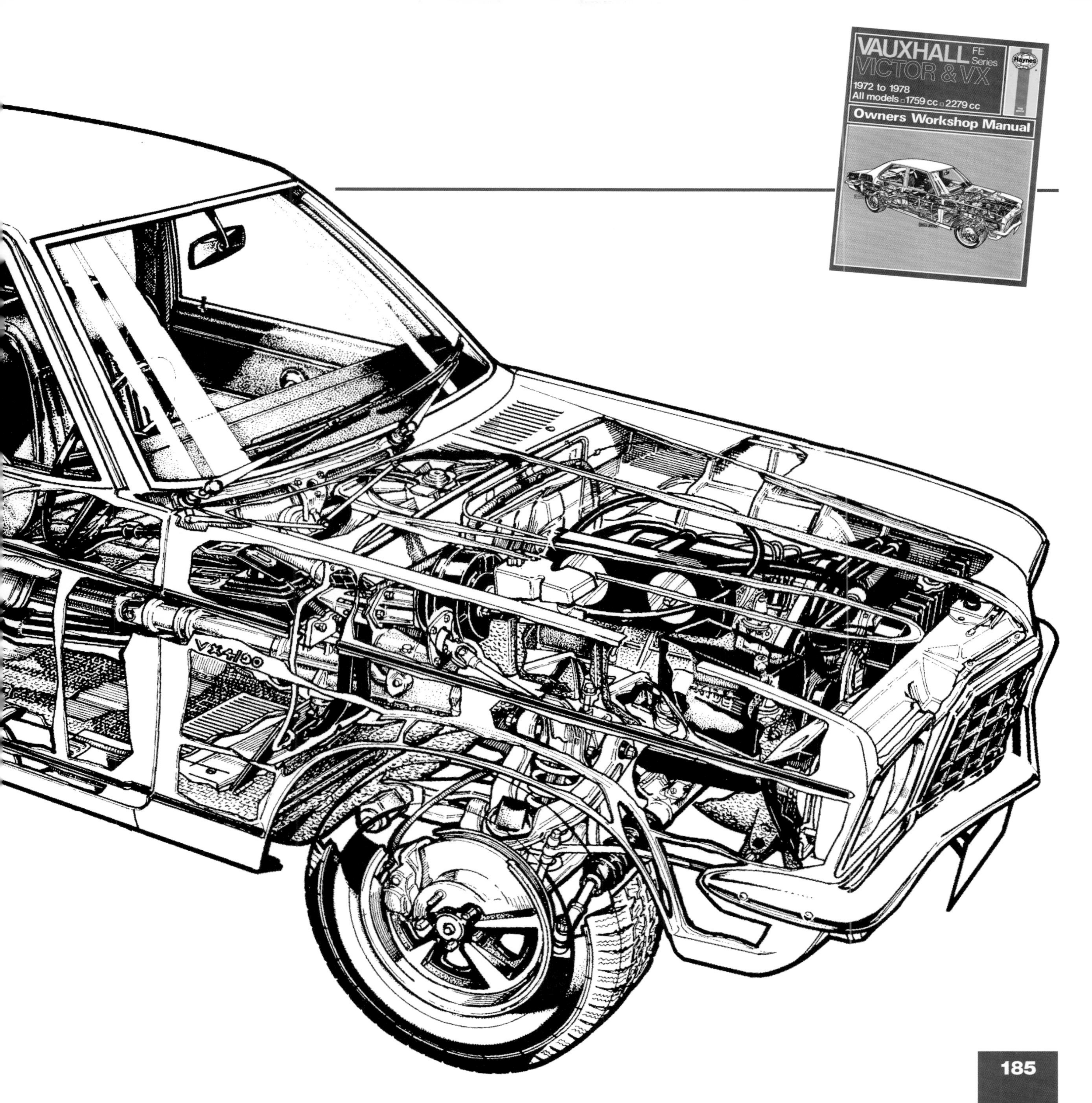
VAUXHALL FE Series
VICTOR & VX
1972 to 1978
All models 1759 cc 2279 cc
Owners Workshop Manual
Haynes
VX4/90

VAUXHALL CHEVETTE

YEARS MADE
1975–84

NUMBER MADE
415,608

ORIGINAL PRICE
£1,650 (three-door L in 1975)

MECHANICAL LAYOUT
Front engine, rear-wheel drive

RANGE OF ENGINES
1,256cc, four-cylinder

MOST POWERFUL ENGINE
59bhp (1,256cc)

FASTEST VERSION
91mph (1,256cc)

BEST FUEL ECONOMY
35mpg (1,256cc)

WHEELBASE
2,392mm

LENGTH
3,962–4,165mm

NUMBER OF SEATS
4

It arrived in Vauxhall showrooms in May 1975 and immediately caused a stir, because the Chevette was Britain's first compact hatchback to rival the Renault 5 and VW Polo. Vauxhall even stole a March on Ford, as its Fiesta arrived a year later, and BL's Metro was five years off. Parallel editions of the Chevette went on sale at the same time, from the Opel Kadett in Germany to the Holden Gemini in Australia, as General Motors rolled out its globe-spanning 'T Car' project.

Quite a lot of the Chevette was unique to Britain, actually, from its 'droop snoot' front styling to the 1,256cc engine and four-speed gearbox straight out of the faithful British Viva. The Chevette, like other T cars, stuck with old-fashioned rear-wheel drive, with independent double-wishbone front suspension and a live back axle. A two-speed heater fan, radial tyres, reversing lights, heated rear window and reclining front seats were standard even on the base model – the best-equipped, aside from the numerous special editions, being the 1976 GLS with velour upholstery, sports wheels, overriders, a centre console and front door pockets.

While there was only one engine choice throughout the Chevette's nine-year life (not counting the 'homologation special' 2300HS, mind), there were several body styles. In June 1976 came two- and four-door saloons, while four months later a two-door estate was added.

VAUXHALL
CHEVETTE
1975 to 1984 □ 1256 cc
All models including Chevanne
Owners Workshop Manual
OWM 285
OWM 285

VAUXHALL CAVALIER MK1

YEARS MADE
1975–81

NUMBER MADE
238,980

ORIGINAL PRICE
£2,746 (1300L in 1975)

MECHANICAL LAYOUT
Front engine, rear-wheel drive

RANGE OF ENGINES
1,256–1,979cc, four-cylinder

MOST POWERFUL ENGINE
100bhp (1,979cc)

FASTEST VERSION
111mph (GLS, 1,979cc)

BEST FUEL ECONOMY
32mpg approx (1,256cc)

WHEELBASE
2,520mm

LENGTH
4,445mm

NUMBER OF SEATS
5

In 1977, when Vauxhall built its first Cavalier in Britain, the heyday of the hard-driving, jacket-off and sunglasses-on company rep was in its early years – the M25 wasn't even built and the best he could expect at Toddington services was chicken'n'chips and a cup of watery Nescafé.

Many early Cavaliers were thrashed up and down the M6 by their shirt-sleeved masters, had a 'retirement' as minicabs, and then headed for a grateful death in the scrapyard.

For the first two years of its life, from 1975 to 1977, the Cavalier was made only in Antwerp, Belgium. The car was designed by Opel, and sold as the Opel Ascona in mainland Europe, but for UK-bound – and then UK-made – Cavaliers there was a typical Vauxhall slant-nosed restyle at the front for the neat two- or four-door saloon (no estate was ever offered). The 1.6-, 1.9- and later 2-litre engines were all shared with the Ascona, but Vauxhall offered an entry-level Cavalier with its own 1.3-litre Viva powertrain on board.

The Cavalier's true significance is that it was a turnaround car for Vauxhall, reasserting the British marque in the market with quality, value and reasonable dynamism after years of also-rans. It was as good as, if not better than, the Ford Cortina, and for Vauxhall that was a genuine achievement.

VAUXHALL
CAVALIER 1300
1977 to July 1981
All ohv models □ 1256 cc
Owners Workshop Manual
Haynes

VAUXHALL
CAVALIER MK2

YEARS MADE
1981–8

NUMBER MADE
807,624

ORIGINAL PRICE
£4,165 (1300L four-door in 1981)

MECHANICAL LAYOUT
Front engine, front-wheel drive

RANGE OF ENGINES
1,297–1,998cc, four-cylinder petrol; 1,598cc, four-cylinder diesel

MOST POWERFUL ENGINE
130bhp (1,998cc)

FASTEST VERSION
120mph (SRi 130, 1,998cc)

BEST FUEL ECONOMY
46mpg (1,598cc)

WHEELBASE
2,570mm

LENGTH
4,370mm

NUMBER OF SEATS
5

The Cavalier became a British roadscape icon; the 1.7 million sold until the Vectra usurped it in 1995 mean it's among Vauxhall's biggest-selling nameplates ever. And this Mk2 really sparked the sales inferno – the car that made Britain finally take Vauxhall seriously. In 1984 and '85 the Cavalier was the country's second bestselling car after the Ford Escort, an unprecedented feat for General Motors' outpost here.

Why was it so successful? There are three factors. First, it switched from rear- to front-wheel drive, and everyone who drove it was immediately impressed by its sound roadholding, safe handling, and excellent chassis design; power steering was only fitted on the luxury CDi – the others didn't need it.

Second, the Ford Sierra, launched in 1982, disappointed many because of its dated RWD driveline, and many more deeply disliked its 'jelly mould' styling; buyers defected to the Cavalier in droves, especially for its terrific diesel engine.

And third, the Cavalier came as a four-door saloon and five-door hatch from day one – a more popular line-up than the Sierra's hatch or estate choice (a Cavalier estate was added later, and sold poorly).

The Cavalier (the sporty SRi 'sat' for our artist) deserved every ounce of its huge popularity. This 'J-Car' design was sold worldwide under eight other General Motors brands – the most ever for one single car design.

VAUXHALL
CAVALIER (petrol)
1981 to 1988 1297 cc
1598 cc 1796 cc 1998 cc
Owners Workshop Manual
Haynes
SR

VAUXHALL NOVA

YEARS MADE
1983–92

NUMBER MADE
446,462

ORIGINAL PRICE
£3,496 (1.0L three-door in 1983)

MECHANICAL LAYOUT
Front engine, front-wheel drive

RANGE OF ENGINES
993–1,598cc, four-cylinder petrol; 1,488cc, four-cylinder diesel

MOST POWERFUL ENGINE
100bhp (1,598cc)

FASTEST VERSION
114mph (GTE, 1,598cc)

BEST FUEL ECONOMY
40mpg (993cc)

WHEELBASE
2,345mm

LENGTH
3,620–3,955mm

NUMBER OF SEATS
4

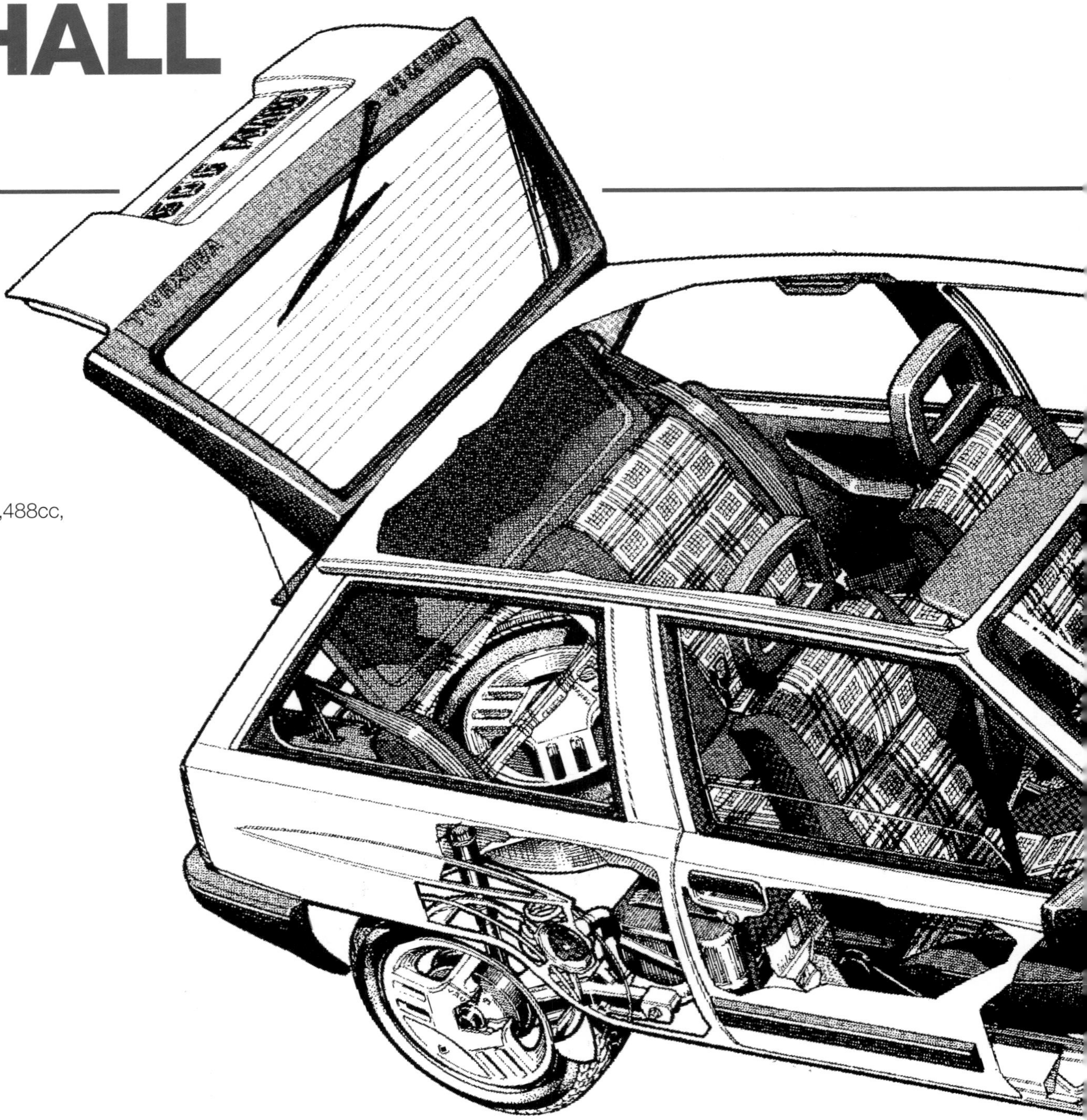

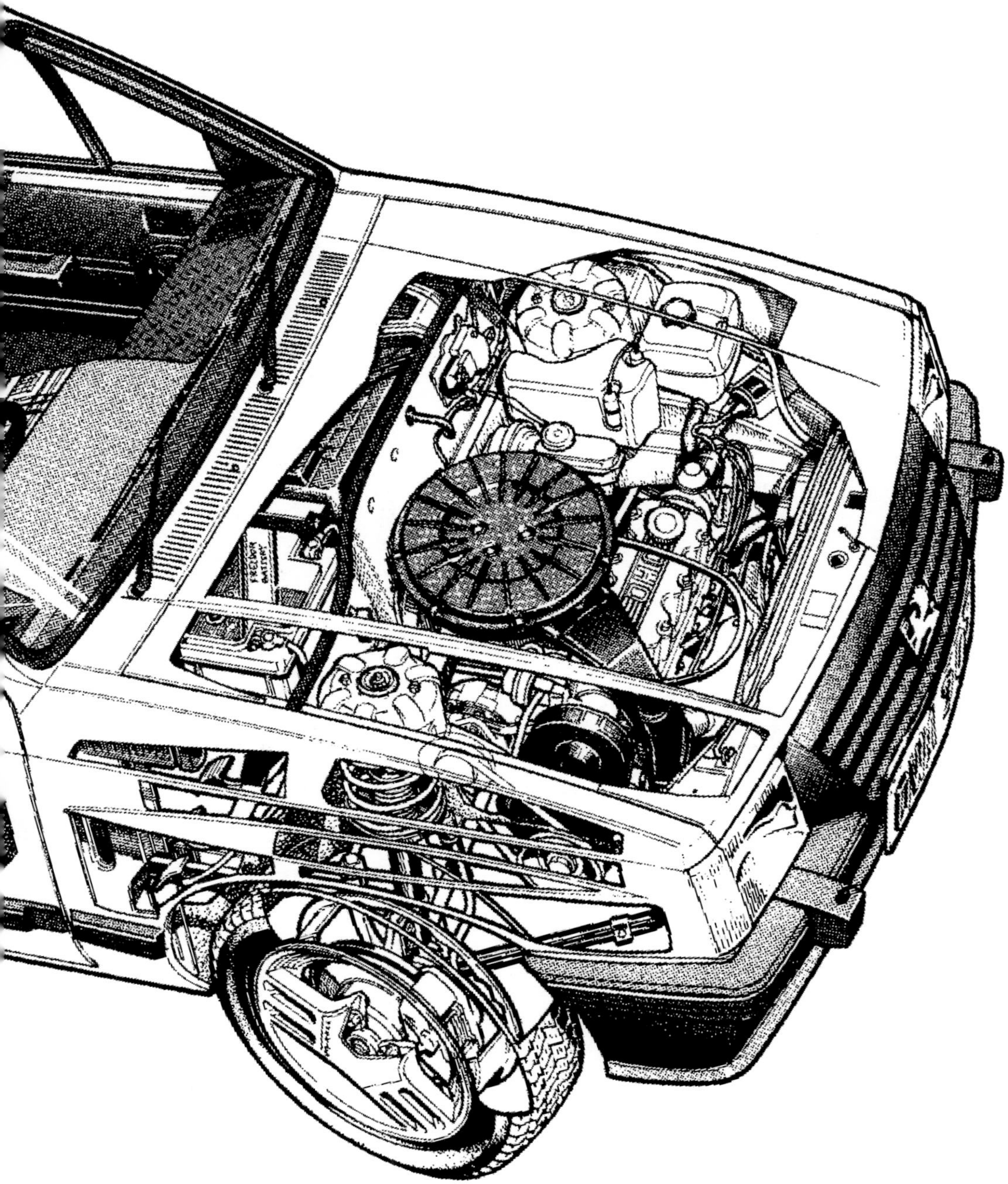

General Motors began with a totally clean sheet of paper for the Nova. It would be the first time the company had created a truly credible supermini rival to the Ford Fiesta, Austin Metro and Volkswagen Polo – and it was one of three highly capable new entries into the sector in 1983, alongside the Peugeot 205 and Fiat Uno. Plus, it was built in a brand new plant in wholly new territory for GM – Spain.

First seen in 1982 as the Opel Corsa, the name was changed for Britain to Vauxhall Nova. The classic supermini package of front transverse engine, front-wheel drive and spacious three-door hatchback was adopted; the smallest engine was a pushrod carryover from the now obsolete Opel Kadett City, although the rest of the engine range, with overhead camshafts, was brand new.

The three-door car had distinctive and sporty blistered wheelarches, although the subsequent five-door did with plain wings and was pretty bland-looking, and the range departed from the European norm with the addition of two- and four-door saloons.

The Nova was no great shakes in the driving enjoyment department, especially beside the sparkling 205 and Uno. Still, this was no bar to its popularity and, indeed, its longevity. It was reliable to own and cheap to run. GM made over three million of these cars, with nearly a sixth of them sold as Vauxhalls.

VOLKSWAGEN BEETLE

YEARS MADE
1939–2003

NUMBER MADE
21,529,464

ORIGINAL PRICE
£650 in 1953

MECHANICAL LAYOUT
Rear engine, rear-wheel drive

RANGE OF ENGINES
1,131–1,584cc, flat-four-cylinder

MOST POWERFUL ENGINE
50bhp (1,584cc)

FASTEST VERSION
81mph (1303, 1,584cc)

BEST FUEL ECONOMY
36mpg (1,192cc)

WHEELBASE
2,400mm

LENGTH
4,030–4,090mm

NUMBER OF SEATS
4

The air-cooled clatter and turtle profile are familiar to everyone who experienced the second half of the 20th century…for vastly different reasons. In both pre- and post-war Germany, the Beetle represented contrasting outlooks on how to motorise a nation; in 1960s America, the car was a symbol of free spirits and an antidote to consumer gluttony; and in South America in the 1970s and '80s, it was an attainable workhorse for school run or taxi rank.

And in Britain? The car was hugely popular from the moment the first 'Volkswagen Export 1200' saloons went on sale in 1953 to the last Beetle sold in December 1978. We bought 424,052 of them.

Ferdinand Porsche designed the original rear-engined saloon in the 1930s to a Nazi party brief, but production only began properly – under British auspices – in 1945 with a truly austere 1,100cc model that offered cable brakes and no chromework. However, people rapidly came to prize its solidity and unburstable nature.

The flat-four pushrod engine grew to 1,200cc in the 1950s as the range expanded to include a cabriolet. Calls for more power and modern driving standards in the 1960s resulted in 1.3- and 1.5-litre editions equipped with an all-synchro gearbox, front disc brakes and an optional semi-automatic transmission. And on it went. Intrinsically, though, it was still the same old noisy, slow, lovable Beetle.

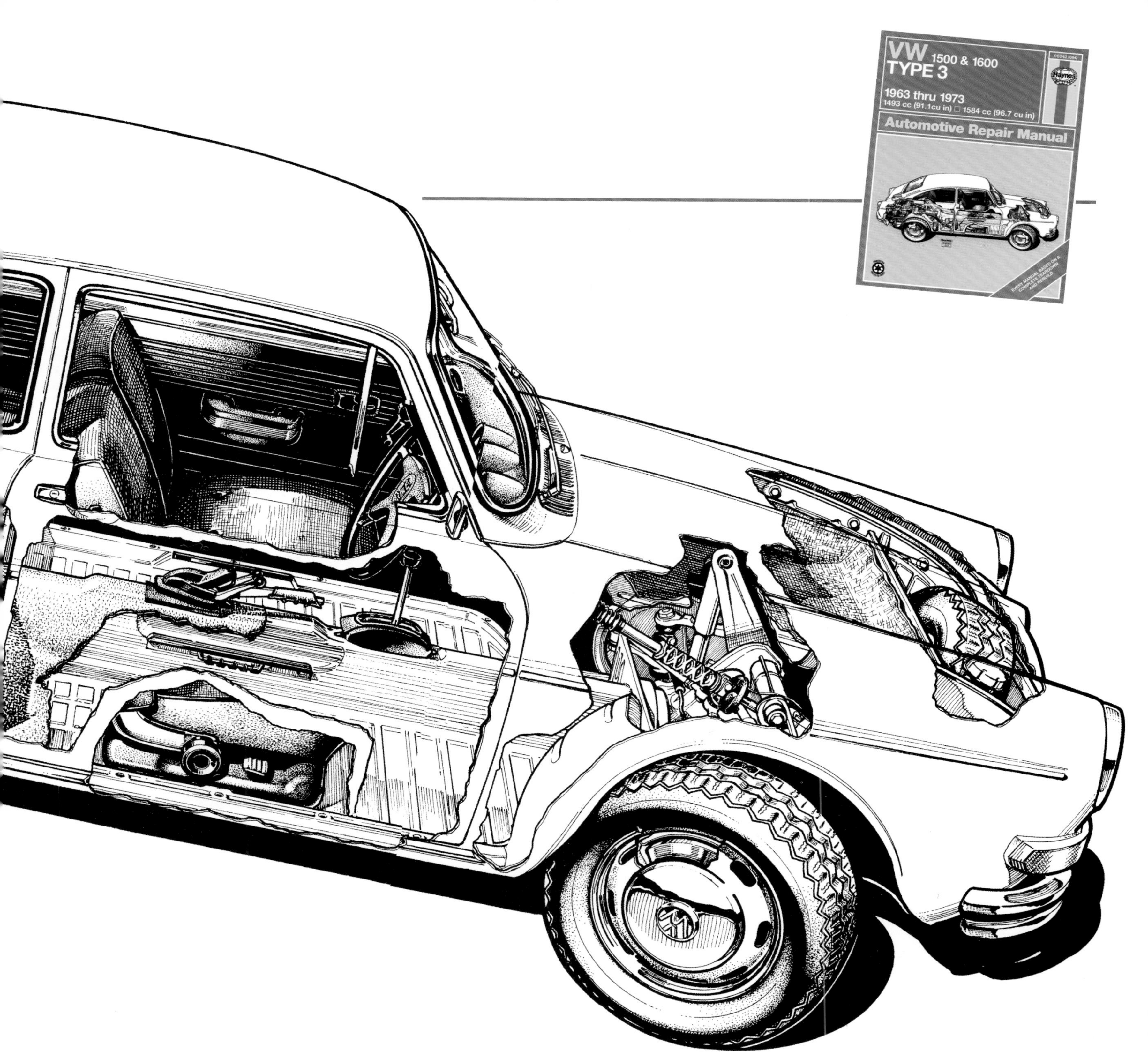
VW 1500 & 1600
TYPE 3
1963 thru 1973
1493 cc (91.1cu in) □ 1584 cc (96.7 cu in)
Automotive Repair Manual
Haynes

VOLKSWAGEN POLO MK1

YEARS MADE
1975–81

NUMBER MADE
768,200

ORIGINAL PRICE
£1,798 (0.9 L in 1976)

MECHANICAL LAYOUT
Front engine, front-wheel drive

RANGE OF ENGINES
895–1,272cc, four-cylinder

MOST POWERFUL ENGINE
60bhp (1,272cc)

FASTEST VERSION
95mph approx (Polo GT, 1,272cc)

BEST FUEL ECONOMY
34mpg (895cc)

WHEELBASE
2,335mm

LENGTH
3,150mm

NUMBER OF SEATS
4

Here's a little-known fact: the original Polo wasn't a Volkswagen at all.

The car was designed by Audi, which put it on sale in 1974 as the Audi 50; intended to replace the old NSU Prinz, engineered by the man behind the NSU Ro80, Ludwig Kraus, and styled in Italy by Bertone, the car was deemed such a sound piece of work that a Volkswagen version was created in 1975. The Polo was born, and the little supermini went mass-market.

Always with a lower profile than rivals from Fiat and Renault, *Motor* magazine had this to say in March 1976: 'We regard the Polo as the best small car in the world today… If the Polo can be summed up in one word it would have to be refinement… The engine is remarkably smooth and quiet… Other qualities include outstanding roadholding and handling, excellent interior space, a slick gearchange and astonishing fuel consumption.'

In short, it was the small car to go for. The 1.3-litre engine was never sold in the UK, although it did appear in the dinky saloon spin-off, the Derby, which was. The Audi original was axed in 1978, that marque aligned henceforth only to upmarket cars. The Polo, meanwhile, has continued to this day in four different styles, always in the shadow of the bigger Golf but equally as competent.

VW
POLO & DERBY
1976 to Jan 1982 □ All models
895 cc □ 1093 cc □ 1272 cc
Haynes
Owners Workshop Manual
VW 1302 & 1302S
BEETLE
1970 to 1972
All models □ 1285 cc □ 1584 cc
Haynes
Owners Workshop Manual
Continental
560-15
OWM 110

VOLKSWAGEN GOLF MK1

YEARS MADE
1974–today

NUMBER MADE
6,950,000 and ongoing in South Africa (all Mk1s)

ORIGINAL PRICE
£1,517 (1100 L in 1975)

MECHANICAL LAYOUT
Front engine, front-wheel drive

RANGE OF ENGINES
1,093–1,272cc, four-cylinder

MOST POWERFUL ENGINE
60bhp (1,272cc)

FASTEST VERSION
92mph (three-door, 1,272cc)

BEST FUEL ECONOMY
29mpg (1,093cc)

WHEELBASE
2,400mm

LENGTH
3,705–3,815mm

NUMBER OF SEATS
5

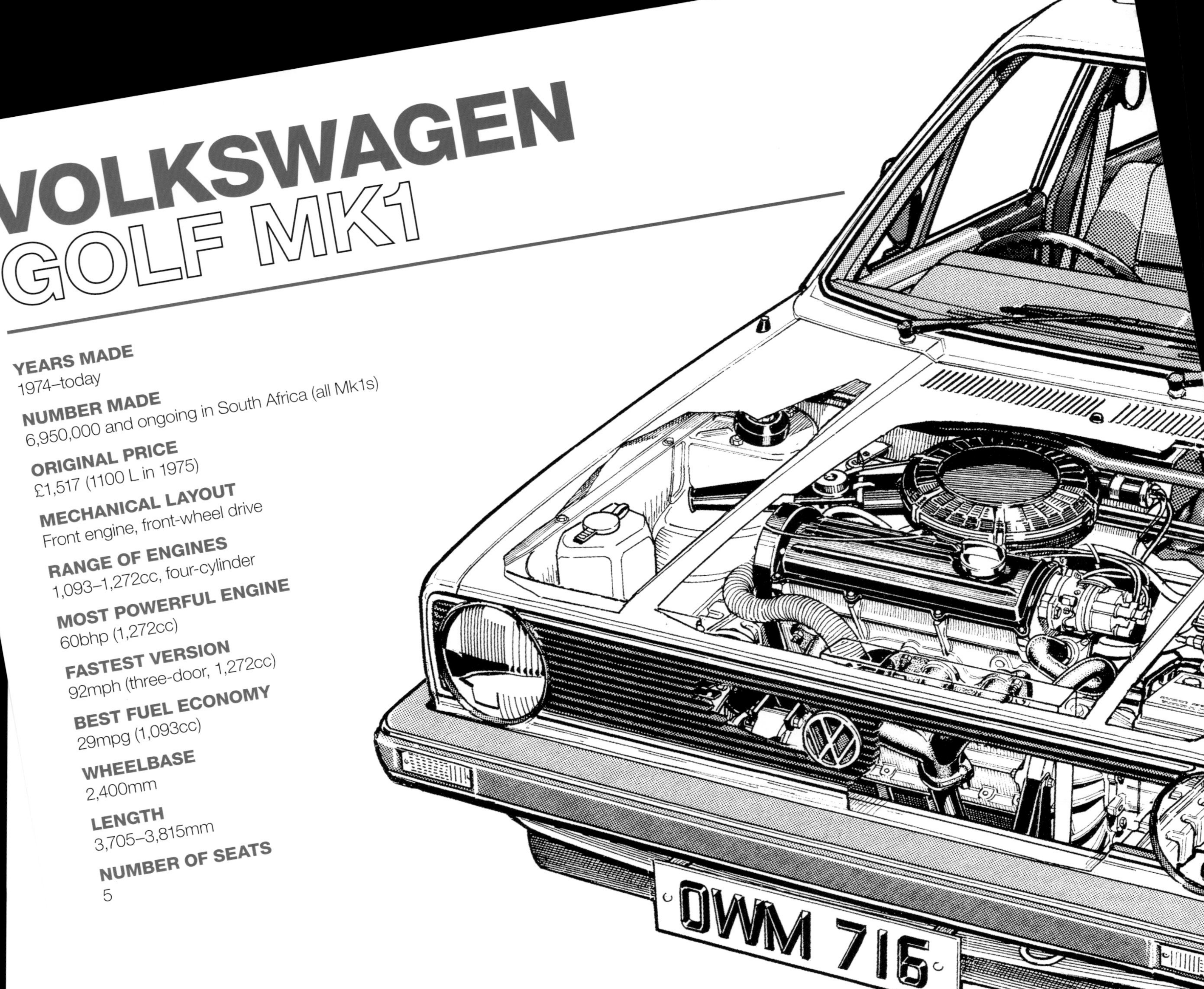

… the straightforward reason that, after the Beetle and the Transporter, it was the third new model range to come from the German manufacturer, the official title of this stylish Fastback was the Volkswagen 1600.

The basic car had first appeared in 1961 as the 1500 saloon with a conventional 'three-box' profile, although it was mainly Beetle underneath, except with torsion bar suspension in place of torsion leaves. After five years on sale the car was redesigned as the Fastback to give it a sporty persona, and to spearhead a sales push in the USA, where the visually unchanged estate model was known as the Squareback; they even hired a pimply Dustin Hoffman to star in TV commercials for it. This was helped by specifying the 1.6-litre engine fitted with twin carburettors, ably attended by front disc brakes, which made it a more willing performer than the equivalent Beetle, if not exactly a firecracker.

The optional automatic gearbox offered from 1968 onwards blunted the urge yet further, but the 1600 TE of that year could give much better acceleration thanks to its standard Bosch electronic fuel injection; it was one of the first mass-produced cars to have such a sophisticated fuel delivery system, even if the top speed of 85mph was still extremely modest beside conventional British rivals.

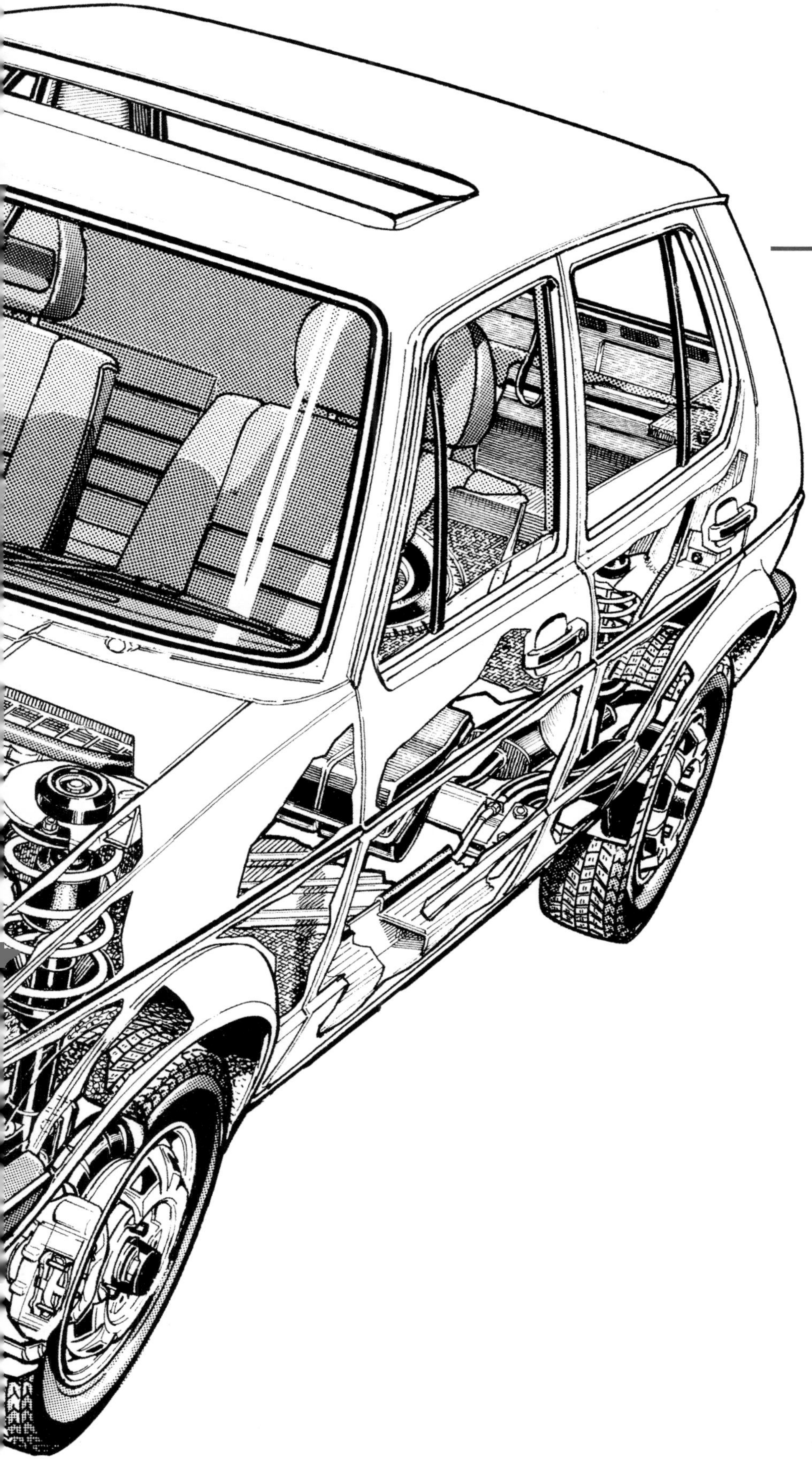

When masterful Haynes Manuals artist Terry Davey created this artwork for the first Volkswagen Golf, he was not actually thinking of the utterly exhilarating GTi – the single variant of the Mk1 that's achieved immortality among enthusiasts. For when the Golf was launched, there was no GTi, and moreover no official thoughts of one.

In fact, the GTi was developed by Volkswagen engineers in their spare time; policy-makers at VW would not sanction a 'Sport Golf' because they could see no market for such a car. They only changed their mind when they sampled the stunning result of all that moonlighting.

Anyway, our Terry chose the least powerful five-door family models, which in 1974 were entirely representative of the cars Volkswagen anticipated selling. Excellent in every way with transverse engines, front-wheel drive, water-cooling, brilliant Giugiaro styling, safe and responsive performance and capacious cabin, it's still easy to overlook the fact that these Golfs actually got off to a slow start in the UK. British family car buyers were so accustomed to the dated and uninspired products of domestic manufacturers, or value-packed but technologically stale imports from Japan, that they viewed this radical German interloper with suspicion.

Although today's Golf is five generations away from the Mk1, the original 1974 car is – amazingly – still made in South Africa as the Citi Golf, and remains a strong seller there.

VOLVO 144/145

YEARS MADE
1966–74

NUMBER MADE
1,251,371

ORIGINAL PRICE
£1,415 (144S in 1967)

MECHANICAL LAYOUT
Front engine, rear-wheel drive

RANGE OF ENGINES
1,778–1,986cc, four-cylinder

MOST POWERFUL ENGINE
82bhp (1,986cc)

FASTEST VERSION
120mph (GL and E, 1,986cc)

BEST FUEL ECONOMY
22.5mpg (1,986cc)

WHEELBASE
2,620mm

LENGTH
4,630mm

NUMBER OF SEATS
5

Big, square, solid, safe: all adjectives that became synonymous with Volvos from the 1960s to the 1990s. Here's the car that began the Swedish company's reputation for comfort and passenger protection. Direct descendents of the 144, moreover, would be on sale for 27 years, and would really establish the marque in the UK and North America.

Passengers were certainly surrounded by plenty of metal in the 144, but the front and rear sections had energy-absorbing, in-built crumple zones and the steering column was collapsible. The car's braking was split on a triangular pattern, guaranteeing 80 per cent of braking capability for the driver even if the system failed. More safety innovations followed later, including three world firsts as standard: rear seatbelts, front seat head restraints and rear door child locks.

Despite accounting for over a third of the series' output, the two-door 142 was sold in the UK only between 1967 and '69. In contrast, the hugely capacious 145 estate became an icon in British suburbia. But all 140-type Volvos felt heavy and slow until the arrival of fuel injection on GL versions in 1971.

By 1973 the cars sprouted prominent rubber-faced bumpers and a padded steering wheel to keep ahead of US safety laws and delight anxious, middle-class buyers, although this was but a prelude to the dodgem car looks of the 240 replacement range in 1974.

VOLVO
140 Series
1966 to 1974
142, 144 & 145 1778 cc 1986 cc
Haynes
Owners Workshop Manual

When Terry Davey retired from Haynes in 1991 things were changing very fast in the world of book publishing. Typescripts and manuscripts were disappearing, replaced by word processing documents which were moved from author to typesetter by floppy disk. (The author who stapled a compliments slip to one had better remain nameless.) Photo-typesetting, itself a marvel to hot-metal men, was superseded in its turn by page make-up on screen. Film cameras gave way to digital, though not without a struggle at the high-quality end of the market. And as already noted, the pen-and-ink cutaways were replaced by electronically-generated images.

For Haynes it wasn't just the publishing technology which was changing: cars were evolving too. European emission control regulations meant that carburettors and contact breaker points became obsolete in 1992, being replaced by fuel injection and electronic ignition systems – computer-controlled, of course. Doomsayers immediately started prophesying the death of car DIY; Haynes published manuals on the new systems. Diesel cars became increasingly popular, but many mechanics, both amateur and professional, knew little about how they worked: Haynes published manuals on diesels. The decade advanced, the technology with it, but we managed to keep up.

In 2008 car and motorcycle manuals are still Haynes' core products (over 6 million sold worldwide in the last financial year) but the company now also publishes books on an ever-widening variety of topics including aviation, camping, caravanning, commercial vehicles, computing, cycling, health, home DIY, maritime, motorcycling, motorsport and vehicle modification and restoration. The Haynes formula of doing the work, taking the photos and telling the story has turned out to be applicable to an extraordinarily wide range of activities. After all, to paraphrase Clarke's third law, technology which you don't understand is indistinguishable from magic. We've been demystifying technology of one sort or another for nearly 50 years.